THE LONE WOLFF

AUTOBIOGRAPHY OF A BRIDGE MAVERICK

BOBBY WOLFF

MASTER POINT PRESS • TORONTO, CANADA

Master Point Press
331 Douglas Ave.
Toronto, Ontario, Canada
M5M 1H2
(416) 781-0351
Website: http://www.masterpointpress.com
Email: info@masterpointpress.com

Library and Archives Canada Cataloguing in Publication

Wolff, Bobby
     The lone Wolff : autobiography of a bridge maverick / written by Bobby
Wolff ; foreword by Eric Murray.

ISBN 978-1-897106-37-2

1. Wolff, Bobby. 2. Bridge players--United States--Biography. 3. Contract
bridge. I. Title.

GV1282.26W64A3 2008   795.41'5092   C2007-907137-6

Editor   Ray Lee
Copy editing   Suzanne Hocking
Interior format   Sarah Howden
Cover and interior design   Olena S. Sullivan/New Mediatrix
Cover photo   Ron Tacchi

Printed in Canada

1 2 3 4 5 6 7   12 11 10 09 08

Table of Contents

Acknowledgements

I want to acknowledge and thank the following people, who read some or all of the manuscript of this book in an early draft and made helpful comments and suggestions:

Martha Beecher
Blair Fedder
Bobbie Gomer
Robin Kay
Carol Pincus
Jeff Polisner
Gloria Rabinowitz
Evie and Burt Rosen
Jane Segal

Author's Tribute...

SINCE MY INTRODUCTION TO THE GAME on that train ride in 1944, my life has been positively touched by thousands of incredible people whose memories I will always hold dear. Obviously, time and space does not allow me to detail all those associations, but I would be remiss if I did not recognize the following individuals who so generously impacted my life and in some measure played a major role in *The Lone Wolff*:

Johnny Gerber, *Ozzie Jacoby* and *Tobias Stone* who recognized the talents of a young enthusiast and helped further my career;

Joe Musumeci who was my first mentor and with whom I started a bridge club in San Antonio in 1960. He later joined the Aces as Coach and whipped us into shape so that its founder, Ira G. Corn, could realize the dream of his life — creating the first successful professional bridge team in the world whose players devoted their lives to nothing but learning and enhancing their playing of the game at the highest level possible;

Jimmy Ortiz-Patino (*The World*), *Denis Howard* (*Australia*), *Jose Damiani* (*France*) and *Ernesto d'Orsi* (*Brazil*) who helped me recognize and appreciate the important composition of foreign bridge cultures and most importantly, different types of work ethic, creativity, individuality, and making good things happen.

Nick Nickell, the actively ethical *crème de la crème* of the bridge and financial world, who, when everything is considered, formed perhaps the most successful bridge team of all time (for whom I played from 1991 to 1998);

My late wife, *Debby*, to whom I was married for 17 years, for demanding and bringing out the best in me and encouraging me to pursue my ideals to uphold the high standards of the game, making the bridge world a better place for posterity.

And finally to *Judy Kay-Wolff*, whom I wed late in 2003. Her enthusiasm and vitality compelled me to resume writing the book I had temporarily abandoned — having begun it in 1995. Unrelentingly, Judy stayed on my case till its conclusion — allying me with a delightful publisher, *Ray Lee* of Master Point Press in Toronto, to whom I will always be grateful.

Foreword

An intriguing behind-the-scenes revelation of what's going on in our game and a clarion call to players and administrators alike to right the wrongs and clean up the very best of games.   Who better to blow the whistle than Bobby Wolff, eleven-time World Bridge Champion, United Media Syndicated Bridge Columnist, who served as WBF and ACBL President, member of the ACBL Board of Directors, Chairman Emeritus of the WBF Appeals Committee and co-founder and co-organizer of the first professional bridge team, the Dallas Aces?

I hope that this book leads to beneficial changes in our game and that Bobby's warnings are not *vox clamantis in deserto*!

— Eric R. Murray

CHAPTER 1 FIRING IRA

WHEN I AROSE FROM THE TABLE, I knew it was time. We still had to compare with our teammates, but when that was done, I would be steeling myself for the job ahead — one I had been delaying for months. "Ira," I said, "let's take a walk."

It was a Tuesday in Minneapolis in the summer of 1968. We, the Aces, had been there for five days — five troubled days. As Ira and I weaved our way through the hotel, the chatter of other players comparing scores was audible. I rehearsed the speech in my head, trying hard not to envision the worst-case scenario. Would he blow up? Fire us all? Make a scene? I had no clue. This dreaded task had fallen to me, and I had to get on with it — like it or not! Though the sun was shining, I sensed a dark cloud looming overhead. I was about to 'fire' Ira Corn as a playing member of the Aces.

No one was more enthusiastic about bridge than Ira G. Corn, Jr., millionaire-businessman and founder of the first full-time professional bridge team in history. Ira's odyssey began in 1964, when, as an aspiring bridge enthusiast, he traveled from Dallas to New York to scrutinize the high-level game during the World Bridge Olympiad. After discovering bridge through a friend, Ira had thrown himself into the game with the same energy that had built Michigan General, his thriving business.

Always supremely confident, Ira figured he could master the game through sheer force of will. He was an enormous success in the business world, so why couldn't he apply the same drive and intelligence toward becoming a top bridge player? All he needed to do was study the game, observe some successful players and emulate what he saw. Simple! .

Ira was electrified by what he witnessed at the Olympiad in New York. The revered Italian Blue Team won comfortably against a good American team in the gold-medal round, and Ira returned to Dallas with a vision. He approached Dorothy Moore, the friend who had introduced him to bridge, and set his plan in motion.

"What would it take for us to put together a team in Dallas?" Corn wanted to know. "What do we need?" Money was no object at that point, but Ira had no idea how to go about fielding the right players. Eventually, Dorothy put Ira onto me. She knew me because we had both played professionally in Texas. I was living in San Antonio at the time, and she respected my bridge ability and my evaluation of the talent in the bridge world.

When we finally got around to recruiting players in 1967, we started with Jim Jacoby, who was right there in Dallas. Two down, four to go. Ira, however, was thinking in terms of three more. He was planning on being a member of the team — and I was going to be his partner.

Ira did a lot of things right after we got the Aces together. Our lineup (besides myself) was Jacoby, Billy Eisenberg, Bobby Goldman, Mike Lawrence and, of course Ira. In the early days, we were involved in a lot of practice matches against competent players in the Dallas area. Eventually, for these sessions, we imported even stronger opposition from out of town. Ira was absorbed with his business, which had just gone public. He had neither the time nor the inclination to work at bridge but he still wanted to play, and his indomitable personality could be a problem. Ira was about the level of an average club player — at best. He never read a bridge book but he was thrilled by good results and he was eternally optimistic. He loved to play. It was like cake and candy to him.

One incident will always loom large in my memory. I was playing with Ira in a practice match and my right-hand opponent, the dealer, opened 1♣. I held:

♠ A Q J   ♡ K J 7 2   ◇ K 10 7 5   ♣ A 3

I doubled for takeout. My left-hand opponent passed (though many would have bid 1♠ on his cards) and Ira bid 2♣. This was followed by 5♣ by the opening bidder. Given Ira's cuebid, 5♣ sounded like an advance save. I had a good hand but it was more defense-oriented than offensive, so I doubled for penalty and everyone passed.

West

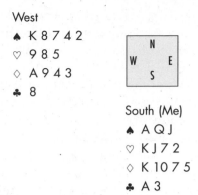

♠ K 8 7 4 2
♡ 9 8 5
◊ A 9 4 3
♣ 8

South (Me)

♠ A Q J
♡ K J 7 2
◊ K 10 7 5
♣ A 3

I started by laying down the club ace to look at dummy; Ira played the ♣4 and declarer followed. It immediately occurred to me that we should take our heart tricks before declarer could establish the spade king for a heart discard...so I switched to the ♡2. To my wonderment (not to mention displeasure), this rode around to declarer's queen. Soon declarer extracted my other trump, conceded a spade trick and scored up +550 by making 5♣ doubled. The full deal:

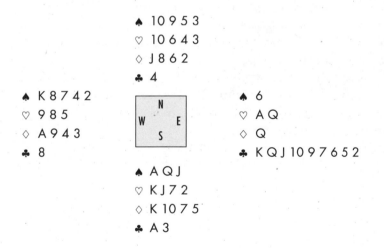

♠ 10 9 5 3
♡ 10 6 4 3
◊ J 8 6 2
♣ 4

♠ K 8 7 4 2　　　　　　　♠ 6
♡ 9 8 5　　　　　　　　♡ A Q
◊ A 9 4 3　　　　　　　◊ Q
♣ 8　　　　　　　　　　♣ K Q J 10 9 7 6 5 2

♠ A Q J
♡ K J 7 2
◊ K 10 7 5
♣ A 3

It turned out that Ira's 2♣ bid was his idea of a brilliant bid, something he saw once on Vugraph — "I'll just cuebid, Bobby will pick one of my majors, I'll pass and everything will be fine". Never mind the implications of the cuebid if the auction became competitive, as it always will. The post mortem was enlightening in the extreme!

　　Ira asked, "Couldn't we have set the hand?"

　　"Yes," I told him. I thought so.

"How?" he asked.

I replied I could have switched to the diamond king at Trick 2.

Ira snarled, "Why did you switch to a heart? You blew the setting trick!"

"Yes," I agreed, starting to question my role in this situation.

Ira did not begin to comprehend that the only cards he could hold which might possibly justify a cuebid were the ace and queen of hearts and probably the diamond queen. Eventually, he calmed down and realized he was out of line in the way he was talking, but he still didn't get the picture. As smart as Ira was, he had no idea how much there was to bridge — particularly at the level where he was striving to play.

For example, much is gleaned about the other hands once dummy is tabled. I am not always exactly correct but I can approximate the distribution of the other hands at that stage and have a better idea than most players about where the high cards lie. Then, after the next few tricks, the distribution becomes a virtual certainty and the high card information falls into place. Is this unusual? No! Not only is it *not* unusual, but there would be no way you could be among the top one hundred players in the country if you didn't do this on every deal. You must count each deal, which requires concentration, work and more work, and then you must possess the discipline to work some more after that. Envisioning the unseen hands is second nature to an expert.

You will soon learn that we are talking about the essence of the game itself. And only with such reasoning is the high-level game of bridge as beautiful an art as it is. Of course, what I'm really talking about is time. I didn't become a world champion overnight. I played and played and played, made mistakes, learned to concentrate, learned to count and learned to read the table action. This didn't happen in two weeks or two months or two years. There's no magic pill you can take to develop the kind of judgment that is essential if you are going to hold your own among the big boys.

One important factor which cannot be overlooked: I began in my teens. I was resilient enough to take my lumps and bounce back. I didn't have to unlearn a million bad habits. I've seen it time after time — men and women who take a fancy to bridge late in their lives. Some are smart people, often ultra-successful in other fields, with great determination and motivation, but I can count on one hand those who have made it to the top without starting in their youth.

There wasn't much point in telling stuff like that to Ira. Despite his fervor to be a top player, he just didn't come close to possessing the mandatory attributes of a world-class player. Few do! The game didn't come naturally to him. He had all the confidence in the world from his business success, and he saw no reason why he couldn't succeed in bridge to the same extent, but it didn't work that way. Don't get me wrong here. Ira was a good guy. I loved him. The people who knew him loved him. However, on occasion, he could be absolutely infuriating. Sometimes it seemed his ego was as big as Texas, which is part of the reason we ended up with him as a playing member of the Aces — at least at the outset of the venture.

We had practice matches and played in a few Regionals. Our results were okay at the Regionals, but the competition wasn't really what you'd call stiff. Our first NABC appearance was in the Vanderbilt in the Spring of 1968 in New York. We won two matches, then lost to another Texan team.

Now... here we were in Minneapolis in the Spingold, the other major knockout team event on the national tournament scene. When Ira and I played as part of the Aces, we were always behind at the half. In Minneapolis, we had barely squeaked by teams in the first two rounds that we should have trounced. Now in the third round, we were trailing again. Without Ira in the lineup, we probably would have been up by about 50.

The Aces had been assembled only months before, so we really hadn't formulated a personality as a team in any real sense — and we hadn't discussed the 'Ira Situation' as a unit. If the subject was keeping me up nights, it had probably also crossed the minds of my teammates. If Ira continued to play, we were fated to be merely an ordinary team. How were we going to dominate as we wanted to — as Ira dreamed we could — if we were actually no better than all the other monkeys in the zoo?

I didn't consult any of my teammates, and I knew I was going out on a limb, but I felt I had no options at this point. It was time for Ira and me to go for that walk. We compared scores with Billy and Bobby. Yes, we were trailing again — and Ira and I left the playing area. We meandered down a side entrance to the hotel, away from the crowds. Ira was puffing on one of those gigantic cigars he enjoyed so much. It seemed to fit his personality and accentuate his intimidating persona. I was not thrilled to be in the vulnerable position in which I had placed myself, but the job had to be done.

"Ira," I said, "we've been practicing and working and we're at a point now..." I was fumbling for words, about to lose my nerve. Suddenly, I just blurted: "There's no way in the world the Aces can be anywhere close to what you want them to be if you continue to play." Ira puffed on his cigar and regarded me coldly.

"What do you mean?" he queried.

"Ira, I know you love the game, but you are so far away from where you should be as a player. It's like we're a Class D Bush League team trying to win the World Series. Actually, it's even worse than that. We can't hide you in right field. You're right there." I couldn't believe I was saying all this to Ira G. Corn. "If you feel that you have to play," I went on, "maybe we should disband the team. Everyone knows your intentions were stellar. It has nothing to do with that. It has to do with..."

I couldn't say any more. I was finished pleading my case, and Ira understood exactly what I was saying. If he threw me off the team or abandoned the whole Aces idea, I figured I could always go back to San Antonio. I was in a haze of sorts, mentally playing out the rest of the impending self-imposed debacle when Ira's voice hauled me back to reality.

"Well," he said gruffly, "you better win." We lost the next day.

As I reflect on it, it was terrifying for me to try to break it to Ira Corn that he wasn't good enough to play with the Aces, but winning back to back world championships in 1970 and 1971 more than justified the potential suicide course I embarked upon. It was well worth the gamble. I was thinking of how much time and effort had been devoted to trying to mold the Aces into a world-class team and how it would be such a waste to let it all go down the drain. Of course, there was also the dream of a world championship that had seemed so real at first, but started growing dimmer and dimmer. Those were some of the thoughts that motivated my taking the stand with Ira.

I don't hold myself up as any kind of noble character or hero for biting the bullet and taking on the 'Ira problem'. Certainly, back in the summer of 1968, part of my motivation was selfish. But today, even with six decades of playing bridge behind me, I am still compelled to take a position when I am troubled by actions I feel are inappropriate. Perhaps it is having the courage of my convictions that has earned me my reputation as 'The Lone Wolff'.

Through the years, I have been a player, administrator and 'politician'. Bridge has taken me around the world and I have played with and against the best — and against some of the worst. I've seen how decisions are made behind closed doors, for wrong reasons and right ones, and I've formed some strong opinions about the way things *should* be in the bridge world.

My opinions are not shared by all. Far from it! I have made enemies when I have spoken out because I have initiated action where I was convinced it was needed. I've stepped on many toes, and this book will no doubt generate more animosity. There are individuals and groups out there who have strong reasons for zealously guarding the status quo. I hope my voice will serve as a clarion call for change. A person's opinions and beliefs are, in large measure, formed from life experiences. That is certainly true for me. What I have seen and heard over the course of a long career has inspired and fortified me to strive to effect the changes that I feel are necessary if our game is to survive.

From my perch, the world of bridge is comprised basically of four groups:

Social players, who play solely for recreation, relaxation and sheer enjoyment of the game;

Professionals, both top experts and expert 'wannabes' who prefer to cash in on their bridge talents rather than hold down an equal or lesser-paying real 9 to 5 job (and who can blame them for that?);

Sponsors, many with unlimited funds, who are unlikely to achieve stardom playing with their peers;

Administrators, who shape the fate and conditions of bridge, the majority of whom are not top players but get their kicks from being around the game they love, volunteering, and probably most of all, enjoying the limelight and authority to make decisions affecting the game.

It is this mix of bridge activists that will be examined as you read on. My intention is to share my experiences and enable you to understand both my motivation and the tactics necessary for achieving my goals. At times, these methods may appear to be extreme. I assure you my sole objective has been and always will be to preserve the dignity and beauty of the game and have it assume its rightful station in the scheme of things. No one can argue that the best position to be in is on the side of the angels.

CHAPTER 2

TRACING MY ADDICTION

WHEN WE RETURNED from the train station, my father rushed to turn on the radio. The ride from Chicago had taken a couple of days and he was anxious for updated news of the war. It was November of 1944. D-Day was long past, but World War II wasn't over yet. My father, who was Chief Air Raid Warden of San Antonio, was often glued to the radio, eager for the day's reports from the front, and my mother, brother and I listened along with him. The war would soon end, but in a military town like San Antonio, with US Air Force bases everywhere, it was all anyone talked about. I was twelve years old, so the war didn't have the same impact on me. Besides that, on that infamous train ride I had acquired a brand new interest — something called *bridge*.

Before that exposure, I knew in a vague kind of way that my parents played bridge — whatever that was. My father, Walter, was the eldest of three brothers, and they were all hooked on the game. One of my uncles, Melvin, had a drug store in San Antonio, but he went broke because he was always in the back room playing bridge. People would enter his store, see no one there and leave. He later moved to Los Angeles and became the chief pharmacist at the famous Owl Drugstore at Hollywood and Vine. He continued playing bridge until his death at age ninety-four and is no doubt still pursuing his addiction from above.

My parents, Walter and Elma, were not particularly good players, but they were the stars of our neighborhood — and my father was a positively ferocious competitor. He hated to lose at anything. From the time I was six years old, my father and I played 'pitch', a game of trumps and tricks — as it happened, a good prelude to bridge. My father always played for blood, even during our kitchen table interludes, and I guess that 'training' imbued me with the competitive spirit that has served me well over the years.

Bridge — pitch — you name it. Whatever my father played, he spared no one's feelings. On more than one occasion, bridge games at our house were known to dissolve in acrimony. The bridge get-togethers allowed for socializing, to be sure, but make no mistake about it — my father was out for one thing: to win.

Dad was an attorney who was kept on retainer by a number of meat-packing plants in San Antonio. In the fall of 1944, Ed Auge, an executive at one of the plants, asked my father to accompany him to Chicago on a business trip. It was decided that my parents would go with Ed and his wife, Ella. My seventeen-year-old brother, Walter Jr., was away at college and the Wolffs weren't about to leave a twelve-year-old home alone, so reluctantly they decided to take me out of school for the nine-day trip. The three of us visited the school to inform them of my parents' decision. That was over sixty years ago and still echoing in my ears are the uncannily insightful words of consolation offered to my parents by the schoolmarm: *"Oh, he'll learn more on the trip than he could in school."* Brother, was she ever right!

During the train ride to Chicago, which took a couple of days, the Wolffs and the Auges played bridge non-stop. I was an intensely fascinated kibitzer. In fact, at the trip's conclusion, I had the bizarre notion that, although I had never played the game, I could do better at it than the adults. I remained silent as the games on the train continued, but as I watched, I could envision situations that they had overlooked — endplays, for example, and above all the importance of establishing tricks in a long side suit. It was fascinating. As I reflect on it, it seems to me that I had a pretty highly developed sense of how to play the game even before I touched a card. I didn't know any of the nomenclature such as 'tenace' or 'finesse', but I knew there was an advantage to playing last to a trick, and I understood the overall concepts and theories, possibly better than the adults who were playing on that train. I couldn't wait to play myself, and after we returned, I was invited to join the adults in the family bridge games. That was the start.

From the time I was seven years old until 1958, when I left home to get married, my family lived in a duplex in north San Antonio. My father had the home built by one of his clients for $6,000. It was a duplex with identical floor plans — top and bottom. For the entire time I lived there, we resided on the first floor and rented out the second story. During the time when rent controls were in effect, the typical rent for our tenants was $15 a month. It was in this house that I learned many games, including bridge. I was extremely shy and a loner as a child, playing baseball games with myself and keeping statistics. I was fascinated by numbers, sports, logic problems and table tennis. In fact, I got to be reasonably good at the latter, thanks to a neighborhood contemporary, Meyer Scharlach.

My buddy Meyer had an air-conditioned room which housed his table tennis set-up. It was quite refreshing to play there, as air conditioning was almost unheard of in San Antonio in the forties. Meyer's father, Louis (a state champion himself) was friendly with a Hungarian fellow named Tibor Hazi, who was a former world champion. I enjoyed playing against Tibor, who would spot me 10 points and then go on to whip me something like 21-13. What I learned from this carried over to bridge — *playing against the best at whatever you're doing is the fastest way to improve.* My sessions against Tibor deflated my ego but strengthened my game and helped me make it to the finals of the State Junior Table Tennis Championship one year. I believe that the courage to play over my head in all games was one of the driving forces which eventually prepared me to win eleven world championships at bridge.

One of my first bridge partners was my brother Walter, who was (and still is!) five years older. He continues to flourish and practice law in San Antonio. Walter was always the serious type. He enjoyed sports and competition, but he didn't have time for them. He was almost always number one in his class, even in the accelerated program that got him into college at the age of seventeen. He was High School Valedictorian and second in his class at the University of Texas Law School. In fact, he earned his law degree at the age of twenty and had to wait another year until he was old enough to practice. He joined my father in his law practice and excelled immediately.

I played my first duplicate bridge game in 1949 at the Gunter Hotel, which still stands in downtown San Antonio. Every Friday night all the top businessmen and the most respected people in the community would appear at the Gunter for the Unit game. In the late forties and early fifties, bridge was *the* thing to do. Television was far from perfected and cyberspace not yet thought of. All of my parents' friends played bridge, and local tournaments were underwritten by the businessmen. I still remember some of the prizes donated by a local jewelry store — silver worth $500 to $1,000, quite a lot back then.

My partner in my duplicate debut was Richard Goldsmith, whose father was considered one of the best players in town. Richard and I later became roommates at the University of Texas. As I recall, we did respectably that night at the Gunter, although we didn't win. That was one of the few times I played bridge before I matriculated at the University of Texas in 1950. Once in college, I played all the time. It's the age-old story of addiction and it was a conservatively fair assessment to say I played too much.

I stayed at Austin for only a couple of years. My grades were barely average and my father wasn't enthralled to be footing the bill at U. T.

for such a mediocre performance, especially compared to Walter, who got straight A's. I was a C+ student. To tell the truth, I wasn't all that keen on being there either. I was enrolled in a pre-law curriculum, but deep down I knew that practicing law wasn't my life's ambition, so when my father told me he wanted me to transfer to Trinity University in San Antonio, I was happy to oblige. I did finish Trinity, with a degree in business.

Once back in San Antonio, Walter and I started playing regularly. While I was in Austin for two years, Walter had gotten into bridge pretty seriously, so he was ready for me when I returned to San Antonio. From about 1952 to 1956, we were one of the best local pairs around — and it wasn't clear at that point which one of us was the better player. Walter was an extremely disciplined performer; he is a perfectionist who has lived his whole life by the letter of the law. In fact, he gave up bridge because he couldn't be perfect. He married a lovely girl, Sondra, a graduate of Bryn Mawr, and, as did all the young couples of that day, they played bridge together. When they played, however, they tended to fight. Playing bridge together was the only time they had any trouble in a marriage which has spanned fifty years, so Walter gave up the game completely. Although he has retained his ACBL membership, he has not played a single deal in more than forty-five years. He became Life Master No. 937 and there is no telling what heights he would have achieved had he continued to play.

In the early days of our partnership, however, things were different. Walter was a real student of the game. He even wrote a book about it. His habits as an attorney spilled over to his bridge game. By that, I mean that no one was ever better prepared for a task than my brother. When he joined my father's practice, it was Walter Sr. who got all the clients but Walter Jr. did all the work. Our bidding system was pretty much the standard of the day — four-card majors and the other accoutrements of the Goren system. One of our big experiments was using the Solomon 2◇ opener, a bid that shows a long suit and asks for specific cards in responder's hand. It was quite the rage for a time, but it faded out pretty quickly for one important reason — it almost never came up.

Those were exuberant times. Walter and I were one of the few real partnerships around Texas then, and as a result, were ranked among the most successful players. I can remember train trips to Shreveport for bridge tournaments and drives to Fort Worth and Dallas. At other times, we would motor to Houston. In those days, the Sunday game was the Open Pairs. We would play a two-session game and then drive throughout the night to get back San Antonio in the wee hours of

Monday morning, catch a wink of sleep and be ready at sun-up for either work or school.

I liked the intensity of the game, and even from my early days, I was — and remain — an aggressive bidder. I guess it's my natural optimism and confidence. In 1989, at the Spring Nationals in Reno, Dr. Marty Seligman, a Philadelphia area bridge player and world-celebrated psychologist and author, conducted a test to determine various bridge players' levels of optimism. He asked questions about how people felt in certain situations, and he tested all the players who made it to the round of 16 in the Vanderbilt Knockout Teams. Marty told me that of all the people he had ever tested, I scored the highest in optimism. It's hard to explain how that translates to winning bridge, but here is my credo:

I don't expect to win every bridge competition I enter and since I don't believe the world will come to an end if I lose, I never get nervous in critical situations.

At the time Walter and I were playing, there were bridge games all over town. There was a club at a converted apartment house, games at country clubs, at the Gunter Hotel and at the Officers' Club at Fort Sam Houston. The game at the Officers' Club was somewhat different since guests were required to play with one of the soldiers or airmen or their wives... rather like having a sponsor. During this period, I was so involved in bridge that I even served as Secretary of the San Antonio Bridge League for a couple of years. I couldn't get enough of the game.

Walter and I had become a regular partnership and our success earned us respect. I also played with a host of other people — usually a different person every week. I knew I was pretty good, especially compared to most of the club players, and I won frequently, so I was in demand. I was riding high and enjoying my newfound stardom — a far cry from being that hibernating loner I had been as a child.

I also played some with my father. I remember partnering him in the Open Pairs at a Regional in San Antonio. These tournaments were a big deal back then, and on one occasion we had the legendary Al Sobel as the Director in Charge. The tournament was at the Gunter Hotel and always featured a big free dinner between sessions of the pairs game (which might have been the *force majeure* responsible for attracting so many). The mystery and intrigue surrounding the names of the qualifiers and leaders made it more exciting than the later era of burner sheets or today's lightning fast computer printouts. As was the custom, sometime during the dinner break 'Uncle Al' Sobel would stand up and announce the names of the qualifiers as well as his predictions as to the eventual winners. I recall on this particular occasion how

Dad beamed when Sobel announced that Walter Wolff, Sr. and Robert Wolff were among the qualifiers and added that they'd be reading the name of young Robert Wolff and be hearing about him in the future. Alas, we didn't win that day, finishing the event about average.

I remember one club championship in which my brother and I played. Our score was 137.5 on a 108 average — and there were three pairs tied with 137. That was a heady experience. Our confidence was soaring. In those days, they gave trophies for winning and Walter and I had amassed more than a hundred of them. Individually, each of these trophies no doubt represented excellent judgment, decent performances and more than our fair share of good luck, but to my way of thinking, this pile of mementos at some nondescript point in time was, in the end, only a place for dust to collect. I vividly recall, while at the border town of Del Rio, Texas, for a tournament, my friends and I deciding to venture into Mexico for dinner. My collection of trophies (for some reason tossed helter-skelter into my trunk) was confiscated by the border authorities for fear that we were smuggling gold (little did they know!). We were promised it would be returned when we came back. A few hours later, true to his word, the border guard approached the vehicle with my trophies in tow. I can still picture the shocked look on his face when I waved him off, saying, "Keep them. They're yours." So ended the problem of the dust collectors and the alleged contraband!

One of the players I saw a lot of and came to respect was Joe Musumeci, then an Air Force officer stationed at Kelly Field. Joe, later tabbed 'Moose' by his close friends, was known as one of the best players in the area. Walter and I liked him because he was always very friendly and helpful. Joe eventually was transferred overseas, but he would rematerialize as a major factor in my life after he retired and returned to San Antonio.

I was drafted into the US Army Reserves in 1955 and then later into the Army in 1956. I served my basic training at Fort Chafee in Arkansas and then was sent to train for the Counter Intelligence Corps at Fort Holabird in Baltimore. At that time, although the Korean conflict was over, it was still very much a part of the political landscape and paranoia over communism was a grave reality. Strange as it may sound to you, my being in the Army Reserve and training at Fort Holabird involved its share of cloak-and-dagger matters. Times have changed, but fifty years ago one aspect of security that was a sensitive issue to the government and the military related to homosexuals. At that time, homosexuality was still a 'closet' issue, and gays were considered to be potential targets for blackmailers and therefore high security risks. I was trained to join a special unit whose job it was to process out the gay people in high-level jobs which required top security clearance.

Near the end of my training, I filled out a form that asked for my preference — no, not sexual, but rather my choice of locales for my next assignment. We were instructed to itemize three choices in the order of desirability, and the standing joke was that no one should list as number one what he *really* wanted because they always gave you your last choice. I was so naïve and disbelieving (or call it defiant if you will), that I named Fort Sam Houston in San Antonio as my first choice. As luck would have it, that's where I ended up — eight blocks from my parents' home. Incidentally, the choices ranged from Hawaii, SHAPE Headquarters (Paris, France), and IDF (Icelandic Defense Forces) down to other more mundane places in the United States like Fort Sam Houston.

Back in San Antonio, I was putting in my time with the Army and playing lots of bridge. I was popular because I was getting better and better as a player, and one of the people courting me as a partner was a colonel — the head of the Judge Advocate's Office at Fort Sam Houston. One day, I was surprised to see the colonel's name on a file that hit my desk. He wasn't gay, but someone had informed the Army that the colonel's wife, a Hawaiian, was in the pornography business and that her enterprises were at fever pitch on the Islands. I was supposed to investigate without letting the colonel become aware of it. I had played with him a couple of times, and he seemed like a regular sort. I was uncomfortable at the prospect of invading his privacy. Luckily, I was able to pass the case along to someone else, and pretty soon that distasteful segment of my life was over.

One of my most interesting experiences early in my bridge career was helping put together a television show for the NBC affiliate in San Antonio. The show, called 'What's Your Bid?', aired on Sunday afternoons from noon to 12:30. It actually lasted thirteen months, and was syndicated briefly in places like Harlingen (in the Rio Grande valley) and Amarillo (in the Panhandle).

Walter and I, together with a friend named Perry Zeller, would invite two guest panelists to compete against us. The guests were quite often celebrities or politicians. We once showcased the Mayor of San Antonio and the Governor of Texas on our show. Even Oswald Jacoby came down from Dallas to appear a few times. We attempted to make it humorous with clever chitchat, and we always had a good-looking woman as a hostess. At one point, we got a bite from a national TV producer who talked about turning our show into a nationwide attraction, but what did we know? We thought his offer was too low and we stupidly refused. No one else ever expressed any interest in it. The show eventually petered out despite our attempts to get TV stations in other cities to come on board.

My theory of the importance of learning bridge in one's youth is substantiated by many factors. I was one of those lucky ones. The record books bear out my conjecture that few who start the game after their mid-twenties ever develop into top players. There's just too much involved, and you have to be young so that your ego can withstand the punishment it has to absorb to make it to the world level. You must play thousands and thousands of deals and learn to count automatically and with routine ease, to recognize when a key play is necessary and make it without having to think about it. When you're playing at high levels, you aren't going to get any help.

In the early days of television, there was a show hosted by Groucho Marx called 'You Bet Your Life'. If you ever watched it, you may remember that at a certain point a duck would descend from the ceiling and signal the secret word. Well, that just doesn't happen in bridge. No one is telling you, "Hey, kid! A key play is coming. Get ready!" You must be mentally ready at all times, much like a cornerback in football, who never knows when the receiver he is covering is supposed to catch the game-breaking pass. No one sends the cornerback a telegram to be on the lookout for something special, so he has to be alert on every play. You've got to be a cornerback in bridge, with total focus so that you can handle the big play when it happens along.

In my bridge infancy, I was lucky enough to play against some of the best. In San Antonio, there was Joe Musumeci, who was a star when I first started playing. Harold Rockaway wasn't well known outside Texas, but in his heyday — which was when I was playing — he was one of the best around. He was a hustling Roth-Stone player who was stationed in San Antonio during a military hitch. Benny Fain was another Texas player who could have held his own at any level when he was playing at his peak. He was a gambler who ran a bridge club in San Antonio. I sat across the table from Sidney Lazard and Curtis Smith, both great players and I also played with the legendary Oswald Jacoby when he was at his best. Of the many people I've met and had close dealings with in the bridge world, Ozzie Jacoby might have been the most memorable — certainly he was one of a kind. I must indulge myself and share that experience with you.

He was possibly the only true genius I have ever been close with, capable of multiplying three- or four-digit numbers in his head without benefit of paper, much less a calculator. The quality that set him apart, however, was his mercurial habit of bouncing from one totally unrelated subject to another. He could be contemplating a serious decision such as choosing a bridge partner and/or teammates for the next Vanderbilt, Spingold, or Reisinger and within a microsecond would leap to an irrelevant hypothetical question like "What would one call a Baseball World Series between the Texas Rangers and the Houston Astros?" He labeled it a Southwest Airlines Series, like the Subway Series between the Brooklyn Dodgers and the New York Yankees. Ozzie was unlike anyone I had ever met!

At one time, probably in and around the late 1940s and early 1950s, Ozzie was unquestionably in the top ten worldwide as a player in bridge, poker, gin rummy, backgammon and even canasta, a new game at that time, having written enjoyable, bestselling and accurate books on all of those games. He was best remembered for doing (and completing) *The New York Times* Sunday crossword puzzle, *in ink, moving straight across, rarely bothering to check the 'Down' clues.*

When we talked about gambling or the art of winning, Ozzie would often recall Damon Runyon's famous line, "The battle does not always go to the strong, nor the race to the swift, but that is the way to bet". However, despite his multi-faceted talents, his Achilles heel became apparent when he could not resist playing games other than bridge for high stakes against stronger players. Invariably Runyon's words would ring true — he lost.

Ozzie hated to lose. I well remember accompanying him to one of the many illegal gambling houses in Texas. He would always hand over his wallet to me for safekeeping and made me swear that *under no circumstances* would I release it to him while we were there. Invariably, he would change his mind (after he lost a shekel or two) and request his wallet. Ozzie was always a man of his word and I took him at face value, which proved to be a fatal mistake. The first time I was put to the test, I refused to hand the wallet over but I lived to regret it as he humiliated me by shouting for all to hear what an idiot I was (and perhaps I was — to believe he wouldn't weaken).

Having Jake (which was what he was called by people close to him) as a friend, mentor and early partner was one of the highlights of my life. It showed me, in spades and at a young age, the vast capabilities of the human mind. It definitely made me sharper and faster-witted at arithmetic, the single most important component in winning at bridge. It also taught me with convincing clarity the necessity for intense concentration if I was to succeed at the highest levels. Jake's self-confidence was off the charts (as is that of Warren Buffett and Bill Gates, who are both social bridge players) and by observing this characteristic in living color, I was awakened to just how important it is. Self-confidence was important not only in my becoming successful as a player but also in learning how to transform myself into the intimidator rather than the intimidated. Mindset is a powerful tool, especially at the bridge table. Oswald Jacoby had a tremendously positive effect on my life and I will always look back on our friendship with special pride.

Bridge is an education in itself, though some of the practices you adopt at the bridge table in your formative years aren't necessarily laudable. Playing with Walter in my youth, he and I had a natural advantage over most of the players at the clubs and in small tournaments — simply because we were *better*. I learned later that you can augment 'better' with what you might euphemistically call 'moves'.

Many of the players I came to know, especially from the fifties, had lots of so-called 'moves'. In today's world those same 'moves' are considered 'histrionics', and completely unethical. In fact, some fairly dubious practices were considered standard operating procedure in those days. For example, you are declarer and someone makes a lead right into your AQJ. If you're on the wrong side of the morality curve, you frown a little — maybe just enough to be barely perceptible — to indicate you didn't like that lead. You want them to do it again, don't you? When the lead was not so good for your side, you came alive, as though you wanted them to lead it again. Got the picture? You could pick up on these baited moves, of course, but the smart players varied them so you couldn't always rely on their extra-curricular activity.

All this is wrong, of course, and this isolated form of chicanery doesn't even scratch the surface of what I've seen in my travels through the bridge world. It's gratifying to say that this is one area where the high-level bridge community has seen the light, at least for the most part. A small step forward!

CHAPTER 3

PLAYING PRO
VERSUS A REAL JOB

MOOSE AND I INTRODUCED professional bridge to San Antonio in the very early sixties. We had no choice. For me, it was that or selling insurance, a distasteful alternative. During that period, I was stationed in San Antonio and while serving in the US Army, one was rewarded with an inordinate amount of spare time. In 1958, I was being processed out of the service, and fortunately for me, I was stationed in San Antonio which was a hotbed of bridge activity — though practically devoid of top players.

One of the regulars at the games I frequented was a lovely woman by the name of Frieda Yuill. She played bridge five or six times a week so our paths crossed quite often. A year or so before I was due to be released from the Army, Frieda, a perky, attractive blonde in her late fifties with a cameo-like face, told me she had a daughter, Betsey, who was coming home for a break from college. Betsey, Frieda said, was a student at North Texas State University in Denton, near Dallas. Betsey had developed an interest in bridge, and Frieda wanted to know if I would play with her. I liked women, especially nice looking ones, so I had no trouble taking her up on the offer. I don't know if I realized it at the time, but Frieda was matchmaking.

Betsey Yuill was a delight — five-foot-two, blonde and very vivacious, not to mention smart. She seemed to like me, although not as much as I liked her. Betsey enjoyed having a partner with whom she could win — thus, the mutual attraction. Betsey returned to North Texas State, but we kept in touch while she was away and saw each other when she wasn't in school. I was discharged from the Army on June 2, 1958 and Betsey and I got married in December of that year.

It's worth noting that after we married, we played a lot of bridge together. Walter had given up the game and Betsey and I shared a common passion. The truth is that we won a lot. The curious thing is that, as I remember it, no one ever gave Betsey any credit for our good showings. It was always, "Bobby won! Bobby won!" They never said

'Bobby and Betsey'. I was always uncomfortable with that because bridge is a partnership game and Betsey, who was beginning to show some aptitude for the game, was really improving. If anything, she should have been given more credit than me. It's not worth going into the psychology of why people say the things they do, but it seemed they didn't want to give Betsey her due, and people would fantasize that if they were playing with me, they'd be winning too.

I did reasonably well in the insurance business, mostly because my father helped steer some clients my way. My insurance career was lackluster, to say the least, but life got better — certainly more interesting — when US Air Force Lt. Col. Joseph Musumeci, recently retired, returned to San Antonio. This was 1960, and I was ready to do something involving bridge. Bridge was where I shone. It was what I was known for among my friends. It was a game that brought me prestige and nurtured my ego. Moose and I had met while he was stationed in San Antonio, had played bridge together and grown to like and respect one another. We kept in touch while he was overseas on his various Air Force assignments. Before he was discharged, we decided to go into business together.

We were rebuffed in our first effort, which was an attempt to buy the existing major bridge club in San Antonio, the Bridge Studio. The owner, a close friend of mine by the name of Burt Gideon, refused to sell. Hastily, and in a state of frustration, we did a foolish thing — in a town hardly big enough for *one* bridge club, we started a *second*.

In the seven or eight years that Moose and I ran the club, it had several locations. We learned many lessons the hard way. One of them was that bridge players show up at a place to play bridge, not to admire the architecture or interior decorating. It turned out to be a costly venture when we decided to move from a smoke-filled 1200 square foot location to the basement of a luxurious new building. We quickly realized the error of our ways. It mattered not how chic the place was as long as it was adequate for playing bridge.

During this time, I was teaching bridge, playing rubber bridge for stakes, playing duplicate bridge for a fee and playing assorted other games, such as gin and pitch, for money. I still had my insurance license, but I had stopped selling, so it wasn't really much of a business. I tried to earn money every which way I could. We did lots of things to promote bridge in San Antonio, including running Calcuttas, where players and others bid on and buy 'shares' in the various contestants (who can buy themselves, too). The proceeds of the auction go into a prize pool and everyone — winning players and those who own 'shares' of winning players — splits the booty when the scores are tallied.

It was fun being in the bridge business, although my father wrung his hands in despair and looked worried whenever we discussed it. My father's dream was for me to go to law school. I had actually been considering it when Moose reappeared, and my destiny was changed for ever and ever. Unfortunately, fun didn't pay the bills, and the income we got from the club was truly peanuts. At one point, we figured that with all the work we put into the club, we were making about 11 cents an hour. Even in 1960, that wasn't much! That's when we started playing with people for pay. It started on a small scale — $5 per session at the local duplicate. Eventually, we branched out to Sectionals and Regionals. I never really went on the circuit like some of today's traveling professionals, but I had a stable of clients whose fees were the income that kept me afloat.

The forerunner to my real professional bridge career was 'Miriam'. I played my first game with Miriam at our bridge club in late 1960. Miriam was a divorcee who had been married to a wealthy businessman. It seemed like he had owned half of Mexico City. I met Miriam, a cute redhead in her fifties, when she came into our club with a friend. We took an instant fancy to each other, and fortunately for me, she was looking for a good player to help her become a Life Master. She knew of my local bridge acclaim, so we struck a deal. I was paid $5 a session to play with her. It was the start of a long relationship that, at times, was surreal. I came to care very much for Miriam, despite her foibles. She didn't have a clue about how to play bridge. Nevertheless, she was a fine woman and a good friend, and it was hard not to enjoy her as she provided surprise after surprise. Some of my strangest experiences at the table occurred sitting opposite Miriam.

Once, at a Regional in Lubbock, Miriam and I were playing in a Consolation Game. Most Open Pair events back then started with a qualifying session, and non-qualifiers (losers) played in this event if they didn't make it into the final. I remember that we were defending a suit contract and I led the king of a side suit. In those days most players had never heard of ace from ace-king, and Miriam followed with the ten. I continued with the ace of that suit and Miriam showed out. There were still some of that suit in dummy, and I led another one. Miriam discarded. When the hand was over, I politely asked, "Miriam, why didn't you trump?"

"Bobby," she said with a sigh, "I was too tired to trump."

That was my Miriam!

Miriam was a charming lady who loved life and was fun to be around, but she was the exact opposite of what a bridge player should be. For instance, she never once noticed a card that I played as a defender. If she was third hand, and I made an opening lead through the queen in dummy and she held the king-jack, she often played the king. I still yearn to wring the neck of the person who introduced her to the theory of 'third hand high'. However, every cloud has a silver lining. One problem I never experienced with Miriam was her getting endplayed, because she always stripped herself of aces and kings early in the hand.

Despite her lack of understanding of bridge, Miriam loved to play the game. She thought bridge was one of the most fun things she could do. One time at an NABC, certainly in a side game, Miriam and I had a 238 on a 156 average (76%). She had no clue that she had scored so well. In fact, she could have had just as much fun with a 46% game since she was totally oblivious to what went on around her.

There were times when Miriam and I experimented. When we played together, we announced to the opponents that we were playing an unusual system. *Unusual*, indeed! For example, if I opened 1♣, Miriam had a choice of bids — *five* bids... either 1◇, 2◇, 3◇, 4◇ or 5◇, depending on how many high-card points she had. The big decision would come later. We had auctions where Miriam responded to show an opening hand, I bid 3NT and she transferred to her six-card major. That way, I played every hand when the partnership bought the contract.

That system, of course, was not really fair to the opponents, but no one was policing the sport in those days. For example, if I opened a minimum 1♣ and Miriam bid only 1◇, showing a poor hand, I often psyched my rebid because I knew it was the opponents' hand. You can't get away with actions like that today, but remember, bidding was pretty primitive back then. Even though we announced what we were playing, the system was so ridiculous that it made the game a lottery. I did it, but I'm not proud of it and I wouldn't countenance it today. Bridge should not be played that way. Back then, however, I was more enthusiastic and ambitious than wise, and I needed some help playing with Miriam... all the help I could muster up!

I told Miriam when we played that she should *never* underlead an ace against a suit contract, but she didn't listen. On one occasion, she underled an ace in a suit and the trick was won in declarer's hand. Declarer then played trumps. Miriam, holding the ace of trumps and one or two others, jumped up with the trump ace, dropping my single-ton king, then cashed the ace of the suit she had underled on the go, beaming broadly.

"See, Bobby," she said, "you told me never to underlead an ace, but this time it didn't cost." She never saw my king of trumps. In fact, she usually determined who had won a particular trick by watching to see who led to the next one.

She rarely played a hand, but one time in first seat she held ten solid spades and three singletons. Since we were not playing Namyats (where an opening 4♦ bid shows a strong 4♠ hand), there wasn't much she could do but open 4♠. How could anyone blame her for that? I had no aces, so I went quietly. 4♠ was passed out. Her left-hand opponent led one ace, then another and tried to cash a second card in that suit. Miriam ruffed, but she still had a loser. All her singletons were low cards. Miriam ruffed the third trick with the ace of trumps and started running spades. It was obvious that she had started with ten spades and another card. I was dummy and playing against people I knew. They looked bewildered, as though to say, "Why are we wasting all this time?"

Miriam plowed on, another trump and another and another. Then one of Miriam's cards fell on the floor. I told her, and she picked it up. It turned out that it was from the discard pile — another trump. At Trick 13, Miriam still had two cards. She played the trump which she had picked up from the 'played' pile and the opponents discarded the ace and king of clubs in turn. Miriam then faced her final card, the ♣2.

I said, "It's good, Miriam."

She said with a look of true amazement, "It is?"

I said, "You don't see anything higher, do you?"

"Bobby," she said breathlessly, "is this what they call a squeeze?"

Just another routine +650 (though I scored it as +620!).

Another time, I was playing with Miriam at a tournament in Corpus Christi on a team with Moose and another woman comparable to Miriam (although admittedly, she would be pretty hard to clone). On one round, the opponents bid to 6♠ and Miriam, with a collection of kings and queens, doubled. Of course, they made it. Miriam enjoyed keeping score, although she didn't know what any of the odd scores were — such as 6♠ doubled, making — so she said, "Bobby, how much is that?" It was just another day at the office for me, but I was feeling a bit churlish over this particular result, so I looked at my watch and said "Twelve twenty-four". Miriam wrote it down without flinching. The opponents must have been equally unfamiliar with the scoring, because they didn't question it either. As we compared scores after the round, Moose came to our 'interesting' board.

"Plus 980," said Moose.

"Minus 1224," said Miriam.

Moose looked up in surprise, caught my eye, nodded and went back to totaling up the IMPs.

One day at the club in 1965, Miriam showed up early for her scheduled game with me. She had just achieved Life Master status in the ACBL and perhaps wanted to strut her stuff and be available for handshakes. Before any of the other regular patrons arrived, she confided in me.

"Bobby," she said, "Our San Antonio players are probably much better than those in other cities."

"What brings you to that conclusion?" I asked.

"Well," she replied, "since I became a Life Master, I thought I should play with some other people occasionally so I could help their game — but up until now, no one has taken me up on my offer."

I contained my initial reaction, bit my tongue, thought a moment and enthusiastically replied, "They will Miriam. Probably they are too embarrassed to ask for your help. Just give them time." She seemed encouraged by my remarks.

Miriam was my first real client, but she wasn't the only one. Bridge playing clients were on the rise. There was another lady from Shreveport, with whom I never played, who wore a hearing aid. There is an oft-told story about her untimely sequence of calls on one occasion that always makes me laugh — perhaps a bit from sympathy — because, who knows, one day it could happen to you, too! Playing in a pairs game, the woman opened the bidding with 3♣. The next person to bid was considering his hand when the opening bidder chimed in again with 5♣.

Everyone was looking at each other and considering what to do when she spoke once more: "Six clubs." She had made the first three bids at the table! It turned out that her hearing aid had been tuning in what was going on at other tables, and she thought she was participating in a very lively auction. Funny though it appeared at the time, I, more than most, can readily appreciate the frustration and embarrassment of having a hearing disability. Bidding boxes have gone a long way to prevent such hard-to-handle episodes.

I have had sessions with clients that left me counting the minutes until the game was over, and I don't know how some of the touring pros can do it day after day and night after night. I never went out on the trail and never wanted to get involved to such a degree. Moose and I played professionally so that we could pay the bills, but we didn't want to build our bridge careers on that kind of foundation.

I would like to share another memorable experience which I filed under 'All in a Day's Work'. After reading it, you will understand why, in good conscience, anonymity must be respected. I was attending Trinity University in San Antonio, teaching bridge and in the process of being drafted into the Army Reserve. My teaching schedule included a foursome of ladies. They were some of the wealthiest in San Antonio and among the *crème de la crème* of the city's high society. Their average age must have been early sixties while I was just a wee lad of twenty-one. We usually lunched at the exclusive San Antonio Country Club first and then the ladies would play the prepared hands I had brought along for the lesson. It was a ritual they seemed to enjoy — having several drinks both before and during lunch to fortify themselves for their afternoon of bridge. It went on for three or four years and hardly a week went by without a lesson.

One day I got a mysterious telephone call from one of the women — inviting me to her home for what I thought was going to be a private lesson. Never wanting to miss an opportunity to pick up another six bucks (the cost of one lesson), I hurriedly made my way to her house. The door was opened by her butler and I was ushered into a magnificent living room. The butler told me his mistress would be down shortly and to make myself comfortable (whatever that meant). He then disappeared!

I waited what seemed like an eternity, probably only ten minutes or so, when I noticed prominently displayed on the coffee table about a foot from my knees two books featuring the Kama Sutra. To save some of you a mad dash to your encyclopedia, let me fill you in. The Kama Sutra deals with Oriental methods of love-making and the many extraordinary secrets of satisfying women. As I pondered what to do next, my hostess appeared for the lesson — sauntering down a spiral staircase in a flowing negligee. Suddenly, it all became clear — instead of being the teacher, I was going to be playing the role of the student. Since a gentleman never tells, I won't either, but I guarantee you it was an afternoon I'll never forget.

Back to the real world and the world I understood. I knew early on that I had the ability to play at high levels in bridge, and I was lucky enough to be able to get some good partners and win some important events so that I could rise from the level of a hack to the status of a genuine player. Of course, I didn't always make the best decisions when it came to choosing partners and teammates, although some of it was dictated by financial need.

In the Spring of 1967, I passed up an opportunity to be on the team that eventually won the Vanderbilt Knockout. Jimmy Jacoby had invited me to be on the team that consisted of Lew Mathe, Ron Von der Porten, Mike Lawrence and Lew Stansby. Instead, after I had turned them down, Jim got Bobby Nail and proceeded to win the title. There was no pay involved, and I had received another offer to play professionally with Charles Goren — yes, that Charles Goren, who by then had slipped dramatically and was very near senility. My pro deal turned out to be lousy because the team wasn't very good and the pay wasn't all that much. Goren, the sponsor, was pretty much of a cheapskate. Shelling out took too much of a toll on his bank account as well as his pride.

Only a few months later, I played on another team with Goren in the Spingold Knockout at the Summer NABC in Montreal. It was Goren's last tournament, and he went out rather ignominiously. My teammates were Dan Morse, George Rosenkranz, Paul Hodge, John Gerber and Goren. In our second-round match, we played against a team that included Frank and Diana Schuld, a lovely couple from New York, who, although decent players, were very much the underdogs. Going into the fourth quarter of the match, we led by 70 IMPs. The Schulds tried early on to generate some swings, but they backfired and everyone at our table knew the final margin was going to be in three digits for sure. Diana and Frank were basically just throwing cards on the table. They wanted to get it over with — and who could blame them? We were floored when we finished the set and went back to compare. We won by only 9 IMPs.

We learned that Goren had been having trouble seeing, but also had just about bottomed out mentally as well. He had gone to the table half shaven and utterly disoriented. Kibitzers were actually crying as they saw him playing queens under kings and kings under aces. That session turned out to be his swan song — Charles H. Goren's final appearance at a bridge table. Gerber, the team captain, benched the famous player to shield him from further embarrassment. Later on during the tournament, he disappeared from the hotel and was found early one morning wandering around Montreal in the financial district, unaware of where he was. Fortunately he was spotted by Norman Kay who whisked him into a cab and escorted him back to the hotel and into the care of Harry Roth who was looking after him. Apparently, Charlie quietly slipped out of the room shortly after dawn while Roth was still sleeping and took off for parts unknown.

Goren is a legendary figure in bridge, but the truth be known, he was never considered a top flight player by his peers. His real gift was *salesmanship*. He was a handsome man, always well dressed, with a great booming voice and an imposing persona. His natural charisma made him a phenomenal promoter of bridge. At the table, his bidding was good, and he had fine judgment in competitive situations, but he was otherwise mediocre.

There are many wonderful Charlie Goren stories that circulated even during his heyday as the greatest promoter of bridge who ever lived.

One of his regular partners was Helen Sobel. Helen enjoyed a rather exciting existence. A native Philadelphian (as was Goren), she moved to New York, became one of the Radio City Musical Hall's legendary Rockettes and appeared in several movies, including *Animal Crackers* with the Marx Brothers. While backstage one day, another chorus girl taught her to play bridge to kill time between acts. Helen was a 'natural' and eventually became universally regarded as the greatest woman player of all time, a title to which, in my eyes, she still lays claim. One time she was playing in a tournament with Goren when one of her opponents, impressed by the gallery bursting with kibitzers which surrounded the table, turned to her and inquired, "How does it feel to be partnered by the world's greatest player?"

"I don't know," she fired back. "Why don't you ask Mr. Goren?"

However, had it not been for Charles H. Goren, 'Mr. Bridge' himself, who knows what any of us would be doing today — and, moreover, in which direction the game would have been steered. There is no doubt he shaped its destiny, and we are grateful to him for the ingenious insight and brilliant marketing which put the modern game of bridge on the map.

CHAPTER 4

THE BIRTH OF THE ACES

THE DISTRACTIONS OF GOREN'S DEMISE notwithstanding, I laid considerable groundwork for the formation of the Aces at the Montreal NABC. It's hard to pinpoint where the original idea for the Aces came from, but it is safe for history to recognize three people: Ira Corn, Dorothy Moore and Bobby Wolff.

As I told you in Chapter 1, the germ of the idea unquestionably was conceived in 1964. Ira went to New York to view the latter stages of the World Team Olympiad, in which the Italian Blue Team triumphed over a group of six US players. I hesitate to dub the US players a *team* as they represented the country strictly by virtue of their finish in the Pairs Trials as One-Two-Three, constituting automatic qualification. Incidentally, the Pairs Trials gave way to the Team Trials in 1969, a procedure which has continued to gain momentum over three and a half decades, definitely favoring sponsored teams. There is no doubt that cohesiveness is an important factor in any team's success. However, the present system of Team Trials has to recognize and confront a far more serious problem which will be dealt with later in this book — the agonizing dilemma of having a sponsor and his or her partner on the team.

The actual team in '64 were veterans Sam Stayman/Victor Mitchell and Robert Jordan/Arthur Robinson — with relative newcomers Bob Hamman/Don Krauss. Anyway, the front four, so to speak, were easily handled by the Marconi-inspired Italians in New York. Ira noted the way the Blue Team performed and began dreaming a dream — that the United States could put together a similar well-oiled machine and reclaim the world championship. Easier said than done!

Ira was not considering any of the issues presented by the prevailing method of team selection. His focus was zeroing in on how to get the Aces idea off the ground and he didn't have a clue where to start. That's where Dorothy Moore and I came in. Ira was a strictly social player. He met Dorothy through business — he chaired a company involved in acquisitions and for a period of time did very well.

At the Spring Nationals in St. Louis in 1963, Ira and Dorothy had won a Mixed Pairs event. This had the dual effect of tremendously enthusing Ira about the game and instilling in him a sense of confidence in Dorothy. That trust was well placed, particularly where bridge was concerned. Dorothy, a Texas native, was quite underrated as a player, in no small measure because she was a woman. She was, in fact, a very solid player. She and I had met many times at tournaments around Texas. She played professionally and was good at her trade. I first met Ira at the Summer Nationals in Chicago in 1965, where he was playing on a team with Dorothy and my wife Betsey in the Spingold. However, it was not until the 1966 Pittsburgh Fall NABC that the Aces venture seriously came under discussion.

The idea was singular, for sure. It was to be the world's first full-time professional team. There were, of course, many professional players at the time, but the concept Ira was promoting — a squad of players whose *only job* was to be part of a team — had never been attempted. Interestingly, although Ira was a successful businessman, he didn't have nearly as much money as people conjectured. That worked to his advantage, of course. Being considered a man of considerable wealth opened many doors for Ira that otherwise might have been slammed shut had the truth been known.

The reality of the situation was that Ira enjoyed the challenge of putting the team together, and he was attracted by the glory and acceptance that would be his — should the project succeed. I recall a conversation with him after the Aces had been formed that typified his outlook. We were at his home, talking business, when he surprised me with a question.

"You play backgammon, don't you?" Ira said to me.

"Yes," I said.

"Why don't we write a book about how to play backgammon?" Ira said.

"That's an interesting idea," I allowed.

"Well," he continued, "you know enough about it, don't you?"

"Maybe I do," I said. "I'm certainly not one of the best backgammon players, but I could get some advice, and I might be able to write a book."

"I want my name on the book," Ira said.

"But," I countered, "you don't even know how to set up the pieces."

"Bobby," Ira grinned, "you don't understand — *that's what makes it so great!*"

Ira's view was that people who wrote about the stock market or World War II or hundreds of other subjects didn't really know diddley squat about them, but they were still writing their articles and books *in spite of that!*

Once I signed on with Ira to help form the Aces, it was necessary for me to leave San Antonio. It really wasn't a difficult decision and actually I jumped at the opportunity. For starters, by 1966 I was pretty frustrated in San Antonio. I was still begrudgingly attending law school — mostly because my father wanted me to — and not far away from taking the bar exam, which seemed like an exercise in futility as I had no desire or intent ever to practice law. My daughter, Wendy, was born in March of 1966, which increased the financial pressure on Betsey and me. Between law school and trying to run the bridge club with Joe Musumeci, I was going pretty much non-stop from 6 a.m. until after midnight every day.

My typical day was to arise at six, head for a café for breakfast, review my law book cases while I ate, attend law school from 7 a.m. to 11 a.m., then go on to the bridge club. I had to be there to greet the rubber bridge players and to begin my classes. There were 'playing lessons' with several clients. At one point I had ten women and three men in my stable. I had doubled my regular club game fee to $10 for 'Masterpoint Night'. In those days, there was one special game where you could earn a whole masterpoint for winning. It wasn't anything like the grotesque masterpoint inflation we see today.

Moose and I had opened our bridge club in 1960, operating it at three different sites over the years. By the time 1966 rolled around, I could scarcely say where the time had gone but one thing was certain — I didn't have a lot of money to show for it. I never took the bar exam, and, if I wasn't going to practice law with my father and my brother, I was going to have to make it *somehow* in the bridge world. Despite my outer confidence, my future in bridge was pretty much of a question mark. Perhaps Ira and the Aces were the break the Puppeteer sent my way. (Bear with me for now — I'll explain my Puppeteer theory of the universe later in the book!)

The Aces experiment seemed to represent an unparalleled bridge opportunity (if it actually went on to succeed) and I gratefully seized it. I suppose if the Aces idea had failed, I would have tried my luck as a touring pro, although that life did not appeal to me and, by choice, was not an option I wanted to consider.

Once we decided to move ahead with the Aces project, the question was whom we were going to recruit for players. I was one. Jim Jacoby — already conveniently situated in Dallas — was another. To Ira's way of thinking, we needed merely one more person because he was planning to play himself. Needless to say, that was not what I had in mind. Despite the love for him the team shared, Ira could be most exasperating at times. And despite all his positive attributes, including his incredibly upbeat nature, he was never going to become a good enough player.

As noted earlier, I firmly believe that, with very few exceptions, you must start very early in life to develop into a great player — the kind who can play at the world level and have a chance to win. However, there were others like the great theoretician Al Roth, who believed that your only chance to get to be a top-flight player was to be decimated at the rubber bridge games in New York, getting your brains bashed in for higher stakes than you could afford. I am proof that you don't need that kind of training ground, but the basic idea is sound — you've got to play against top players to become one. At any rate, we did finally settle on recruiting five besides Ira.

Our initial thrust was discouraging — all of our first-round draft choices turned us down, notably Chuck Burger, Sami Kehela, Bob Hamman and Eddie Kantar. Burger was actually my first choice. An attorney living in Michigan, Chuck was — and still is — an absolutely terrific player, with his feet on the ground. Chuck didn't want to leave his law practice and move to Dallas for what seemed like an oddball experiment. Similarly, Kehela — one of Canada's all-time great players, who had a fine partnership with Eric Murray — didn't want to leave home. Hamman thought the plan had no chance of success and wasn't interested. In Montreal, we tried to recruit Eddie Kantar, who at the time was playing frequently with Hamman in Southern California and didn't want to break up a partnership that was looking pretty good. Two players who did buy into the idea in Montreal were Mike Lawrence and Billy Eisenberg, both of whom were shocked and delighted to hear that someone actually wanted to pay them to play. It was a new concept indeed.

When we finally got the team assembled, the Aces were yours truly, Jim Jacoby, Eisenberg, Lawrence and, until we 'fired' him, Ira. Our 'pro' lineup was Eisenberg/Lawrence and Jacoby/Wolff. We still needed another player, and Lawrence, whom we had imported from California, wanted us to hire another San Francisco-area resident, a talented Canadian-born player by the name of Hugh Ross. In later years, Hugh was to enjoy three wins in the Bermuda Bowl, two of them as my teammate. Another candidate was Bobby Goldman, a quiet, young, little-known player from Philadelphia. The other person being considered was Dan Morse, a solid expert player from Houston. I played with him in Montreal and in the 1967 Team Trials in Atlantic City and he has been my partner in major events since Hamman and I went our separate ways in 1998.

Although I liked Dan a lot and it was no secret that I preferred him to Goldman, the decision was not mine alone. In the end,

Eisenberg prevailed, and we did decide to go with Goldman. However, adding Bobby to the Aces turned out to be great strategy. Of all the Aces, Goldman worked the hardest. He taught himself how to program a computer and, using time Ira purchased for the team on some giant machine, he wrote a random deal generator and learned to use the computer competently for hand analysis. He was a dynamo, and very serious about his role on the Aces. He was not a naturally gifted player, but he made up for that in spades with a work ethic that put the rest of us — especially Jim Jacoby and me — to shame.

Jim and I did very little to improve the Aces, with our 'go as you please' bidding system — something loosely based on Standard American — and slack work habits. Jim and I won our share of Regionals, but we had limits because we weren't ready for really good competition. At one point, Edgar Kaplan journeyed to Dallas from New York and helped us learn and adopt a modern version of the Neapolitan Club, pretty much what Hamman and I went on to play for more than twenty-five years.

One advantage Jim and I had was that I could read him like a book. We weren't blatantly exchanging signals or anything close to that, but I could always tell by Jim's demeanor whether he had a good hand or a bad hand and whether he liked the way the defense was going. I'm not proud of this, and I believe that today, through the use of screens and bidding boxes, we have managed in large degree to eliminate antics such as eye contact and body language from serious bridge competition. Oh, but how much easier it is to play when you know what your partner has! In terms of ethics and playing bridge the way it should be played, Bob Hamman is the all-time best. He is absolutely impossible to read. His demeanor gives away nothing.

On February 1, 1968, the assembled team moved to Dallas where Ira owned a large two-family dwelling. He lived on the ground floor and Betsey, Wendy and I enjoyed a lovely apartment on the second story. The other Aces resided elsewhere but were available whenever we needed to get together. In the beginning, I spent many hours wondering whether I had made a wise decision to get involved in this extremely tenuous venture.

Bridge players, as we all know, can be ornery — present company included. At one point, well after we got started, Ira sent Eisenberg and Goldman to a shrink to see if they could get their partnership act together. What was going on was that Goldman was a very meticulous, disciplined bridge player. In those days, Eisenberg frequently liked to shake and bake, doing what turned him on regardless of whether or not it was part of the system he and Goldman were playing. This drove Goldman crazy, and eventually Goldman switched partners, playing with Lawrence instead.

Of course, Goldman could be difficult, too. An incident at Ira's house looms large in my memory. Obviously, Ira had invested heavily in the Aces, but he also had raised money from other sources. One night, after an Aces practice session, Ira instructed the team members to don their jackets because he had accepted an invitation on behalf of all the Aces to visit the home of Marian and Lenny Schaen. The Schaens were investors, and they were hosting a get-together for some people who wanted to meet the team.

"I'm not going," Goldman firmly proclaimed.

Ira was nonplussed and it took him a moment to recover from this unexpected act of rebellion.

"But the Schaens have invested $100,000 in the team," appealed Ira.

"I don't care how much they invested," Goldman resounded defiantly. "This wasn't part of the deal. I'm not going."

Ira chomped on his cigar for a few more minutes, and I thought we were headed for major trouble, but he let it pass. Goldman did not attend the party.

In the beginning, it seemed situations like this were constantly popping up, and I thought there was serious danger our team wasn't going to make it to mid-year. However, most problems righted themselves when Moose was hired as our coach. No more fooling around. No more go-as-you-please for Wolff and Jacoby. Although Moose underwent considerable scrutiny from our team initially, he impressed us with his no-nonsense approach and gained our respect. He knew his limitations and his responsibilities... but most importantly, he knew his place. *He didn't try to tell us how to play bridge.* His primary job was to adjust our work habits and see that everyone toed the line. Ira loved it and, as the Aces began to make their mark on the bridge scene, the players came to realize Moose was an integral force in the Aces' success.

At the 1968 Summer NABC in Minneapolis, Goldman and Eisenberg won the Life Master Pairs, and Jacoby and I were second. Even more momentous — at the Spring NABC earlier that year in New York, the Aces had won the Men's Board-a-Match Teams, playing together for the very first time.

Don't think that this team victory didn't catch Hamman's eye — after he had turned up his nose at the Aces because he thought the cast wasn't good enough. There were also two different occasions when the Aces had journeyed to Los Angeles and both times whacked a top L.A. bridge team including Lew Mathe, Meyer Schleiffer and Hamman himself. In fact, our strong showing made such a huge impression on Hamman that by January of the following year he had succumbed and was prepared to jump upon our bandwagon. By then, Ira had been thoroughly convinced that we couldn't win if he insisted on playing, so our lineup was now Eisenberg/Goldman, Hamman/Lawrence, Jacoby/Wolff.

The Aces were on their way!

CHAPTER 5

THE DEATH OF THE ACES AND THEREAFTER

GETTING BEATEN AT TABLE TENNIS in the Sharlack home as a kid impacted my bridge career immeasurably. Meeting and competing against the best players around taught me a valuable disciplinary lesson which has served me well with the pasteboards over the years. I don't think I ever won a game at Meyer's house. In fact, the scores were usually on the order of 21-4 or 21-5 against me. Playing against outstanding players, however, made me pretty tough when I took on kids my own age (eleven or twelve). It was a marvelous training ground — preparing me for what lay ahead.

One Saturday afternoon in November of 1944, I found myself in the gymnasium at the San Antonio YMCA, facing a young chap named Virgil Steele, Jr. in the finals of the state table tennis tournament. Virgil was a terrific player, perhaps a little older and bigger, but at one point I was ahead, 20-15, in the first set of a best two-of-three match. At that point, my father and brother entered the gym to watch, and I spotted them. I'm not sure what happened, but I lost, 24-22, in that game and lost the next one, 21-16. It was over. I don't remember if I got nervous when my family arrived, but I do remember promising myself after the match that I would never again let the pressure of the moment get to me.

You may think it's unusual for a twelve-year-old to recognize such a situation and make that vow as I did. However, it is now well over sixty years since that incident in the gym — and I have been true to my word. To this day, I never get nervous about bridge games or matches.

I always try to do my best but bridge competition to me has never been a matter of life and death. I play hard, whether it's a routine duplicate, a practice match, a meaningless exhibition game or a world championship final. Obviously, I don't always play my best — and, admittedly, there have been times when I've played badly — but it is never from lack of effort. And win or lose, life goes on.

I say all this as a means of imparting to you how I was looking at life as things seemed to be coming together for me as a bridge player. Yes, the Aces had won the world championship in 1970, and each of us had seen our individual stature in the bridge world climb a notch or two. We won again in 1971 in Taiwan, and it was a much more gratifying victory. For one thing, the field was much stronger. For another, we defeated a super team (France) in the final. It felt good to be a world champion for the second time.

Back in Dallas, however, change was in the wind. Right after we won in Taiwan, Billy Eisenberg and the Aces parted ways. His partnership with Hamman had gone south and he was yearning to get back to his life on the West Coast as he had not been enamored with Dallas from the start. In fact, in the final against France, Hamman and Eisenberg played only one segment (16 boards). Billy departed for California more or less happily. Not long after that, Lawrence also went back to Berkeley, although he remained part of the team.

After Taiwan, the Aces' office remained open, but things were in a state of flux. We were busy with various little projects such as rubber bridge tournaments and other minor promotions, but Hamman didn't have a partner for the rest of the year. Our lineup was Jacoby/Wolff, Goldman/Lawrence — and Bob. In early 1972, I played some with Hamman, but mostly my partner was Jacoby. The shakeup of the lineup and eventual disbanding of the Aces, as people knew them, deeply affected the lives of several players as they took off in different directions.

Though Billy was no longer an Ace, it is worthy of note that 'Broadway Billy' went on to lead an enchanted life and enjoyed the many roles he was destined to assume along the way. His friendship with Hugh Hefner (of *Playboy* fame) provided an exciting lifestyle few have experienced. Known as a terrific raconteur and replete with charm, wholesome boyish good looks, personality and an impish sense of humor, Billy's *savoir faire* opened many doors.

Permit me another digression to talk about the late Jim Jacoby, my partner on the Aces for over four years. Jim was a 'people person' — good looking, popular, fun-loving, highly intelligent and blessed with a self-deprecating sense of humor. He was my friend. For just about all of his bridge life, Jim suffered in the gargantuan shadow of his father, the great Oswald Jacoby. I don't know this for a fact, but my vibes tell me that Ozzie, perhaps unconsciously, imparted to Jim the notion that he was a good bridge player — but would never be quite as good as his father. Ozzie also lionized the stars of the day to his son, with the result that Jim was always intimidated by them, or indeed by anyone he considered his superior. Ozzie's tremendous persona plus his obvious conception of Jim's game took a devastating toll on his son. There was no denying this. Jim did great against palookas, but he tended not to measure up against the top players.

In the early years of our partnership, Jim and I were undisciplined and not very effective, but things brightened up when we started playing a system similar to the Neapolitan Club. He also benefited from the discipline Moose enforced upon the Aces. In 1971, Jim played the best bridge of his life — better than he ever had before and, sadly, better than ever would again. I played a lot with Ozzie, and I can tell you, with unyielding conviction, that Jim, in 1971, played better than Ozzie *ever* did, although you would have had a tough time convincing Jim. Being relegated to the role of Ozzie's son and trying to follow in his dad's legendary footsteps negatively affected his game.

There were a couple of turning points in the unusual saga of Jim Jacoby. One was in Stockholm in the 1970 Bermuda Bowl. In the final, the Taiwanese had surprised everyone by winning the first set, so it was important for us to pick up some momentum in the second.

This was the tenth deal of the second segment.

Dealer: South
Vul: East-West

	♠ A Q 2	
	♡ K 8	
	◇ 3 2	
	♣ A Q 10 9 5 2	

♠ 8 5 4 3		♠ 10 9 7 6
♡ Q 10 2	N	♡ 9 7 3
◇ Q 10 9 5	W E	◇ A 8 7 6 4
♣ J 4	S	♣ 8

	♠ K J	
	♡ A J 6 5 4	
	◇ K J	
	♣ K 7 6 3	

In an uncontested auction with Jacoby as South, the bidding proceeded:

North	South
Wolff	Jacoby
	1NT
2◇[1]	2♡
3♣	4♣
6NT[2]	

1. Forcing Stayman
2. In an effort to 'rightside' the final contract, I bypassed the best contract of 6♣.

West led a spade, and Jim won it in his hand and rattled off six rounds of clubs. West tossed three spades and the ◇10. It was up to Jim to interpret this card. No one flags an ace unless he's trying some kind of double bluff — messing with your mind. More likely, he was trying to help his partner in his discarding, say if he had the ◇K. The ◇10 would let East know it was all right to throw his diamonds in case he had to keep four hearts to the jack.

So Jim had to work out what was going on in diamonds. He studied the dummy a little bit longer and cashed the ♡K. His troubles would have been over if the queen had been singleton — but it wasn't. Then he played a diamond from dummy. East followed low and Jim went up with the king. When it held, he had his twelve tricks and the slam — and a huge boost in confidence. I could almost see the transformation taking place at the table. Lesser players would have guessed wrong. All of a sudden, Jim was confident, and when he was confident he could play a helluva game of bridge. We went on to win that set with ease, and before we knew it we were world champions.

Jim continued to play well during 1972 and then reached the second turning point in his bridge career — at least from my perspective. We had gone to Bal Harbour, Florida (just north of Miami) for the World Bridge Olympiad and had put together a squad for the World Master Mixed Teams, which preceded the main event. Our team was me, playing with Betsey, my wife; Jim playing with Heitie Noland, a long-time friend and client of his; and Bobby Goldman partnered by Nancy Alpaugh. We got into the event at the last minute. In fact, the directors reopened entries to accommodate us, with the stipulation that we had to find another team to enter so that there would still be an even number in the field.

I have to admit that winning that event remains one of my biggest thrills in bridge. Not only did we win from the underdog position — no one gave us a chance — but we needed a good last round to take the championship, and we delivered. It was a magnificent win for Betsey, Heitie and Nancy and a great start to the tournament for the Aces — which at that point was Jim and me, Goldman-Lawrence and Hamman playing with Paul Soloway.

Following the Mixed Teams, the Aces made it to the final of the main event — the World Bridge Olympiad. Our opponents were the famous Italian Blue Team, out of retirement once more. We were up against Garozzo, Belladonna, Forquet — the whole crew — with a chance for a third straight World Championship. We also had a point to prove: that we were not flashes in the pan, good enough to win only if the Blue Team wasn't around.

Our captain was Lee Hazen, ACBL's legal counsel of many years and a legendary bridge figure himself. Hazen started Jim and me with Hamman and Soloway. There was only one problem with that scenario: with this important match on the line, Jim had stayed up all night drinking and playing backgammon. He always carried his backgammon set with him. It was his trademark. He loved to play and he excelled at it, but the night before this important match was not the time to indulge himself. As I headed for bed about midnight after our semifinal match against Canada, I spotted Jim going out the front door of the hotel with his backgammon set. I was told later that he did not go to sleep that night.

Predictably, the next day against the Italians, Jim was all over the place. We stunk, and the Aces finished the first set down 42-7 to the Italians. The Blue Team still had their reputation, but this was a beatable team, and we had tossed them a significant advantage for no good reason. Hazen, apparently oblivious to all this, pulled Hamman and Soloway after the first set and left us in! We didn't do any better. Jim and I should have been benched after the first set, but Hazen missed the call. It was grim.

Finally, Hazen took Jim and me out, and we didn't play again until the last of the six sets. By then, the contest was decided. The other four had mounted a valiant, though short-lived, comeback midway through the match, and ultimately fell back again when the Blue Team asserted itself.

Looking back, I feel that Bal Harbour was the day Jim's bridge career died. I felt that he never really played competitive bridge again after that, although our team — invited as the defending champions — did make it to the final of the Bermuda Bowl the next year in Guaruja,

Brazil. We were absolutely crushed by the Italians, 333-205. It was a total embarrassment.

From there, Jim went back to the Regional circuit, where he could reign as king. He once told me he always liked to go down an hour before game time when he had won the previous day — he liked to call it the 'Jacoby Strut' — so that he could be seen and enjoy the handshakes. He won a lot of Regionals playing against lesser opposition, and he raked in the masterpoints, but he did not enjoy the respect from many of the top players which every bridge expert yearns. It was sad, really. For the next fifteen years he was not asked to join any important teams. Even the fact that he was on the only US team to win the World Bridge Olympiad (in 1988) didn't make a difference. Jim was overlooked by the other top players, even at the Regional level. It hurt... it had to hurt. In the end, as much as I hate to say it, Jim Jacoby had fallen on hard times at the bridge table.

In 1990, partly for old times' sake, but also because Jim could be fun to be around and was a friend, I made some dates to play bridge with him — first in the Cap Gemini in the Netherlands, followed shortly thereafter by the London *Sunday Times* Invitational Pairs tournament. Both usually took place in January. What I discovered in those two tournaments with Jim left me saddened even further. We were about average in Holland and below average in London. There was no sign of the confident, expert player I remembered from 1971.

I recall one hand in particular from the *Sunday Times* tournament. We were playing against Gabriel Chagas and Marcelo Branco, when I picked up

♠ 6 ♡ A 6 5 ◇ A Q 4 3 ♣ Q J 8 5 4

I opened 1◇ and Chagas, on my left, jumped to 2♠. The only way I can describe what happened next is to say that Jim went out to lunch. He hemmed and hawed and finally passed. Of course, the natural thing to do with my hand on that auction was to double, but after all that action (or lack of it), there was no way in good conscience I was going to do that. So I passed, and we beat it four tricks. Jim had a 14-point hand with five spades, and he was thinking about whether to pass and hope for me to reopen with a double — or just to go straight to 3NT.

After the session, Jim asked why I hadn't balanced, and I lit into him. I couldn't believe he didn't understand the ethical dilemma he had created for me by hesitating and then passing. After he cogitated that long, he had to *do* something — *anything* but pass, so as not to punish me and place me in a no-win situation. I had been campaigning far and wide for improved ethics, especially in situations like this. Perhaps he didn't realize the consequences of his slow pass. I guess he had missed the speeches, or maybe he just wanted to play the old way, where people 'hesitated' to the right spot and no one said anything. I didn't know what was behind his action, but I didn't want any part of it. Balancing in this situation would have been against everything I have always preached against and believed in.

Jim and I had made a date to play in the World Open Pairs in Geneva in 1990, but after the tournaments in Holland and London, I broke the date. Near the end, Bob and I would often see Jim when we were playing in major team events. He hovered like a vulture, obviously rooting for the other team, and he would needle Bob when he got the chance. They had become friendly at one point when Jim started dropping by Bob's office to play backgammon for high stakes.

Bob and I won the Spingold Knockout Teams in Chicago in 1989. Later on, a friend sent me a series of bridge columns by Jacoby who had taken over his dad's column which was syndicated by the Newspaper Enterprise Association. For a whole week, Jim delighted in featuring hands from the Spingold — all highlighting mistakes by Bob and me. Jim had changed, or perhaps his tailspin had changed him. I cherished and shared many lighter moments of success and glory with him, and I prefer to remember the delightful Jim Jacoby of happier days.

Jim died in 1991, ironically within a few weeks of the death of Heitie Noland, his steadiest client for years. Jim thought he had pulled a muscle in his back, and he went to see a doctor. He was sent to the hospital for some tests, but he died of a heart attack during the procedure. It turned out that he was riddled with cancer, so the heart attack may have been a blessing.

Every player in every sport dreams of winning a world title, or at least getting to the big dance. Some think that becoming a world champion will change their lives, and in some cases that's true. For professional athletes, the endorsements often follow the title, as do new and bigger contracts. In my world, the two championships didn't seem to change things a whole lot. After winning the Bermuda Bowl in 1970 and 1971, the members of the Aces were regarded more highly in the bridge world than they once had been, but other than that the titles didn't really do anything significant for me (nor, I suspect, for any of the others).

What I worried about most at the time was making a living, and the outlook seemed bleaker each day in regard to the Aces as a team being able to earn a steady enough income for me or anyone else. My concerns became a realization pretty soon after we won our second title. (Incidentally, it may be of interest that the average annual salary of the original Aces back in the late sixties and early seventies was $12,000 with the unmarried players receiving somewhat less — a pittance compared to today's professional market.)

In early 1972, Ira announced that the well had run dry and he was officially closing the Aces' office. The paychecks would become a thing of the past. That didn't mean, by the way, that we were all heading for the unemployment line. For some time, we all had been developing different sources of income. Bob was running an insurance business (at one time, early in the Aces' history, it was called the Wolff-Hamman Insurance Agency), Goldman was doing a lot of teaching and Jacoby had returned to the pro circuit. Eisenberg was gone and Lawrence had been back in Berkeley for months, although he remained a part of the team. Soloway, also a member of the Aces for a time, had never lived in Dallas. In the fall of 1972, I went to work for Michigan General, Ira's company, and I ended up staying until 1981. Although we weren't being paid to play as the Aces, any team that included Bob and me was known as the Aces for some time after the paychecks stopped.

My partnership with Hamman started in 1972. Soloway, no longer being paid by Ira, had no incentive to continue with Bob. Paul was very active as a professional, was much in demand and had made other engagements. Jim had announced that he was returning to the circuit, so Bob and I were both free. Although we had played a few times previously, our partnership did not officially kick off until the Fall NABC in Lancaster in 1972 (we played together in the Reisinger with clients and were not impressive).

Alas, the Dallas Aces were no more. However, their talents and the groundbreaking foray into professional bridge were recognized. With the exception of Mike Lawrence, all of us (including Ira) have been inducted into the Hall of Fame. For personal reasons, Mike has declined to be placed on the ballot, although it is my opinion he would have made it hands down the first time he was nominated.

Life was always interesting working for Ira and, even after the Aces were no longer on the payroll, he still played when he could and occasionally sponsored teams. He also enjoyed the political aspects of bridge. Ira had been elected as First Alternate to the ACBL Board of Directors from District 16 in 1972, so when John Gerber resigned from the District 16 position in 1972, Ira took his place. I can't prove it, but I think it's possible, more likely probable, that Ira made some financial arrangement with Gerber to step aside and make room for him. We'll never know.

Ira was elected to a full term in the early '70s and served on the Board until 1981. One of Ira's campaigns for re-election was something of a turning point for me. One day in the early summer of 1978, Ira called me into his office at the Michigan General building. "I need your help," he told me, referring to the pending election to pick the District 16 Representative to the ACBL Board of Directors. Ira had been re-elected a couple of times with no problem. This year he was being challenged by a high-profile opponent — one Walter Jenkins, an Austin travel agent who was a former associate of the late President, Lyndon B. Johnson.

Jenkins was a frail man who appeared somewhat battle-worn. He had an attractive, vivacious wife — always an asset. Walter wasn't an exceptional player, but he had enough money to hire some pros, so there were influential players in his corner. One of them, Barry Hagedorn, of Houston, was no fan of Ira's. Hagedorn, who lived in Dallas during the Aces' formation, had wanted to be on the team and resented the fact that Ira never considered him. Hagedorn, therefore, was pleased to try to unseat the great Ira Corn. There were others with similar sentiments. There were few people who were neutral about Ira.

Jenkins was pushing hard to get the necessary votes, promising all kinds of incentives to secure the support of the wide variety of factions you would expect to find in a state as large as Texas. For example, despite the fact that tournament directors in the state were prohibited by ACBL rules from being involved in the political process, Jenkins was promising the TDs that if they supported his candidacy, he would ensure they got their hands on some special coupons that would make them money whenever they traveled to tournaments.

The election process for the ACBL Board, by the way, does not involve a vote amongst the membership. The electors are members of the various Unit Boards, with the electoral votes of each Board weighted mathematically according to the number of ACBL members in the Unit. In other words, District 16 might have 50 total votes. A smaller Unit within the District might get two of those votes, a larger Unit, 12. If there are six members of a Unit Board and that Unit's vote total is two, each Board Member's vote is equal to one-third of a vote in the District. As you will see, this became very important in the latter stages of this curious campaign.

Things were so bad for Ira that even he recognized that his re-election chances were just about zero. It was at that point he summoned my help. I believed we could salvage the election for him, but I may have been the only person with that outlook. The only option I saw was to hit the road. I visited Units in Tyler, in northeast Texas; in San Antonio, where I was still known as the hometown boy who made good; in Houston, where Jenkins seemed to have the election sewn up. I even went to Harlingen, in the Rio Grande valley.

I told everyone who would listen that I thought Jenkins was a fine fellow, but that Ira, with his business experience and long service to the District, was better. "If you vote for Walter Jenkins," I told them, "you will be missing out." I found that my stature as a bridge player gave me tremendous clout. People listened to me, and they respected what I had to say. I also discovered that speaking out for another person or for a principle can and will always make enemies.

For example, I was outraged to find that tournament directors, despite clearly spelled-out rules against it, were actively campaigning for Jenkins. I've never been good at pussyfooting and I made no secret to the ACBL of my dismay concerning Jenkins' promises of additional perks for the tournament directors and their defiant campaigning for him. Of course, word leaked out to the directors, and they wound up hating my guts. Over the years since then I've had a number of administrative confrontations with the TD fraternity. The result is that there is still a lot of animosity towards me today among TDs, especially from those old-timers who remember being thwarted in an effort to get their own way.

That's unfortunate, but that's who I am. What you see is what you get! It distresses me when someone makes a pretense of caring about something he or she really despises. In many situations, I may not have been right, but in my heart, I thought I was. I've never been beholden to anyone, and even later when I sat on the Board of Directors, I never voted for someone's measure for the sole reason that he or she wanted me to. If it was good on merit, I voted for it. Otherwise, I was not supportive and as far as I was concerned, the subject was closed. I do not believe in the reciprocation process — you scratch my back, I'll scratch yours.

Anyway, the trips all over the state paid off. Ira went from having almost no votes to having just enough. The way the voting was done (where each eligible person's vote was but a fraction of his Unit's vote share), there were bound to be fractions at the end. In the final tally, Ira came out ahead of Jenkins by less than a tenth of a vote. I further angered some of the Memphis staff by dashing to ACBL Headquarters to be there when the votes were counted. When Richard Goldberg, the CEO at the time who was personally above suspicion and beyond reproach, asked what I was doing there, I was brutally honest. "If the ACBL won't enforce rules about tournament directors campaigning," I retorted, "how do I know they're going to give an honest count in the election? I'm here to help see that the voting is done in the proper manner and assure that Big Brother is watching."

Sure enough, Ira won by an incredibly small margin — but now another problem arose. The election was to have taken place between certain dates — I believe August 15th was the first official date — and it was determined that the Tyler Unit Board had voted on August 14th. Furthermore, after they had voted, Jenkins somehow got to them and now some of the Board members wanted to change their minds after the fact. Jenkins' lawyer wanted all the votes (most of them for Ira) discounted. What a mess! The issue eventually went before the full ACBL Board, which voted to uphold the early Tyler vote and thus Ira's margin.

That was my first real experience with making enemies, but I've never been good at ignoring injustice or wrongdoing and pretending it doesn't exist. When the whole episode started, just about everyone liked me. During and after the campaign, lots of them made 180-degree turns. Through the years, more people have added their names to that list. It's not something I want, but I refuse to back down when I believe I'm right. A quiet, peaceful existence in my old age was not in the cards for me. Because I want things to change for the better, I have been willing to do whatever it takes to get there and I have the scars to prove it.

CHAPTER 6 REFLECTIONS

BEING A MEMBER OF THE DALLAS Aces was a fortuitous experience for me, and though the togetherness of the team was rather short-lived, it afforded many unique experiences that would not ordinarily have come my way. My exposure to the real celebrity world is worth relating. I would like to share some one-of-a-kind vignettes, mostly from the seventies, which I will always fondly remember.

Ira was quite resourceful and through his dynamic public-relations person, Jean Carpenter, had secured a daily syndicated bridge column appropriately entitled *The Aces on Bridge*. Upon Ira's death in 1982, I purchased the rights to the column and changed the byline from Ira Corn to Bobby Wolff. Some twenty-five years later, it still enjoys the popularity that Ira introduced.

Every Tuesday in the column, we tried to feature a deal played by a celebrity personality. In order to get actual deals, Ira conveniently arranged to have a Sunday brunch at his house. The timing was to accommodate road show attractions who loved bridge and would agree to accept invitations to brunch when their shows were passing through Dallas. Big name stars such as Phyllis Diller and Meredith Baxter were two of the 'fun' people who accepted Ira's invitation; their guest appearances encompassed a three-hour bridge session which followed an outstanding specially catered Sunday brunch *chez* Corn.

George Burns was another of the famed entertainers who accepted. One day I had the pleasure of playing with him as my partner against Ira and Charlie Weed. Charlie was in charge of Mergers and Acquisitions at Michigan General — Ira's put-together multimillion-dollar conglomerate. That particular afternoon playing with George was special, primarily because of one incredibly great bridge defense directed by George. It was rather spontaneous, which made it even more memorable. Our opponents had bid a game. The actual auction was:

West	North	East	South
Wolff	Weed	Burns	Corn
		pass	1◇
pass	1♡	dbl	3◇
pass	3♠	pass	4◇
pass	5◇	all pass	

From George's vantage point with dummy on his right, he could see:

```
        dummy
        ♠ Q J 5 3
        ♡ A Q J 6
        ◇ 6 2
        ♣ 9 8 3          Burns
        ┌───────┐        ♠ K 10 8 6
        │   N   │        ♡ 7 3
        │ W   E │        ◇ A 5
        │   S   │        ♣ A 7 6 5 2
        └───────┘
```

I led the club queen. George overtook with the ace and Ira's king came tumbling down. What next? After about ten to fifteen seconds, George came up with the only defense to beat the contract by leading a heart into dummy's AQJ6. Declarer won it in his hand with the king and led the king of diamonds. George won his ace and without a moment's hesitation, persisted with his original line of defense, leading his other heart — and he did it for the right reason.

The entire deal was:

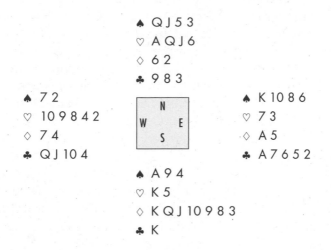

```
                    ♠ Q J 5 3
                    ♡ A Q J 6
                    ◊ 6 2
                    ♣ 9 8 3
♠ 7 2                                   ♠ K 10 8 6
♡ 10 9 8 4 2          N                 ♡ 7 3
◊ 7 4           W           E           ◊ A 5
♣ Q J 10 4            S                 ♣ A 7 6 5 2
                    ♠ A 9 4
                    ♡ K 5
                    ◊ K Q J 10 9 8 3
                    ♣ K
```

When the club king fell at Trick 1, George realized that the declarer had denied both three hearts and four spades with his 4◊ rebid and, since he dropped the king of clubs at Trick 1, his hand had to be almost exactly what the auction purported it to be (including Kx of hearts). George's imagination and arithmetic ability had enabled him to conjure up the winning defense.

He thereby killed declarer's heart entry (not allowing him to pitch his two losing spades on dummy's two good hearts while trumps were still out because George would ruff the third heart). Declarer could no longer make the minor-suit game. If declarer won the second heart and took the marked spade finesse, George would refuse to cover (so as not to create an entry to dummy with the jack), and he could not just pitch the other spade loser because George would have foiled his plan by ruffing the third heart. With any other defense, the game would have succeeded.

When friends ask me what kind of player George Burns was, this deal will always allow me to answer with no reservation, "A very good one and someone who could have been a top player if he could have devoted the necessary time it took to do it." However, his love for show business and his many decades of success and popularity triumphed over his fascination for the game.

Believe it or not, this hand gave me quite a thrill as it focused on a 'sometime' bridge player who could use detective work and counting to his advantage with the best of them and gave him the opportunity to show off his skills in front of the right audience. It was obvious George got a big kick out of the afternoon, playing with the big boys.

Furthermore, after the session George, believe it or not, asked me for my autograph. I was so thrilled by his gesture — George Burns asking *me*, Bobby Wolff, for *my* autograph — that it caught me off guard. I am appalled to this day that I did not have the presence of mind and courtesy to ask for his in return. I suppose I lack those social graces as that kind of thought doesn't even enter my mind, but every time I think of George or see his image on TV, this hand flashes before me as I recall the expertise of his lightning fast analysis. *Oh, God!* What fond memories I have of that delightful afternoon with George Burns as my partner.

George's California schedule afforded him the luxury for many years of playing rubber bridge almost every day at his favorite haunt, the Hillcrest Country Club. Of course, his trademark was his famous cigar and many years later, when our paths crossed again, he confessed to me that the Club Management displayed a prominent sign in the card room where his daily games were held. It read: 'Smoking prohibited for anyone under 95'.

Another bridge-loving celebrity was Tommy Prothro, the famous football coach. While George Burns loved playing rubber bridge, Tommy preferred duplicate. He always had a hand for me when we would run into each other at bridge tournaments. I attended a University of Texas-UCLA football game, as his guest, in the early 1970s in Austin when Tommy's UCLA almost ended a very long Texas winning streak during their glory years, but lost in the last few seconds. Seated in the UCLA section, I was surrounded by hordes of enthusiastic California fans but I was secretly pulling for my beloved Longhorns. I have rooted for them since I was seven years old and some things will never change.

Bridge often glues people together because of their mutual love for the game. Of course, two of the richest guys in the world, Bill Gates and Warren Buffett, are both bridge lovers. About ten years ago I visited Omaha to play with Warren at the Lincoln, Nebraska regional. He is so passionate about both bridge and, of course, investing. I enjoyed a challenge he posed to me on that occasion. He showed me three dice, one of which was a regular specimen with the numbers 1 through 6. The other two had very strange-looking numbers on their six sides. Warren then asked me if I would accept a proposition wherein I could choose one die and then he would choose another and we would have a 500 time throw-off; whoever's die won the most times (over 250) would win the contest. I hemmed and hawed, stalling for an answer, recalling Damon Runyon's warning not to bet a man who was offering this kind of proposition no matter how much it tempted you. Seeing my wheels churning, Warren took me out of my misery. I quickly learned from him that if we call the three dice 'A', 'B' and 'C', then 'A' could beat 'B', which in turn could beat 'C' while 'C' could then beat 'A'. So, regardless of the die I chose, he could pick a winner.

Bill Gates has always sung the praises of the fun and challenge of bridge. The press conferences he has conducted over the years about bridge always stress the beauties of the intellectual challenge and the healthy competitiveness which the game exudes. Despite his heavy schedule, he frequently pops up at NABCs. In fact, at the recent Nationals in Nashville, I caught a glimpse of him departing The Palm restaurant in a limo. It is amusing to note that if his image had not been plastered all over magazine covers and TV screens for decades, Bill Gates would fade into the crowd at a tournament as being just another boyish lad enamored with and fascinated by the game.

No twosome has ever been more supportive of our hobby. Bill and Warren between them have recently donated $1,000,000 to develop young people's interest in the game itself. Use of the funds is overseen by their very good friend, world champion Sharon Osberg. The bridge world has never been blessed with three better allies than Buffett, Gates and Osberg as their administrator, and we are lucky to have them on our team.

This chapter would not be complete unless I shared some unforgettable memories of a special friend of mine — Omar Sharif. Omar entered my life in the late sixties when the traveling Sharif Bridge Circus (which showcased several of the Italian Blue Team's top stars) came to Dallas and then New York to do battle with the Dallas Aces. These matches were then followed up in early 1971 with a seven-stop tour (spending one week in each of seven cities — Chicago, Winnipeg, Los Angeles, Dallas, Minneapolis-St. Paul, Detroit and Philadelphia).

Our week always kicked off with a press conference on Monday. This was followed by the first segments of the ongoing Aces-Circus match played in private on Monday night and then all day Tuesday. In the middle of the week (Wednesday and Thursday) the Circus featured Open Pairs and other bridge events in which local bridge players were encouraged to come and play against their famous opponents. The weekly tour concluded with a three-cornered match on Friday, Saturday and Sunday when members of the Circus, the Aces, and a hand-picked star-studded team of local experts competed against each other with huge audiences looking on.

It was during the mid-week Open Pairs events, when I (and the other Aces) would play with members of the Circus as our partners, that something began to distress me. My partner (regardless of who it was) almost always suggested that we play a particular carding method which he was accustomed to using — and I, too, soon fell in love with it. It is known as *odd-even signals* and it can be used when following suit or discarding. Using this method, a 'discouraging' *even* spotcard (like a two or an eight) also had suit preference overtones, allowing the tempo (obviously not discussed) to suggest just how much partner wanted that suit. Thus, playing an *odd* card would be 'encouraging' — but only an even card could have a dual meaning.

It was at this point in my bridge career, with the discovery of odd-even signals being employed by a band of top players, that I received a sadly rude awakening. It was an enlightening educational process for me, bringing about the painful realization that illegal messages can be transmitted by breaks (or rather 'differences') in tempo and are easy for a partner (especially a regular one) to interpret. This epiphany prompted me to write a series of stories about two fictional characters named, appropriately, Crypto and Telltale. These fellows won every local duplicate they entered but their results belied their ability. In each article they always encountered several duplicated boards wherein Crypto was looking at the exact same defensive situation at Trick 2 after retaining the lead with his opening thrust. Both the bidding and the dummy were always identical, as was Crypto's hand, but in each case Crypto would do something different at Trick 2, depending upon his partner's timing, and, not too surprisingly, it turned out to be the winning action. They did not have prearranged carding signals, but rather communicated beautifully through the tempo of the play. Years later that series, by popular demand, was reprinted in the ACBL *Bulletin*. It shows just how effective the Telltale tempo can be in giving a partnership an illegal advantage. In my opinion, the reaction of an individual reading those articles was pretty much a telltale as to which direction his conscience was leaning. Innuendos were not intended to be part of the game.

The Aces wound up playing the Circus a total of 840 boards on the tour (probably the longest official bridge match ever played). When the Philadelphia contest ended, we were ahead by 101 IMPs in a duel that was up and down with several lead changes during its course. Besides himself, Omar's team consisted of Benito Garozzo, Giorgio Belladonna, Pietro Forquet, Claude Delmouly (a great French player), and Egyptian bridge promoter Leon Yallouze. Omar himself was a very intuitive player, with a lot of table presence. He had a gambler's instincts, and was extremely good at reading his opponents.

It was during this time that the Aces gained invaluable experience — learning what it took to compete with three of the world's finest (Garozzo, Belladonna and Forquet). We witnessed firsthand both the advantages and disadvantages of various systems, conventions and treatments, the value of consistency rather than attempted brilliance, and the necessity for intensity and effort even when not necessarily feeling up to par. We learned the psychology of always being a tough opponent rather than adopting a relaxed attitude which, in turn, made one easily readable, especially by these opponents. The competition was exhilarating and I might add that having played against the 'world's finest' for well over four decades, I sincerely consider Benito Garozzo to be the best player ever — and I do not stand alone.

The Circus emerged during the time of Omar's screen heyday, not long after he made such incredibly successful films as *Dr. Zhivago, Lawrence of Arabia, The Night of the Generals* and *Funny Girl*. Omar was a household name! This huge popularity necessitated his traveling through airports in disguise, ever cognizant of his surroundings. Otherwise he would be helpless prey, mobbed by throngs of fans, mostly women — both young and old. In Chicago I was lucky enough to get to play with him successfully in an Open Pairs. Directly behind his seat at the table, the security team had cordoned off a designated area where at least seventy-five people stood and watched. My guess is that only a very few of the kibitzers even knew how to play bridge, but rather were just aiming for glimpses of Omar's deep brown eyes and his sexy European style.

The early birds for the game, who arrived hours in advance of the start, had the best opportunity to opt for an East-West entry in the same section, enabling them to play against Omar and his partner (who was a very minor part of the equation). Obviously, we were advantaged since many of our opponents were focused on stargazing at Omar and not concentrating on their hands. On every round Omar was always charming to our opponents. He was a number one attraction wherever he went.

I recall hearing a story about a conversation which took place on an elevator at a Nationals at the height of Omar's popularity. Two gentlemen were engrossed in a heated bridge discussion at the rear — oblivious to their surroundings. However, their booming voices made it difficult not to eavesdrop. As a woman passenger curiously turned to see the pair speaking, she recognized Omar and asked her husband if he knew the other person's name. "Oh, him?" The man shrugged, thought a moment and replied, "That's some guy from Italy. I think his name is Garozzo." *Some guy!* So much for priorities.

Another unusual happening on the tour occurred during our second stop — Winnipeg, Canada. When we arrived in mid-January the pilot welcomed us to sunny Winnipeg where the temperature was 36 degrees... and then added '*below zero*'. The Winnipeg bridge promoters met all of us at the airport and presented Omar with a beautiful (not to mention warm) authentic buffalo coat to ward off the too-cold evil spirits. Omar was delighted both with the warmth of the coat and the warmth of the presentation. He proudly sported the coat all week — at least until we left the following Monday, when this same entourage relieved Omar of the coat, belatedly explaining that it was just a loan.

In St. Paul, at the hotel where both of the traveling teams were staying, it was not the only time that I noticed that in the evening outside of Omar's quarters there were always three or four attractive young women lined up at the door hoping for a glimpse (and who knows what else) of their hero.

Our final stop was Philadelphia. It was particularly noteworthy because of the history of Philadelphia bridge, the cradle of so many of our top bridge personalities. The city has produced such impressive superstars as B. J. Becker, Johnny Crawford, Bobby Goldman, Charlie Goren, Bobby Jordan, Norman Kay, Peter Pender, Arthur Robinson, Sidney Silodor, Helen Sobel, Charlie Solomon, and Sally Young. In the fifties and sixties when bridge was gaining in popularity, an unusual statistic surfaced: there were more top players *per capita* in the Philadelphia area than in New York City or any other metropolis in the world. The final stop of the Circus in Philadelphia also fostered a romantic happening. It enabled Benito Garozzo to meet Lea Dupont; eventually that introduction created a twosome and led to the blossoming of a love story which is still going strong after nearly four decades.

For the record — we dealt with overflow crowds in Winnipeg, Detroit and Philadelphia while the other four cities had reasonable attendance but nothing spectacular. It may also be worth mentioning that the Philadelphia experience did not draw the greatest throng just by accident — it was chaired by none other than my current wife Judy, who seems to have more big splashes to her credit than even Esther Williams. I hardly knew her then but I have come to learn that she does not believe in half-hearted efforts. Thirty-six years after the fact, as I am finishing this book, we have had the opportunity to compare notes about our respective contributions to the Circus in totally different capacities.

A series of circumstances found her at the temporary helm of the Sharif event. Bob Jordan, a close friend of the Kays, was the local organizer and contact, and called Judy. He explained he had been asked to do all the advance legwork for the event, but had prior commitments to tour Australia with the Precision Team in the weeks before the Circus' scheduled appearance at the Drake Hotel in Philly.

He confessed he needed some help. That was where Judy came in. In desperation, on his way to the airport a day or two later, Jordan dropped off at the Kays' home detailed instructions listing what had to be done prior to the arrival of the two visiting teams. Bob had a very engaging manner and it was difficult to refuse him. He did, however, assure Judy he'd be back in time to play with the local team, which was composed of Arthur Robinson (his longtime partner) and Judy's husband Norman (with his partner, Edgar Kaplan of New York, who was being imported for the occasion).

Someone else might have been intimidated by the long hours and uncharted waters ahead, but Judy proceeded forthwith. She industriously gathered the names of all the Philadelphia area Country Club women's bridge team captains. She then prepared a flier mentioning that Omar Sharif was coming to the Drake Hotel and that everyone was welcome to play in the afternoon duplicates and kibitz the stars in the three-way matches on Vugraph at night.

Her phone began to ring off the hook. Judy smiles, recalling one particular conversation. When she questioned a caller as to which direction she preferred (North-South or East-West), she received a bewildered halting response. "What's that?" pondered the voice on the other end. Obviously, she knew Omar — but not a heart from a spade.

Judy also alerted the local newspapers and notified all the duplicate bridge clubs within an hour's drive. Her hustle and resourcefulness paid off. The Drake was overflowing for the entire week that the Circus was in town. Another of Judy's jobs was to arrange for the pick up of the visiting dignitaries (the Circus and the Aces) at the airport. The willingness of the locals was not surprising and a tremendous reception committee awaited the guests at the Philadelphia International Airport to transport them to the host hotel. Recruiting individuals to help with the Circus project was a simple chore. After arranging the motorcade from the airport, she turned her attention to procuring help for the actual bridge functions. For the actual bridge matches she secured monitors and recorders, who were thereby allowed to sit beside not only Omar, but the other world-class bridge personalities of the Blue Team and the Dallas Aces. All went smoothly and there was a steady stream of recruits always waiting in the wings to relieve or replace. However, even Judy did not anticipate all the problems that might occur during what seemed to be a pleasant, routine assignment.

The Mike Douglas Television Show had scheduled an early afternoon interview with Omar, and Judy needed someone to escort Omar to and from the studio. There was also another scheduled appointment about four short city blocks away after the TV stint. The sponsors of the Circus (Hamilton-Cosco and Stancraft Playing Cards) had publicized an autograph session to be held near the Eagle, a famous Philadelphia landmark located on the first floor of Wanamaker's, an old-line department store. For the job of 'escort', Judy had selected a lifelong bridge friend (who happened to be an old movie buff), someone she trusted to handle the assignment with efficiency and aplomb — unobtrusively shuttling Omar from one public appearance to another without incident. Wrong! It turned into a harrowing experience for both Omar and her friend Marleen.

After the viewers saw the live TV broadcast, hundreds of fans immediately converged upon the entrance to the studio, blocking access to the street. Marleen and Omar were virtually attacked by throngs of wild, raving fans who practically mauled him, savagely ripping buttons from his jacket and sleeves as souvenirs and pilfering his pocket handkerchief. It turned into open season on Omar — an afternoon neither will ever forget, especially the soft-spoken celebrity who had come to play bridge in the City of Brotherly Love. No two ways about it — Omar was a happening!

Back to the Omar I had gotten to know and enjoy. Since our numerous encounters at the Circus, I have had the pleasure of Omar's company on many subsequent occasions. During elegant bridge tournaments in Monaco, Omar and I had frequent opportunities to exchange stories over cocktails. We have often competed against each other, usually in London at the famous *Sunday Times* tournament (which later became known as the Macallan).

He once came to Dallas to appear at a special tournament at the posh Mansion at Turtle Creek. Coincidentally that happened to be the same period the traveling King Tut Egyptian Exhibit stopped in Dallas, and Omar's presence was acknowledged by adoring crowds. He also graciously traveled to Laredo, Texas to visit my good friend Seymon Deutsch. This enabled Seymon to show Omar off at his elegant department store, 'Joe Brand', and at the same time provided the charming and historic city with an opportunity to honor the star's appearance. Both at the happy times in my life, which have been many, and on the very sad occasion of my wife Debby's death, Omar was ever the gentlemen, ever the compassionate friend, ever the real superstar he has always been.

Omar has now moved back from Paris to Cairo, returning to his roots, while at the same time still staying active in movies and travelogues. His roles are different, but his looks and, above all, his overwhelming charm cannot be denied. To me he will always be an unforgettable character and our association over many decades has enriched my life. One cannot help but admire his loyalty to his friends and his affable manner — but most impressive is his humility. World acclaim and incredible success have never gone to his head. He continues to be the proverbial 'regular guy'. Omar has been well respected and loved in the bridge world since he first appeared on the scene. However, the modest Sharif views himself as just another lover of the game.

My memories of the Aces cover a huge spectrum of emotions — success and failure — happiness and disappointment — downs and ups. One of those early adventures along the yellow brick road to Oz occurred not long after our inception when the Aces arrived at the popular Americana Hotel in New York City for the 1968 Spring Nationals. We were awed by the Big Apple. All of us, except Ira, were clustered in the lobby — resplendent in our team uniforms of bright red jackets and gold trousers — bursting with pride as the newly formed future stars of the bridge world. I was standing near the check-in counter when a handsome, middle-aged man approached, placed his luggage at my feet and handed me his room key. It was a most leveling experience. He had mistaken me for a bellboy! In retrospect, it was rather funny... but at the time it caused me to come tumbling down Mount Everest posthaste.

CHAPTER 7

'SERVING TIME' ON THE BOARD

JIM ZIMMERMAN, one of the shrewdest and most adept members with whom the ACBL Board of Directors has ever been blessed, inadvertently paid me a compliment one time. The occasion and context in which the remark was made eludes me, but his words still reverberate in my mind: "Bobby Wolff has the least number of political skills of anyone I've ever met." Diplomacy and tact should be high on the list of attributes of a Board Member, but unfortunately they are my short suits. Some might go so far to describe them as voids!

Jim may or may not have meant it as a compliment, but I have always proudly chosen to construe it as positive. I do agree with him whole-heartedly. You may wonder, then, what a person with so little political savvy was doing on the ACBL Board of Directors for eleven years. My answer: I was doing my damnedest to make changes for the betterment of the game. I would like to think I succeeded, at least to some small degree.

I never intended to get involved in bridge politics. Through most of my bridge career, my interests have centered on playing and all the joy that goes along with it. Still, I guess it was inevitable. My entree was at the behest of Ira Corn, for whom I was working in 1981 when he called me to his office at Michigan General headquarters. It seemed that Ira was always doing that, and I learned that the occasions were not always ones I would remember cheerfully. At the time, Ira was District 16's representative on the ACBL Board. He did a good job, but he was coming under increasing pressure and scrutiny from the Michigan General Board. The Aces had not been an official team for nearly a decade, but many of Ira's board members believed he was still devoting too much time to bridge. Despite the fact that Ira himself didn't write the syndicated column — *The Aces on Bridge* — its existence seemed to support the view that bridge was interfering with Ira's role as head of Michigan General.

In truth, membership of the ACBL Board is a demanding job, requiring almost daily attention. Ira really did not have enough time to do the job properly, mainly because Michigan General was experiencing hard times. Full concentration on company business was needed. Anyway, when I got to Ira's office, he had some news. He wasn't going to run again, and he wanted me to keep it in the family and run for the position... perhaps a stretch of the nepotism theory. However, there was no mistaking my M.O. I was definitely my own person — always have been and always will be.

Ira had performed responsibly as District 16 representative, and since I was close to Ira personally and in business, I knew something about the setup. In those days, I often discussed bridge matters with Edgar Kaplan, who was revered by most as an administrative guru and had served on the ACBL Board in the sixties. I enjoyed talking about appeals cases and helping make decisions on Conditions of Contest, all without any political pressure. That's the way it was done way back then — a far cry from much of today's motivation. The decisions of most committees were made with the best interests of bridge as the focal point — not *whose* interests would best be served. Nor were things geared to the pleasure of the sponsors or professionals who, in large measure, had not yet entered the spotlight.

Ira's proposal left me cold. My primary interest in bridge in those days was playing. Actually, playing bridge is what I have always enjoyed most. I was not anxious to take on responsibilities that might interfere with my table time or distract me from the game. I told Ira, thanks — but no thanks. It was as simple and uncomplicated as that! My resolve didn't last long, however.

After I declined his offer, Ira spoke to Charlie Weed, who happened to be my boss at Michigan General, where we worked together in mergers and acquisitions. Weed, an affable, likeable, country-boy type, had been Chief Executive Officer of one of the Michigan General paint companies in Gainesville, Texas, about fifty miles north of Dallas, before he was moved to headquarters. Charlie had also been President of the Dallas Bridge Association, so he knew something about politics. The trouble was, he didn't want to run for the ACBL Board either — a totally unthinkable stance in today's world of lust for power. However, Charlie's refusal to run meant that attention reverted to me.

I don't remember exactly what Charlie said to me, but I was persuaded. I agreed to try to fill Ira's shoes on the ACBL Board. At that time, even though many Texas tournament directors were still unhappy with me over the Walter Jenkins election, I guess I could still count my major enemies on one hand. Everyone knew me and respected me for my bridge accomplishments. By that time I had moved on with my life. Betsey and I had divorced and I was married to the former Debby Polak, a beautiful woman whom everybody loved... especially *moi!* Put that all together, and I guess it was no surprise that I didn't have any opposition in the spring of 1981 when I threw my hat into the ring in District 16.

My election in 1981 was actually not my first brush with ACBL politics or with the ACBL Board of Directors. My baptism, such as it was, had occurred eighteen years earlier, in 1963. At the time, there was a rule that when a Board Member was elected ACBL President, he or she could not continue to serve as a District representative. So for the remaining term of the President's office, the First Alternate took over. To this day I'm not sure how it happened, but when District 16 representative Jerry Lewis was elected President, I was called on to take his place on the Board. I say that I'm not sure how it happened because I was elected First Alternate (for Texas and Mexico) without knowing that I was even on the ballot. One of life's little surprises! At the time, I was just thirty years old and much more interested in playing and improving — and I scarcely had time for that. In 1963, I was still in law school and running the bridge club in San Antonio with Moose. It was tough enough to find time to play, much less take on other responsibilities.

So, guess what? When I arrived in St. Louis prior to the Spring NABC in 1963, I had not done one iota of preparation for the Board meetings, and I didn't pay a whole lot of attention to what was going on. I was much more excited about my team for the Vanderbilt. My partner was the great *Oswald* Jacoby. That's not to say I didn't notice anything that took place in the meetings, however. Several of the board members made an impression on me. Sidney Silodor was one. I listened when he spoke, partly because I looked up to him as a great player, but also because what he said made sense. He seemed logical and sincere. I thought Silodor was an eloquent figure, a real statesman. Eric Murray, a barrister from Canada, was another board nember who caught my eye. Again, I was probably swayed initially by the fact that Murray was a great player, but I sensed that his point of view was influenced by what was good for bridge and the ACBL, *not* what was good for Eric Murray or what might get Eric Murray re-elected. Eric and Sidney, in my opinion, were two of the great standouts on the Board.

As I pointed out earlier, professionalism had not yet come of age. Money objectives were not an issue and many of the newer problems had not yet reared their ugly heads. Today, the successful professionals and even up-and-coming juniors enjoy the fruits of their bridge talents via markedly enhanced lifestyles; how can this not influence the decision-making of the middle-of-the-road administrator — causing resentment and jealousy? These were not considerations back in the early sixties; indeed, no one even realized they were on the horizon.

It seems likely, at least to me, that the type of high-level bridge player sitting on the Board of Directors when I arrived in 1963 was quite different from those on Boards that followed. Since the days of Silodor and Murray, with the exception of Edgar Kaplan, no single Director has combined a great work ethic with Hall of Fame credentials and a totally selfless dedication to the purity of the game. In days prior to the sixties, perhaps Lee Hazen and Waldemar von Zedtwitz would have fit the bill. Mathe and Gerber, according to people who should have known, were probably the two best players in the thirties (and they coincidentally also served on the Board), but they would not have measured up in all three categories. Board members like those from the early sixties, with world-class playing skills, have disappeared from the administrative scene — and there is no likelihood that their combination of talent, purity of motive and above all, love of the game, will ever be equaled or replaced.

Another troubling aspect of those working with the administration of the game, either directly or indirectly, is the background (or lack of it) of some of the Memphis staff. In my mind, the prerequisite for employment as middle management or higher at the League headquarters should be some previous familiarity with the game. Each of these positions should be held by a bridge player, not necessarily an expert but someone who has been there, done it, seen it — and who shares a special appreciation for the game. Without that experience and passion, Memphis becomes nothing more than just another place to hang one's hat. Such a lack of background and motivation leaves a stark void in an employee's job qualifications.

As far as my debut on the Board goes, I could have phoned in my participation in many of the 1963 meetings — not that anyone cared. Everyone was nice to me, but I was just a young rookie who played bridge in San Antonio. They paid little attention to me. I was a nonentity. I felt somewhat like Harvey, the invisible rabbit, but it didn't faze me. For one thing, the rule about the First Alternate filling in for the President was changing, so my first meeting as a temporary substitute for Jerry Lewis was to be my last. I was basically going through the motions.

One issue I do remember had to do with reorganizing the ACBL. The actual headquarters were in Greenwich, Connecticut at the time, but there was a Western Division, with separate staff, in southern

California. The Western Division was headed by Tom Stoddard, a powerful individual with designs on running the whole show. The Board eventually voted to eliminate the Western Division and have just one operation, but it took a lot of discussion and argument.

I guess I let Charlie Weed talk me into running for the Board in 1981 because, maybe without even knowing it at first, by then I was interested. I had seen some distasteful things in the bridge world that I thought needed changing, and I had worked out that being on the ACBL Board of Directors would be a good way for me to effect change. It didn't take long for me to get into trouble. I was the proverbial accident waiting to happen. I should have realized, with my personality and ideals, it was just a matter of time — and indeed, it was.

During the second or third meeting I attended, I was having lunch with several other Board members at Leo Spivack's table. Leo was an attorney by profession, originally from Chicago but living in New York at that time. He was a handsome, elegant man with a knack for oratory and persuasion. As was his wont, Leo was expounding upon something during the meal, and I noticed that he was supporting the exact opposite position to the one he had taken only a few minutes earlier in the Board meeting.

Maybe I shouldn't have, but I spoke up. "Leo, you are an original," I said. He looked up with a frown. "What do you mean?" he asked. I said, "You get up in these meetings, and whichever way the last speaker was going, you take the other side. I think you like to practice swaying people even though you have no interest in the subject yourself." I could sense other Board members sitting at the table nodding in agreement, although there was silence. Leo snorted and tried to change the subject, and I could tell he didn't like what I said, but I had something going for me in 1981 that I didn't have in 1963. By 1981 I had done a lot of winning at the bridge table and was well known. I was also still pretty well-liked, especially in Texas, where native sons who have notches in their belts are held in high esteem. I am reminded of something my father said to me many years before: "You have to be in your forties before people give you the respect that most men need." I found that to be true. Fortunately, by 1981, I was well past that milestone!

I decided early on that I liked being on the ACBL Board — it was a conduit for getting things done, and as some of the more influential Board members left, I gained more and more power and respect. I believe I used those assets for the good of bridge. I can honestly say I never made a move that was aimed toward getting myself re-elected. I made mistakes, to be sure, but my goal was always pure — to serve bridge and to make it better. One of my strengths in getting things done was the fact that I was beholden to no one. I never asked anyone to vote for something I wanted by promising to vote for something they wanted, and believe me, that kind of stuff went on all the time. It was the order of the day and I suspect still is. Plain and simple — it is called *politics*!

At one of the last meetings I attended before I left the Board in 1993, there was a vote to add an annual Regional tournament in Ottawa, Ontario. George Retek (who has sat on the Board longer than any of his peers), capably represents District 1 on the Board, and had put the motion on the agenda. It was meant to solidify his position on the Board by giving people in his District what they wanted. It's nice to have a Regional in your home town every year. It means you and other locals don't have to travel and spend a lot of money chasing gold points. George is a good guy and has made a positive mark on the game, but I heartily disapproved of this particular proposal.

The subject of adding Regionals to the calendar turned out to be a touchy one. Many people believe now, as they did back then, that there are too many Regionals — that all these tournaments really hurt the bridge clubs in the cities where they take place. Local clubs are the grass roots of the game and their existence should be protected. There is no question that is true. Anyway, George's proposal hit the table, and eight straight board members stood up and took it in turn to decry the idea. "This is a ridiculous proposal," said one. "It's killing bridge where it's most important." Said another, "What do we do when we have 500 Regionals? What then?" The feeling in the room was obviously against it.

After the eighth speaker had finished, Jim Zimmerman, who was always bigger than life itself, said, "Let's get on with the vote. Nobody's in favor of it." We voted — and the motion passed, 17-8. It had been a *fait accompli* before the subject even came before the Board! I sat back in total amazement. And almost sixteen years later, things haven't changed that much; the routine is just more blatant — with cliques, camps and alliances. George had done his homework and had lined up his votes before the issue ever came up. I guarantee you, seventeen members were holding markers on George after this one, and he would be voting for whatever they wanted on some other occasion, regardless of merit. That's the way it goes!

Although I never played the game of tit-for-tat — or maybe *because* I didn't play that game — I was able to make changes of which I am proud. One of my best successes was getting the ACBL Board to agree to bar the odd-even signals I alluded to earlier. Odd-even discards are allowed nowadays, but *only on the first discard*. I was goaded to action by my distress over the negative and cheating-like aspects inherent in the convention, when odd-even signals could be employed throughout the deal.

These are the basics of odd-even signals: when you are unable to follow suit, a discard can have two meanings. If you discard an odd card in a suit — a 3, 5, 7 or 9 — that is *encouraging* in that suit. If you discard an even card — a 2, 4, 6, 8 or 10 — that is *discouraging* — and it also has suit-preference implications. An example: you are defending a heart contract. On the third round of trumps, you discard the ♣2. That says you don't like clubs but you do like diamonds, the lower-ranked of the two other suits. Had you discarded your ♣8 or ♣10, that would also be discouraging in clubs but this time indicate strength in spades, the higher-ranked of the two other suits. The discard of an odd card in clubs would indicate you liked that suit.

The problem arises *when you are not dealt the right cards for the message you want to convey*. Suppose you are defending a heart contract and this is your hand:

♠ A 8 6 4 2   ♡ 7 6   ◇ K 8 7 2   ♣ 9 3

You lead a trump and declarer wins and plays two more hearts — with partner winning the third round. You discard the encouraging seven of diamonds, and when partner gets in, he plays the diamond ace and a diamond to your king. Declarer ruffs the third round of the suit and begins running trumps. You want to let partner know that he can let go of his spades to protect clubs. The problem is, how can you say that with a discard? You can't!

All your spades except for the ace, which you certainly don't want to pitch, are even-numbered cards. An even card is discouraging in that suit. If you throw a spade spot, partner will think you are guarding clubs. On the other hand, both of your clubs are odd cards. If you pitch one of those, partner will think you have strength in that suit and throw clubs, making sure he protects whatever spade holding he has.

It's a dilemma, right? Not for unethical players! All they have to do is discard a *slow* ♠8, indicating that, despite the message the card itself is supposed to send, they really do have something in the suit. A *fast* or *in-tempo* ♣3 says, "Partner, you guard spades. I've got clubs under control." An alternative would be to throw a *slow* ♣3, saying, "Partner, this is supposed to be encouraging, but I hope you understand that I have something in spades." Perhaps a *slow* ♣9 would get across the correct suit-preference implications. You can see that there are many variations for getting the right message across with the wrong cards — *and every one of them is unethical as hell.*

Even players without evil intent can fall into the trap. It is easy to break tempo and give unauthorized information simply from facing the quandary of having the *wrong* cards, and taking a pause to consider, perhaps, which 'lie' would be the least misleading (if that is possible). That's why I strove to bar odd-even signals except on the first discard. Of course, the tempo-based problems are always there if you are dealt the wrong cards for this discarding method, but at least the likelihood of a revealing hesitation is reduced when it is used for the first discard only. You do usually have more cards from which to choose.

I count this among my good moves as a member of the ACBL Board, along with establishment of the Recorder System, the promotion of Active Ethics and the formation and development of the Ethical Oversight Committee. These are contributions of which I will always be proud.

In case you don't know about the Recorder System, it is a way for players to address sensitive issues without unpleasant confrontations. Suppose you think something fishy has gone on at your table — say, the opponents' bidding goes 1NT - 3NT - 6NT (making, of course) — you can bring it to the attention of the Recorder. The Recorder will then check out the complaint and, if appropriate, establish a file on the perpetrator or begin an investigation. The Recorder will usually talk to the person and tactfully counsel him or her about the behavior in question.

I got the idea for the Recorder System, in an indirect way, from the late Ron Andersen. Not that he made the suggestion, mind you; rather, his actions strongly suggested the need for its creation. Ron was a colorful character, one of many in the bridge world who make it an interesting realm. From his base in Chicago, he did a lot of playing and winning. When he died in 1997, he had amassed nearly 40,000 masterpoints. He won several major championships and was the author of eight books.

For all that he did at the table, he was perhaps best known as the Moderator of the Vugraph panels that are now regular features at the NABCs and other major tournaments. At the Spring and Summer Nationals, he often wrote under the pen name of the Hideous Hog, predicting who would win each match in the latter stages of the Vanderbilt and Spingold. Ron also was the Vugraph coordinator for world championships and was in demand for other important European Tournaments. His public persona was that of a rambunctious but overall fun-loving character. He could be captivatingly charming.

Ron had a dark side, however. If you became his enemy — and, one way or another, a lot of people fell prey to his wrath — he tried to hurt you. One method was to spread tales about his enemies. You can get into a lot of trouble openly accusing someone of cheating, but Ron knew the ropes. By the time he got through with his subtle campaign, he could ruin a person's reputation. My idea was to short-circuit Ron and others like him by creating a formal, legitimate way for people to express concern without actually confronting another player or openly accusing that person of cheating or inappropriate conduct. I thought this might disarm some of Ron's shenanigans, and maybe afford his victims a way to complain about him in return by an accepted and recognized formal method.

I established the Recorder System in 1985 at the Spring Nationals in Montreal and during the first few years I handled it personally — with virtually little outside assistance. It was not until Bob Rosen came along that I considered stepping down completely. Knowing him (with his impeccable ethics and our shared feelings about making it tough for the bad guys), I felt totally comfortable relinquishing my post. And because of his tireless dedication to the objectives of the system, it is a decision I never regretted.

I am proud to say the Recorder System has proven invaluable in handling a wide variety of problems. I'll give you an example. Many years ago, a highly ranked young player, I'll call him Mr. X, was playing in a side game at a Nationals with a client. On one round, Mr. X and his partner faced two inexperienced players. Mr. X's right-hand opponent opened 3♣ and Mr. X made a takeout double, holding

♠ A 7 4 ♡ K Q 9 7 3 2 ◇ A 7 ♣ K 5

Mr. X's partner bid 3◇, which caused Mr. X to leap to 6♡, which was cold. Mr. X's non-expert partner happened to have 12 HCP (plus excellent distribution) but was too inexperienced to convey to partner he was not broke by making some response other than 3◇.

The opponents suffered their bad board without being aware that they had been *had*. Unfortunately for Mr. X, one of his opponents was married to a knowledgeable player. When she showed the hand record to her husband and told him the auction, he stared in disbelief. "You must be mistaken," he said. The wife insisted and got corroboration from her partner, prompting the husband to file a recorder form. The subsequent investigation revealed that Mr. X had been 'wired' in dozens of games and had been copping boards (casually glancing at scoreslips and players' private scores to see what results were achieved on certain deals).

Caught red-handed, Mr. X admitted his guilt. The punishment was far too light in my opinion (he should have been suspended for three years or more), but at least it had a happy ending as he has cleaned up his act, matured and has gone on to be a respected player in top events. For the above reason, his identity is being withheld.

There were many other cases like this, some of which led to expulsions. The Recorder System has worked extremely well, in no small measure because of the hard work of my former deputy, Bob Rosen, who conscientiously took over for me as Chief Recorder when I stepped down.

Unfortunately, what was perhaps my best idea was voted down by my fellow Board members, largely because, as Zimmerman says, I lack political skill. I brought the idea up in about 1986. In essence, I wanted to create a title for ACBL members called Current Master. The way to earn this status was to play a lot at clubs. If you earned a certain number of masterpoints at the club level — I was thinking about 15 or 20 — each month, your name would be listed in the monthly ACBL *Bulletin* and would stay there as long as you kept winning the required number of masterpoints. I thought this was a great way to draw people back to the clubs again and motivate them to keep going back. Promoting bridge was my sole objective.

I was disappointed to learn that a lovely woman by the name of Chris Wilson, who represented my current home district (District 17, which encompasses New Mexico, Colorado, Arizona and Nevada) had been told that this wasn't a good idea, and she opposed my motion. Chris said that where she lived, the smaller bridge clubs feared that if my proposal were to be adopted, all the players would flock to the top club to earn the maximum masterpoints, leaving them out in the cold. This was bunk, of course, tantamount to saying the idea was so good, it was bad.

Had Jim Zimmerman been in my shoes, he would have gone over to Chris and given her a hug and in a soft voice said, "Let's write those bridge clubs a letter and try to work this out." He would have assuaged her ego, gained her support and gotten the measure passed. Unfortunately, it was Bobby Wolff, not Jim Zimmerman, who made the proposal, and my sorry political mannerisms and tactics dictated a different course of action. "Chris," I blurted, "you wouldn't know your head from a hole in the ground. What are you talking about?" She started to cry. "I don't know; that's just what *they* told me." There was no way I was going to win this vote. It was 16-9 against my idea. I asked for a roll call, but they turned me down. It took a special person to get my idea voted down — *and I was that person.*

However, overall my track record speaks for itself. The fact is, while I was a member of the ACBL Board, I never had an opponent for any election, either as District representative or for any position on a Board committee. This is the theory I believe best explains my achievements: early on, I was liked and admired, while later, I was feared and resented. Further, never did I encounter opposition when I was nominated for any honorary award at any level. Perhaps my greatest vote of confidence was evidenced after I stepped down as WBF President in 1994. In order to be appointed to the Committee of Honour (the highest citation presented in world bridge), one had to receive support from three of the then-seven zones. I was told by Jimmy Patino I was *unanimously* elected by all seven and received all 68 votes from the total electorate — the only such occurrence in history — and I am proud to report that thirteen years later, that record remains intact.

CHAPTER 8

BLUNDERS AND INDISCRETIONS

ONE OF MY LAST ACTS as a member of the ACBL Board of Directors was to get someone fired. It happened in the spring of 1992. In retrospect, it may have been one of my greatest efforts on behalf of the ACBL. Let me backtrack so that you can understand the whole affair fully.

After joining the ACBL Board in 1981, I more or less fell heir to a coterie of warm relationships with many of Ira Corn's friends. It was apparent that his buddies were inclined to try to form the same beneficial bonds with me that they enjoyed with Ira. I didn't recognize it at the time, but there was also a pretty strong 'good ole boy' network on the Board — the inner circle, if you will. For someone with a different mindset from mine, being part of that crowd could be quite intoxicating. I'm not saying they were evil or malicious. It's just the way things worked, and I had come to realize they routinely assumed I would fall in line with their practices and do things the 'good ole boy' way. I flunked the membership test in their club — with flying colors, to say the least!

One of Ira's friends on the ACBL Board was a gentleman named Dick Hewitt, who represented District 3 (New York). Dick was a prominent estate attorney at a large law firm in New York. He had been on the Board for some time and was well liked and well respected. He and his wife, Shirley, were popular among the other Board members and their spouses. They joined the ranks of the vast majority of the ACBL Board members who attended the NABCs primarily for the social aspects rather than serious bridge play. I am not demeaning that approach, and it need not be a bar to honoring one's responsibilities; it certainly was not in the case of Dick. I, of course, was part of the minority who, after the meetings were over, got down to the serious business of trying to capture major championships.

Another Board member with a similar standpoint to mine was Tommy Sanders, an extremely successful Nashville businessman who represented District 10. Tommy and his wife, Carol, are both world-class players, besides being good people. Although Tommy and I had many intense disagreements, I have enormous respect for him as a player and a human being. It distressed me that it took so long for him to be elected to the ACBL Bridge Hall of Fame. Through Tommy and Dick's association on the Board, the Hewitts and the Sanders had become close friends.

Not long after I joined the Board — and completely unbeknownst to me — a movement was afoot to find a replacement for Lee Hazen, long-time ACBL Counsel. I thought the world of Hazen, a New Yorker who had once played professional baseball for the Brooklyn Dodgers. An incident of interest, never publicly acknowledged at the time, occurred in the mid-thirties when the ACBL was on uncertain financial ground in its infancy. It was Lee Hazen's out-of-pocket funding that helped put a teetering organization on its feet and keep it afloat. Lee was a class act from start to finish, wanting to preserve the status quo and keep the ship on an even keel.

By this time, however, Lee was getting up in years and there was the perception that it was time for him to move on and let someone younger take over. Along the way, Dick Hewitt made it known that he was interested in replacing Hazen. I must confess that I was blissfully unaware of what was transpiring, so when Debby and I received an invitation from the Sanders to join them at their home shortly before the 1983 Summer NABC in New Orleans, I didn't really attach any particular significance to the occasion.

The Hewitts were also there, and the plan was for all of us to travel to New Orleans for the NABC after spending a few days socializing at the Sanders place. Looking back, the idea may have been for Debby and me to get to know the Hewitts better, recognize Dick's qualifications and, when the time came, cast my vote for Dick to replace Hazen as ACBL Counsel — not an unreasonable expectation and surely not out of line as he was quite capable. I think it was kind of expected that I would not be a problem in the selection process. Indeed, I would be part of the solution. We spent an enjoyable few days in Nashville and left feeling good to have gotten to know the Hewitts a little better. They were lovely people and fine company and Debby and I always had a cordial relationship with them.

It took a while to get Hazen out of the job. He wanted to stay, but he was eventually prevailed upon to step down and in January of 1985, I went to Rye, New York as part of a Search Committee to select a new candidate for League Counsel. Besides myself, the committee included Jim Zimmerman, Chris Wilson from Arizona, Doug Drew from

Toronto, Canada, and Larry Jolma from Oregon. I remember flying into New York City and being picked up by Shirley Hewitt at the airport. We motored to the Hewitts' Country Club in Rye, where I was hosted to an unforgettable lobster dinner. In retrospect, to outsiders it may have appeared like I was being induced to favor Dick in the upcoming selection, but I was always my own person and doing what was best for the League was going to be my only consideration.

The candidates for League Counsel were Hewitt, Californian Jeff Polisner (who was a former Clevelander), and Bill Gross, who represented District 4 (Pennsylvania) on the ACBL Board. I remember musing that Polisner was much better qualified for the job than either of the others and that Gross was a distant third. Gross did, however, impress me with his seeming dedication to bridge and his expressed desire to want to help promote the game. He seemed very sincere and businesslike.

Polisner was the uncontested choice of the Committee, in no small measure because Zimmerman, also from Cleveland, lauded his capabilities and qualifications. Another huge contributing factor, when push came to shove, was the hourly legal fee rate required by Hewitt's New York law firm. Regardless of the attributes of Dick Hewitt, a major consideration favoring Polisner was that his rates were forty per cent less than Hewitt's and the Search Committee had a responsibility to the parent organization, the ACBL, to make the best deal we could. Actually, the vote of the Search Committee turned out to be unanimous in favor of Polisner. Of course, you have to realize that in a five-person committee, when three members go one way, the others, even if they are in disagreement, must pause to think about whether they want to be positioned in the minority when the vote is made public.

Anyway, we chose Polisner but did not announce our pick right away. We wanted to time it for shortly before the Spring NABC in Montreal, where the full Board would vote on our recommendation. At the Board meeting, Tommy Sanders was visibly upset. He obviously had been surprised and chagrined that Hewitt was not the selectors' choice as he sincerely believed Dick was eminently qualified. Indeed he was, and no one could argue that point! But the exorbitant New York rates, by comparison to the California scale, favored Jeff. Sanders suggested the Committee's recommendation be discarded and a new group formed. That didn't happen. Polisner was hired and did a spectacular job for the ACBL until he resigned in 2000 to take a similar post with the World Bridge Federation. At one point during the discussion, after Sanders gave an impassioned but vain speech, Leo Spivack joined in on Sanders' side. But before Spivack could really get any momentum going, I pulled out the qualifications for each of the candidates and ran them off for Leo. Polisner was easily the best. "Leo," I said, "which one would you pick?" He fell silent.

Tommy, of course, was upset with me for failing to go along with his crowd in rubber-stamping Hewitt, and it affected our relationship for many years. To Tommy's credit, he could have blocked my appointment as an ACBL representative to the World Bridge Federation, but he was too much of a gentleman to do that. In fact, after turning down the position himself, he encouraged me to go for it. We disagreed often and sometimes quite heatedly, but there has always been a mutual respect and the passing years have dimmed the memories of opposing views. I consider Carol and Tommy very good friends and Judy speaks glowingly of the warm relationship she and Norman shared with the Sanders over the years.

Recently, in Nashville at the 2007 Summer NABC, Tommy and Carol were honored by the Goodwill Committee for their incredible contributions to their Unit, their District and the game itself. I was delighted to be asked to introduce Tommy and my only regret was that that time restrictions prevented me from sharing with the audience many more tales of Tommy's accomplishments in administration and goodwill over nearly five decades.

Some months after Polisner's appointment, I wrote a long personal letter to Hewitt as I felt badly about the disappointment and letdown he experienced when our decision was made public. Had Polisner not been in the hunt, Hewitt would no doubt have gotten the nod. In the manner expected of a classy gentleman, Hewitt replied, thanking me for being the only one to care enough to take the time to correspond with him and attempt to console him. Over twenty years have passed and perhaps time has allowed some of the wounds to heal. Dick and I greet each other cordially when we meet at the Nationals and the 1985 replacement of Lee Hazen will go down as just another chapter in ACBL history.

The relevance of this story is that it was through the meetings to decide upon the League Counsel issue that I formed a favorable impression of Bill Gross. I didn't think he was right for the Counsel job, but I did surmise he had something to offer the ACBL beyond his service on the Board. It was with this background that I voted for Gross to succeed Ralph Cohen as Chief Executive in 1987. Ralph had been hired to take over for Dick Goldberg when he retired in 1984. Dick had been a marvelous CEO. He seemed to know just how to handle the Board (never an easy task), and the ACBL enjoyed a period of prosperity while he was in charge. Dick also had an uncanny good sense of timing, so when he felt the getting was good, he opted to leave.

Ralph was a great card player, but to his credit he was not much of a politician. Although he had been Dick Goldberg's top assistant for many years, he apparently did not learn a lot about how to cope with the complexities of the twenty-five personalities on the Board — but in all fairness to Ralph, few CEOs who preceded or succeeded him ever met that challenge with success. It is a no-win situation even for the classiest, self-respecting, most discreet and honorable individual, and Ralph was no exception. The honor of being CEO of the American Contract Bridge League is a mixed blessing and few have stepped down from the position without noticeable combat wounds. It goes with the territory, since twenty-five ever-changing bosses are a bit much to stomach.

Less than two years after Ralph Cohen was chosen to replace Goldberg, Tommy Sanders, Herb Smith (the Board member from Northern California) and I met in Dallas to consider Ralph's replacement. Ralph had already been forced out (through absolutely no suggestion or urging from me) and the three of us talked to Gross about taking over Headquarters. After the interview, we had mixed feelings about the attorney from Pennsylvania. Tommy was lukewarm, Herb was neutral, but I had positive feelings about the potential new CEO. I kept remembering his sincerity during the interview for the League Counsel position. Finally, we made the decision to offer him the job.

Gross was an earnest man, but his administration at the ACBL was not a success. Bear in mind, as you read on, that I learned about many of Gross's problems after the fact. I did not consider it my role as a Board member to monitor what was going on in Memphis. As far as I knew, the office was running as it should have. In retrospect, my naïveté was off the charts. Gradually, however, I became aware that things were not right.

One situation involved Becky Rogers, Gross's top assistant as Director of Operations. Becky, an experienced player, was a qualified national tournament director and well-versed in many phases of the game. She was a serious, no-nonsense, hands-on individual, whose primary focus was getting the job done and serving the ACBL and the game to the best of her ability. Sometimes her objectives appeared to put her at cross-purposes with some of the people manning the Memphis command posts. Becky's incredible work ethic undoubtedly made her the prime target of those individuals whose credibility, competence and importance she threatened.

She and Marion Bendersky, the ACBL's liaison with the Board, did not get along. Marion, who got her start in bridge as a club director, was envious of Becky's salary and wanted a raise. She believed she should be earning more than Becky. Their quarreling eventually became so obvious that it was actually affecting operations in Memphis, so Gross asked Jim Zimmerman for help in quieting things down. Zimmerman got me involved, which is how I came to be in Gross's suite at the 1989 Spring NABC in Reno. I didn't have much patience for this kind of nonsense, so I basically just sat them down and told them, with an edge to my voice, "Work it out."

Bendersky went immediately to her friend, Phyllis Burke, the District representative from Idaho, to complain that she had not been treated so rudely since she was a schoolgirl. I had made another enemy, but I didn't care. My *sole* concern was for the efficient operation of League headquarters. Ultimately, a three-member committee was formed to decide whether Bendersky should get a big raise. The Committee consisted of Zimmerman, Gross and me. I didn't think she should have the money, but I was outvoted. That, in itself, was no big deal, but I began to wonder about Gross. What kind of executive would first let himself get entangled in such a web and then be incapable of extricating himself? Why did he need to solicit help from Jim and me?

To digress briefly, it is interesting to note that on two or three occasions I could have had the CEO position in Memphis if I had wanted it. More than once, I was approached to take over at ACBL headquarters. I never really seriously considered it. For one thing, my wife Debby most definitely did not want to go. For another, it would have been necessary to work out arrangements for me to continue playing. Membership on the Board did not significantly interfere with my playing career, which was still going very well. I had no intention of being chained to a desk day in and day out. It simply was not my bag. Of course, it would not have been fair even if we had worked out some way for me to be CEO and continue playing. The Chief Executive's job is a demanding full-time position. I doubt if I would have been able to do it justice and continue to play high-level bridge.

In retrospect, I was very wrong about Bill Gross. He was not the right man for the job by any reasonable yardstick. Clearly, I made a mistake. By the time Gross's problems surfaced, they were too many and too serious to overcome. During 1987, while I was ACBL President, Tommy Sanders recruited an efficiency expert to examine operations at ACBL headquarters, a prudent and necessary move. The expert's report was largely ignored by Gross, which infuriated Tommy and lent credence to his call for Gross's scalp. There were also reports that bills were going unpaid at ACBL Headquarters (telephone service was cut off twice because the bill wasn't paid). In 1989, Frank Stewart, a mild-mannered, soft spoken Southern gentleman, resigned his position as Co-editor of the *Bridge Bulletin*, supposedly in frustration over Gross's administration. Such an extreme action, by a respected bridge columnist who *never* made waves, gave food for thought.

Gross might have survived all of his other problems, but he could not overcome the Board's outrage when it came to light that Audrey Grant was planning to sue the ACBL. Grant had written some bridge textbooks for the ACBL that had become bestsellers, at least in the bridge world. The ACBL owed her a considerable sum in royalties, but Gross was very slow to pay. Gross was always a *gross* procrastinator! In fact, it seemed that he simply didn't want to cough up the money. Grant's lawsuit, which was certain to be successful, would cost the ACBL a ton of money. It was hard to believe, and we never did get a good explanation from Gross about why he failed to pay Grant what she was owed. In the end, the reason was irrelevant. Gross had to go, and he was released in Atlantic City in the spring of 1991. I actually had little to do with the firing other than voting to approve it, so this is not the dismissal I alluded to at the beginning of this chapter.

Helping to get rid of Steve Signaigo, however, *was* one of the most significant and important roles I ever played. I never have had much faith in Search Committees. Their track record has not been laudable. In my opinion, each member of a Search Committee must be honest with himself or herself, cognizant of what is needed, and focused on who is best qualified to serve. A serious caveat which is all too often cast aside is *never, never, never* be taken in by a person whom you like and who likes you, but rather seriously consider which candidate best suits the position. The Committee that selected Signaigo unfortunately fell well short in this regard.

With Bill Gross gone, it was important for the Board to act quickly, so another Search Committee was assembled hastily to produce a candidate. Ads were placed in trade publications and a notice of Gross's 'retirement' appeared in the *Bridge Bulletin*. I don't know how many applicants there were, but the new Search Committee — Barbara Nudelman, Doug Drew, Dave McGee and a few others — came up with a startling recommendation: a Memphis man who didn't know anything about bridge. Their choice was Steve Signaigo, who had inherited a beer distributorship from his father and had subsequently sold it for a tidy sum. When he answered the ad for a new Chief Executive at the ACBL, Signaigo was 'retired' and, according to him, looking for a new challenge for a man in his early forties.

At the time, the idea of a non-bridge player taking over the operation of the world's largest bridge organization may have seemed bizarre and it wasn't very surprising that it worked out exactly the way you might have expected. To others, it no doubt seemed like the kind of 'outside the box' way-out thinking that might produce a real winner. You would never have convinced me of that — but I was a non-factor.

Apropos of this thought, I recently received a telephone call from a woman who worked in the Marketing Department in Memphis. She wanted to ask me questions about Goren, his TV shows and his other contributions to the game fifty or more years ago. I suppose age has its rewards and I was flattered that I was called upon for help. But during a lengthy conversation wherein I filled in a lot of the blanks, I learned she was not a bridge player. Obviously, she was intelligent and well-spoken and no doubt well-qualified in her field. However, it will never cease to boggle my mind that the ACBL does not feel that familiarity with the game is a prime requisite for employment, in addition to other skills relevant to a specific position.

Back to Steve Signaigo. Certainly, the new candidate was attractive. He was a former football lineman for the University of Mississippi, had rugged good looks and exceptional charm. His arrival at ACBL headquarters in Memphis produced an immediate boost in morale. The taciturn, reclusive Gross was rarely seen in the office by the staff. By contrast, Signaigo moved easily among the troops and seemed happy to be aboard. He made a particularly strong impression on some of the women. It was a shot in the arm for the office to see Signaigo's handsome, smiling face on the cover of the new *Bridge Bulletin*.

The Signaigo administration started with a bang. He quickly fired a minor manager who defied his orders not to report her problems directly to him. Next to feel the axe was Marion Bendersky, the ACBL liaison to the Board. Bendersky had worked hard to solidify power by currying favor with certain Board members and she resented her reduced role in headquarters operations. Signaigo had signed an employment contract and he no doubt felt that he had the upper hand with the Board. What did he need with a disrespectful woman who seriously and fatally overestimated her political clout in the new atmosphere? Bendersky was gone in a flash.

This caused a stir among some members of the Board, but not enough of one to concern the new boss. The truth is, Bendersky's firing was a done deal long before any Board member got wind of it. Soon another high-ranking figure in the ACBL management hierarchy was gone. Becky Rogers, who had competed with Bendersky for influence with Gross, was unceremoniously given the heave-ho not long after Signaigo had stripped her of most of her power. The day after she was fired, the locks on the doors at the ACBL were changed. Clearly, the new kid on the block was shaking things up — with no fear of reprisal.

I was clueless what Signaigo was about or what he was like until I met him at the 1991 Summer NABC in Las Vegas. Our first encounter occurred when I went to his suite at the Las Vegas Hilton, where the Board was meeting prior to the tournament. After I had a chance to speak to him briefly, I quickly confirmed the talk that he knew less than nothing about bridge. Right or wrong, I concluded that he was like a lot of corporate types I met when I was working for Ira Corn at Michigan General. He was *slick*.

Some people might consider *slick* to be a good quality in a fellow human being, but I do not, especially when the future of the ACBL is at stake. The slick corporate types I met while working for Corn were all style and no substance. They could talk a good game, but when you added up all they had to say, there was nothing there. That was my impression of Signaigo, and it reinforced my gut instinct that a non-bridge player was not right for the CEO position of the top bridge organization in the world.

Now, you might think that running a business is simply running a business, regardless of what it is. If you're a good businessman, you can figure things out pretty quickly, right? After all, it's all numbers and bottom lines. That might be true of some businesses, although I doubt it, but it's certainly not true of the ACBL. Bridge is an entity — completely unto itself! We are a unique sort of creature (to put it mildly) and the management of most businesses does not have the kind of interaction with Board members that goes on at the ACBL. As it turned out, Signaigo had no chance, and he didn't further his own cause with some of his choices.

One of the worst was his selection of Charles Wilson as the Marketing Manager. Wilson came to the ACBL on the rebound from a company that manufactured medical equipment. In fact, he was laid off as sales manager, reportedly in a downsizing move. Wilson, a swaggering, clownish man who clung to Signaigo's coat-tails like a frightened pup, seemed to me to know almost nothing about marketing, and even less about bridge.

Again, we had someone being hired for a senior ACBL position who had no background in the game. It almost seemed that at that time, with a few exceptions, unfamiliarity with bridge was a prerequisite for infiltrating the management scene at the ACBL. Wilson knew nothing at all about the game, nor did he want to. Mostly he bragged about his gun collection and his interest in flying. If anything, Wilson exhibited contempt for bridge and bridge players, hardly an attribute in such a crucial position. When Signaigo decreed that all his non-bridge-playing managers should take bridge lessons, Wilson went along only reluctantly, and he made it clear he didn't like the idea or the players. Signaigo, at least, was on the right track. Wilson, though, seemed to be a total misfit.

The beginning of the end came quickly — in the fall of 1991. Wilson, with Signaigo's blessing and shockingly, *without the knowledge of the Board*, embarked on a direct-mail campaign that cost more than $300,000. Yes, $300,000! It produced embarrassingly pitiful results — something like sixty new members. That boils down to $5,000 per new member, more than 300 times what they paid in annual dues in 1992.

When Board members learned about the mailing, some of them hit the ceiling. This kind of unilateral expenditure was unprecedented. How could it happen? I was still on the periphery and not completely aware of what was going on in Memphis, but I was not surprised to hear rumblings. Signaigo's first NABC, Las Vegas in 1991, went smoothly. He had just been hired and was not expected to be completely up to speed, and it was still the honeymoon period. By the Fall NABC in Indianapolis, some Board members, including me, thought it was time for Signaigo to do some accounting for himself, especially concerning the expensive mailing that had produced next to nothing.

In Indianapolis, Wilson appeared to be more and more of a liability. He had been directed to prepare a report on marketing efforts and future plans and Signaigo accompanied him to the committee meeting where the report was to be presented. Incredibly, when Wilson was called upon to speak, he was unable to utter a word. He was so far out of his depth that he simply froze. It was both embarrassing and horrifying.

Board members were starting to ask, "Who is this guy — and what is he doing in a key position at ACBL Headquarters?" Like the quintessential Teflon Man, Signaigo himself managed to get through the Indianapolis meetings without serious damage. He was so smooth that he was able to wiggle out of trouble despite the massive waste of money. In fact, although Signaigo still didn't know much about bridge or what was really important for the ACBL, he did recognize the value of recruiting Board members to his side — an absolute essential for survival, in fact tantamount to life or death! It was eerie and frightening from my vantage point, but Signaigo departed from Indianapolis in a better political position than when he had arrived. He was building an empire, currying favor with certain Board members to the point that they would back him — no matter what!

Doug Drew was one of his staunchest supporters. At one of the meetings in Indianapolis, I had pressed the CEO hard about the mailing, and in my view he had failed to provide a satisfactory answer to any of my questions. Other Board members seemed to have a different view, especially Drew. "I've been in business thirty years," Drew said, "and I've never seen a person put in such a position." Later, when I tried to tell Drew about some of the things that concerned me about Signaigo, Doug blew me off. "I don't want to talk about it," he said. "I just don't want to talk about it." No wonder! If I had been on the Search Committee that ferreted him out, I wouldn't have wanted to talk about it either. But that was the position of many Board members, including Barbara Nudelman, Dave McGee and Chuck Wilkinson. They didn't want to know about Signaigo's indiscretions. They liked him and they did not want to face making any hard decisions about him. It was akin to blind faith.

My initial misgivings about Signaigo were strengthened every time I had one-on-one dealings with him. He was astute enough to size me up as dangerous, so he did everything he could to disarm me. Whenever he had the chance, he was flattering and complimentary. "We're so lucky to have a person of your stature," he would say. That was all very nice, but it wasn't hard to decipher these statements as being calculated to catch me off guard or deflect my attention from what was really going on.

Most disturbing to me was that he frequently told me he was going to do something and then failed to do it, or assured me he would not do something and then reversed his position. I remember a conference call with Signaigo regarding Becky Rogers' tenure at the ACBL. Dave McGee and Joan Gerard joined in on the call to discuss Becky's future with the organization. We all believed that Becky, a bright and resourceful Director of Operations, was doing a good job and should stay on. Signaigo agreed and *assured us that her job was in no jeopardy*. To our horror and disgust, we later learned that five minutes after Signaigo hung up, Becky Rogers was unemployed. He accused Becky of spying on him, and perhaps she was. Someone needed to know about the excesses, the stealth, the deceit and the irresponsible behavior of the top management official in Memphis.

Early in 1992, it was obviously crucial that something be done. I resolved to do the dirty deed, but I needed help. Going before the ACBL Board to discuss the Signaigo situation was reminiscent of a scene from the eerie movie, *Invasion of the Body Snatchers*. The once responsible, responsive people I knew in the early days seemed to have been replaced by drones, mesmerized by this charismatic character, and exhibited blind loyalty to him — much to the detriment of the ACBL.

I didn't know where to begin, but I had an idea. The annual Houston Regional was scheduled for February, and the District 16 Board of Directors would be meeting during that tournament. I couldn't get members of the ACBL Board to listen to me, but perhaps the District Board would take notice of the unbridled Horror at headquarters in Memphis. I asked Joan Gerard, then President of the ACBL, to join me in Houston to appeal for assistance to the District Board, and I got Shirley Pagan, of Corpus Christi, Texas, to help put Joan and me on the agenda. Shirley was a vital member of the District Board and a veteran of bridge politics. She was a driving force behind the highly successful Pan American bridge event in Corpus Christi that year. Shirley agreed to help, and Joan and I prepared our presentation.

Of course, we talked about the wasteful $300,000 mailing, but there was more. We had learned, for example, about Signaigo's reprehensible behavior that summer during the World Junior Bridge Championships in Ann Arbor, Michigan. For starters, Signaigo and Wilson (with wives and children) flew to Ann Arbor from Memphis first class. Signaigo made an appearance at the tournament briefly, but then disappeared for a couple of days before returning. It was discovered that he and his entourage had hired a limousine to transport them to Windsor, Ontario, for dinner at a very expensive restaurant. He was living high off the hog, but all the bills were being sent to the sty in Memphis for payment!

I also had Bob Hamman get a quote from a reliable competitor, comparable in operation to the company that Wilson had used for the mailing. The price Bob got was about $90,000 less than Wilson had spent, with Signaigo's approval. What did that mean? Maybe it meant only that Wilson was inept rather than dishonest, but it was worth researching.

To my delight, the information we provided created a sense of outrage among the District 16 Board membership, enough to spur them into action. Prior to the meeting, I had no idea what to expect when Joan and I took our case to that group, but the results exceeded my wildest dreams. The late Mary Williams (perhaps remembered by you as Mary Philley) was particularly strong in supporting our cause. A retired attorney, Mary was tough as nails when she took up a cause. She was on the telephone immediately, lobbying ACBL Board members she knew. Other District Board members followed suit. The tide began to turn against Signaigo when some of the ACBL Board were awakened by the details of the whole sorry Ann Arbor episode to their grave mistake in hiring him in the first place.

The issue of Signaigo's continued employment came up at the Board meetings just prior to the 1992 Spring NABC in Pasadena. He knew he was in trouble, and he was doing all he could to save himself.

Wilson was the first sacrificial lamb, although that move was in itself suspect. Even Board members favorable to Signaigo had wondered why Wilson had been hired in the first place, much less retained after the $300,000 mailing debacle. Clearly Signaigo was desperate, as well he should have been.

Had a vote had been taken at the start of the meetings in Pasadena, Signaigo would probably have survived. I estimate the vote in his favor would have been in the 18-7 range. There was simply too much evidence against Signaigo, however, and I managed to sway some of the fence sitters with a speech about the consciousness of guilt. I told them that Signaigo knew what he was doing was wrong, but he had a total disregard for the rules and, perhaps even worse, for the ACBL treasury. He was spending money like there was an endless supply, and much of it for his own pleasure.

In the end, it was embarrassing to witness his last-ditch attempt to keep his job. He told us that in an effort to cut expenses, he was planning to fire Julie Greenberg, head of the ACBL's Education Department, and he would also be prepared get rid of anyone else we recommended. This was pathetic — coming from a man who took over as CEO bragging that he didn't need the job so he wouldn't brook any interference from the ACBL Board! There he was, practically begging to stay on.

One of the keys to my success in getting rid of Signaigo was that I had a plan for keeping the office in Memphis running while the Board went about finding a new CEO. In fact, my plan would allow the Search Committee (and I blanch when I use that term) to take some time to assure that the next choice was not going to result in an instant replay of the Signaigo regime.

With Shirley Pagan's assistance, I had recruited a former World Bridge Federation President, Denis Howard of Australia, to take over as CEO while the search for a permanent executive was in progress. Denis had recently been forced out as WBF President, so I knew he was looking for some way to renew himself and to show his value as an administrator. Denis agreed to take over in Memphis for expenses only while the search was conducted.

It was a grand coup for me and for the ACBL. Denis, a former player and an attorney by profession, is a serious (some may say *difficult*) man with a strong will and absolute integrity. No one could have been more perfect for the interim role. He would run a tight ship while a successor to Signaigo was found.

All in all, the episode with Signaigo and my well-founded determination to get him fired may have been my shining hour as a member of the ACBL Board. It was draining to face that uphill battle day after day, and the process enhanced my growing list of enemies. Would I do it again? Who knows? I wouldn't want to be faced with the choice. At this stage in my career, *let someone else worry*! My dues are paid up.

Before leaving the subject of CEOs (although I know it is totally misplaced in a chapter entitled 'Blunders and Indiscretions'), I feel I must give a special plaudit to our present CEO, Jay Baum. Jay ranks right up there in the category of class and dignity with another past CEO, Roy Green. I don't know what methods were employed to find Jay, but whatever they were, I blindly salute the final result. In my many interactions with Jay, his demeanor has been that of a perfect gentleman. He is an independent thinker, unafraid to take a position when it benefits the ACBL and with the fortitude to stand up for the betterment of the game he loves. I have witnessed a lot of CEOs come and go and, in my opinion, we are most fortunate to have such an upstanding, morally sound individual at our helm (and a good bridge player to boot!).

CHAPTER 9

THE AGONY OF DE-FEET

IN BRIDGE, DEALING WITH CHEATS can be a tricky exercise. For one thing, the laws of the game were *not* designed or set up to handle cheaters. There is nothing in the rule book about what to do if you catch someone cheating. Leads out of turn, revokes and so forth are right there in the rules, but cheating is considered such aberrant behavior that it is not formally dealt with in the laws. It's as though the rule givers didn't want to consider cheating a possibility.

In fact, according to the *Official Encyclopedia of Bridge*, 5th edition: 'The laws of Contract Bridge are not designed to prevent cheating or to provide redress. The lawgivers have taken the view that it would be wrong to accord cheats a status by providing legal remedies against their activities. This also is the policy of the ACBL: exclusion from membership is the penalty for premeditated cheating, but cases of momentary weakness often are dealt with by temporary suspension.'

So what happens if a player is caught fixing hands or a pair is detected giving hand signals? Students of bridge history will remember the notorious scandal involving the Italian players in the 1975 Bermuda Bowl who were caught tapping toes under the table. That famous case is an apt reference, as it turns out, because it demonstrates with sickening clarity what can happen when politics is mixed in with the adjudication of cheating issues.

In case you are unfamiliar with the 1975 brouhaha, although the Italians were caught red-handed (or better yet — red-footed), they were merely given a slap on the wrist — not even tossed out of the tournament. Off the top of my head, I could rattle off half a dozen similar cases where justice was thwarted because of politics. What politics were at work in Bermuda all those years ago, you ask? Consider the following.

The cheaters, Facchini and Zuchelli, were caught touching toes under the table during the bidding and before the opening lead was made. They were not practicing for the Ballet Russe. The facts were made available to authorities at the tournament, but while the investigation was in progress, one of the ACBL's sorriest politicians, Lew Mathe, blew the lid off what was, at that point, a low-profile inquiry. His actions were strictly political and egomaniacal in nature. When the charges became public, the authorities responsible for the tournament made the disgusting politically motivated decision to go easy on the accused. They felt that the government of Bermuda, which had contributed heavily to the tournament, would not be happy with a cheating scandal on their turf — an appalling, inexcusable and self-serving reason for sweeping it under the carpet. This position was totally unacceptable to those honorable participants who were forced to continue playing under utterly abominable circumstances, but that was the decision of the WBF. Protection of the guilty, one more time. So — what else is new?

I vividly recall listening in disgust as the two cheaters tried to assuage the press by attempting to justify some of their unusual actions in the play, which obviously had been based on their illegal signals to each other. For example, with no help from the bidding, one of them led low from 10xxx in hearts against a notrump contract when he had five spades headed by the K-Q. It just so turned out that partner had a singleton spade but five hearts to the K-Q. Rational observers could not believe these skunks were getting away with this.

In order for you to understand my own outrage, I would like to share my personal firsthand account of the whole affair. The Facchini-Zuchelli incident happened over thirty years ago and its beginnings can be traced back earlier by another six months. It is a piece of history known to very few and it is important that you follow the timeline as you watch everything fall into place.

Bob Hamman and I won the 1974 World Open Pairs in the Canary Islands and then wended our way to Venice to compete in the Bermuda Bowl. Our team (Eric Murray, Sami Kehela, Bobby Goldman and Mark Blumenthal, playing with Bob and me) went into the last segment of the finals and came up short, losing to the Blue Team once again.

Before we entered the room for the start of play, an Italian bridge journalist, in broken English, asked me, "Mr. Wolff, if you had one reasonable wish to make before the finals, what would it be?" What a loaded question!

Spontaneously, I responded for all to hear, "I would wish we could have screens for this match." Giorgio Belladonna, the great Italian player, got so upset with this question (and obviously with my answer) that he offered an unsolicited response: "Why doesn't Ira Corn send over the screens and, if he does, I would be happy to play behind them." The journalist's question could have been part of a script I had penned myself!

It is worth noting that before anyone in the States or anywhere else in the world became familiar with the concept, or could even spell the word 'screens', the Italians employed the wooden boards to assure a fairer contest *amongst themselves* at their own Trials. A pathetic commentary! But isn't there a distinct message there? History reveals that screens were the brainchild of an Italian by the name of Mario Franco and were originally called Franco Boards. That was the first attempt at screens and it led to the version adopted by the World Bridge Federation. The WBF screens later incorporated foot boards as a further precautionary measure, so most appendages were now present and accounted for.

After our loss in Venice, I arrived in Milan for the Cino del Duca. This was a tournament that attracted many contestants not only because of the significant money prizes, but because of the elegance of the venue. It was always held in a palatial setting with thick pile carpets, magnificent furniture and exquisite artwork. In addition, participants in European bridge events have always distinguished themselves by their urbane and elegant mode of dress.

Bob and I had decent scores in the event, averaging around 62%, but didn't get a sniff of the prize money as it required numbers in the very high 70% range to place, with the winner coming in at a rather eyecatching 81%. It was a bit of a putdown for us until we learned how things *really* worked at the Cino del Duca. One of the Italian organizers shamelessly shared with me the pre-tournament preliminaries, namely, the 'arranging' of sections. Those pairs who were preselected to score well had some of their confederates sitting in the same direction and others as table opponents in the other direction. Cino del Duca had always been an elegant annual bridge celebration in glamorous locations, offering attractive prize money. However, this calculating, premeditated scheme (which was also coupled with considerable illegal signaling) caused the original lure to fade to a whisper. The once-exciting Cino del Duca had sunk to the depths and became a dull, unattractive destination for many of the top players who had formerly enjoyed attending.

Following Milan, Bob and I set out for Monte Carlo to play in their world-renowned tournament. Again, Bob and I had decent scores in the Open Pairs but were far out of the money. Emerging victorious were an Italian Pair named Facchini and Zuchelli (later to be nicknamed the

Vegetables). Americans Richard Katz and Larry Cohen finished second, and the famous Garozzo-Belladona captured third — all with monstrous percentage scores!

In the team game Bob and I were playing with the great Brazilian star Gabriel Chagas, my good friend Jim Hooker and another pair. We met our maker early in the matches and though it was disheartening not to go very far, our elimination was transformed into a boon — it afforded me an unexpected opportunity for my detective instincts to swing into action.

I began by watching the semifinals played between an Italian team which included Facchini and Zuchelli (who these days are also facetiously referred to as the Foot Soldiers) playing against Billy Eisenberg and Eddie Kantar. The hand that captured my attention involved a bold overbid of 5◊ by Billy which was doubled by the Italians. Late in the hand (Trick 11), Zuchelli (who was on lead and was in front of Billy) held the equivalent of AQ2 of trumps and Billy held the equivalent of KJ3. There were no other trumps outstanding. I stared in disbelief as Zuchelli went into a stupor. I pondered to myself — is this a way of taunting his American opponents? All he had to do was lead a low diamond and then claim the final two tricks, going on to the next board.

Instead, he laid down the ace, subsequently losing a defensive trick that even the rankest of beginners would not lose. I was standing next to a highly respected Italian player who seemed to be familiar with the top European bridge community. I asked her later, "Why did he make such an awful play?" to which she replied, "He probably doesn't know any better." She then went on to describe their partnership reputation and methods of cheating. Upon further grilling, she elaborated that after this pair were forced to play behind screens (which had been introduced some fifteen or so years earlier in Italy) they moved to foot signals under the table. That was my introduction to the saga of the Foot Soldiers.

In January, 1975, fate placed me on a plane heading to Bermuda (from Dallas) to play in the 25th (Silver) Anniversary edition of the Bermuda Bowl. The maiden event in 1950 had showcased an American Team (Crawford, Goren, Rapee, Schenken, Silodor and Stayman) beating a team from Great Britain as well as a combined group from Sweden and Iceland. I was scheduled to play in the World Championship with my regular partner, Bob Hamman. The amazing background to this was that I had not won anything substantial during that bridge cycle. It is winning major events that usually paves the way to qualifying (or being invited to join a qualified team) for the prestigious championships at year's end. But before the Team Trials, I was asked to join the team sponsored by Bud Reinhold to play with him as my partner and with Richard Katz, Larry Cohen, Peter Weichsel and Alan Sontag. They had won the previous Reisinger playing five-handed and had to complement the team to six players in order to be eligible for the 1974 Team Trials to be held in 1974 in the Washington, D.C. area.

After getting to the finals of the Trials, we lost to the Grand National winning team in an exciting match. The winning group was composed of John Swanson, Paul Soloway, Billy Eisenberg and Eddie Kantar with a California pair (Cohen/Mandel) being the fifth and sixth. Alfie Sheinwold was serving as non-playing captain and he was calling the shots. He wanted Cohen/Mandel to drop off the team and be replaced by Bob and me. His new lineup had to be approved by the Board of Directors to become official, but after much consternation, at the Fall BOD meeting in San Antonio in 1974, Bob and I were officially confirmed to replace Cohen and Mandel.

This chain of lucky events (right place/right time and twice being added to teams when I had not actually won the right to play by normal standards) found me Bermuda-bound (via Philadelphia). Chance continued to play a major role in this story, as Bruce Keidan, then Baseball Sports Editor for *The Philadelphia Inquirer*, boarded the plane. He was en route to cover an Olympic-type sporting event in Jamaica, but wanted to start his odyssey in Bermuda, planning to relax and kibitz the first few days of the 1975 Bermuda Bowl. Because Bruce was an ardent bridge player (and due to the fact that *The Aces on Bridge* appeared in the *Inquirer*), our paths had crossed before and Bruce became my traveling companion on the short flight to Bermuda. Little did we know at the outset of our journey what fruits our conversation was destined to bear.

On the trip down, Bruce and I casually discussed the upcoming event and he inquired what my expectations were for that championship. Suddenly, it dawned on me what a perfect role Bruce could play in what was about to transpire — he could help unveil a bridge mystery in the Bermuda Triangle. Let there be no mistake about it: *it was I, Bobby Wolff, who gave birth, somewhere over the Atlantic, to the original master plan to expose Facchini and Zuchelli and bare their feet!*

I carefully explained to Bruce that since table screens were being used for the first time in a world championship, the organizers were going to need as much experienced help as they could recruit. That was where he came into the picture. I prevailed upon him to have his name put forward for consideration as a monitor in the World Championships. No one could have been more suitable for the role. Bruce is extremely bright, sharp, and knowledgeable, with an obvious passion for the game. I had a lot going for me in Bruce — his instinctive nature as a super reporter, always in search of a breaking story. After he happily consented, I confided in him and revealed my plan — explaining that it would be an exhilarating challenge for him to serve as a monitor in the garden where the Vegetables would be putting on their show. I detailed the conversation with my Italian informant about the suspect pair and her explanation of what they did while playing behind screens. Foot movements had replaced the former hand signals, which were now rendered totally useless by the introduction of screens. Each player could see one opponent, but not his partner, thereby virtually eliminating the ability to draw inference from facial expressions, body language, or other motions. Bruce agreed to cooperate, eagerly anticipating this unexpected assignment, and The Sting was about to begin — Redford and Newman in action!

Two nights later the tournament began. Five countries were represented: Brazil, France, Indonesia, Italy and the USA. The first matches of the Round Robin featured Brazil against Indonesia and France against Italy, with the first bye drawn by the USA. Bob and I sat down to kibitz in the Vugraph room. The Veggies were one of the two Italian pairs prominent on the big screen as they took on France. During an early deal, the French pair playing against Facchini/Zuchelli bid to 4♡ via 1♡-2♡-4♡. Facchini, holding QJ93 of spades and Q965 of clubs, decided upon a club lead — catching partner with the A-K of clubs and nothing in spades. Interesting? Yes. Suspect? *Yes.* But it was nowhere near conclusive of any wrongdoing, and on this hand merely prevented the opponents from making an overtrick.

At halftime (after sixteen boards), I opted to go to the bar. We were not playing that night and it was a perfect opportunity to relax and unwind with all I had on my plate. About five minutes after I sat down, in walked an ashen-faced Bruce Keidan, who immediately spotted me. "They were doing exactly what you had told me they would do!" he exclaimed. "Zuchelli would sit like a Buddha and Facchini would tap his shoes, both during the bidding and then before the opening lead if they were defending." Bruce then shared his notes on the specific times their toes touched, and which player had sent the signal. Obviously we were nowhere close to breaking the code of what the foot movements specifically meant, but we were onto something, no doubt about it!

It took a few moments for me to simmer down from the shock of Bruce's findings and I suggested that he accompany me to an almost empty Vugraph auditorium where Edgar Kaplan was still sitting at the commentators table awaiting the start of the second half. After a very brief description of what Bruce had just witnessed, Edgar phoned our captain, Alfie Sheinwold (Edgar's long time friend and partner), who had already returned to his quarters. We were invited to join him and the three of us headed over.

Upon our arrival at Alfie's suite, we were ushered inside to plush surroundings and comfortable easy chairs. Alfie asked his wife Paula to excuse us, and she graciously departed the room. She left the four of us to speak, but after Alfie's unusual request for privacy, there was no doubt something of major import was happening. During the next half hour, we embarked on a full indoctrination of Edgar and Alfie, including how Bruce and I had met on the Bermuda-bound plane, how I had conceived the plan for Bruce to monitor Facchini/Zuchelli and then detailed for him exactly what to look for. Edgar now took control and formulated the following plan.

Since I was going to begin playing early the next afternoon, I was not to be involved in any way. Edgar would lead the investigation by arranging that important personages of the WBF (various team captains and high-ranking officials) would be available to kibitz whenever the Vegetables were in action — which usually was about two-thirds of the time. With the exception of the Italian captain, they would be told in advance specifically what to look for. It was also decided that since it was only Friday night, and there was no urgency to do anything hasty, our plan would not go into effect until the last match of the first Round Robin on Sunday night when the USA would be facing Italy head on. Bob and I would be there, perforce, and I would be an integral part of proving, without a doubt, what we knew was happening.

Everything was well coordinated, or so we thought. On Saturday, we had arranged for Jim O'Sullivan from Australia, Johannes Hammerich from Venezuela, Lew Mathe (the ACBL President) from California, Tracy Denninger representing the host country of Bermuda, Julius Rosenblum from New Orleans (the current WBF President), and finally Sandro Salvetti, the Captain of the Italian team, all to witness the Veggies playing footsie. Everyone except the Italian captain was briefed on what was happening. However, despite all the key parties being in their respective places prepared to do their thing on Sunday, our sting operation never got off the ground as we originally intended. As a result, the bad guys never got burned in the dramatic and convincing manner that we had planned. Why, you ask? Simply because we weren't intuitive or calculating enough to allow for the 'Mathe Factor' alluded to earlier.

Lew Mathe, who was serving his term as ACBL President, had become a bitter man. In the 1930s he had been one of the two best players in the USA (along with John Gerber of Houston), but according to most knowledgeable sources, Lew had long since lost that status. However, he continued to play top-level bridge through the decades, winning more than his share despite playing with many seriously flawed teams. The competitive strain of playing at this level coupled with the frustration of no financial rewards (this being before professionalism appeared on the scene) probably took its toll. The result? Lew simply turned into a grumpy old man. His unhappiness was evident on several occasions when he was heard to complain, "It's impossible to win anything important with five pieces of shit!" Lew never minced words.

He had already negatively impacted our morale by telling some of us that our teammates would crumble from the pressure — making winning impossible, or unlikely at best. With this type of alarmingly negative mindset, it should have been no surprise that in Bermuda, Lew would undermine our investigative process by jumping the gun. This was the kiss of death that killed our sting: Mathe, completely unauthorized, began spouting off to several fringe people what he knew, enhancing the likelihood that the Italians would be alerted to our operation well in advance and foil our plans for a Sunday exposure. As a matter of record, several years later Mathe again betrayed a similar confidence and singlehandedly bungled an important plea bargain settlement in a well-known cheating case. He deliberately violated an agreement to stay silent, contacting the press and thereby causing a megabucks lawsuit to be filed against the ACBL. Fortunately, cooler heads prevailed and eventually the problem was resolved with no money damages having to be paid — but no thanks to Lew Mathe and his inability to keep his lips zipped.

Back to the Vegetable Garden. Kaplan's plan was to climax our investigation by having Bob and me play against Facchini/Zuchelli on that fateful Sunday night. Italian captain Salvetti and Italian coach Volpe were to have front row seats, surrounded by the entourage of noted administrators who had been alerted to our plan the day before. The idea was that, upon a prearranged signal, I was suddenly to pick up the card table for all to see the Italian version of the 'dying swan' — with toes attached. Mathe's *a cappella* intrusion ruined the element of surprise. So, rather than be thwarted by clever excuses, justification and defenses by the Italians, Edgar decided to come forward himself a few hours earlier than we had planned. Besides, we had an abundance of very strong evidence and no one could even begin to question what the Veggies were doing because we could easily substantiate our claims. Like they say, *if the shoe fits*!

Walter Bingham, a Senior Editor of *Sports Illustrated*, was also on site planning to do a story on the Bermuda Bowl. He was there partly for the story but also was (and still is) a very close friend of Eddie Kantar who was one of my teammates. Walter was also a lifetime bridge player, so this was a wonderful opportunity for him to vacation and cover a world championship at the same time. Walter got far more than he bargained for and penned a classic article for the magazine, entitled something like 'I Get a Kick out of You', that even now is well worth reading.

Perhaps the funniest, and most appropriate, reaction to the news of what was going on at our tournament came from Canadian Eric Murray, a Bermuda Bowl veteran himself, of course. He sent Alfie, as North American captain, the following telegram:

Dear Mr. Sheinwold:

I would like to volunteer for the North American Team. I play a reasonable game of bridge and take a size 14 shoe.

Sincerely,
Eric R. Murray

This message was read out in the Vugraph room, to great hilarity.

Anyway — the story broke, albeit prematurely, and the Sunday evening bridge activity ceased on a dime in anticipation of the Trial. Oswald Jacoby, who was there as a journalist, was slated to be an expert witness. With his genius for mathematics and understanding of the laws of probabilities, his opinions would be well respected and meaningful in the final analysis. The Trial lasted until Monday afternoon. A press conference was held with Facchini/Zuchelli, who didn't speak English and communicated through an interpreter. I remember being seated next to Jimmy Patino, who expressed his thoughts about minimizing the scandal and whether or not the defendants should be disqualified. Jimmy called the shots in world bridge in those days. I know Jimmy did what he thought was best for bridge. He always does. There is no one more dedicated or a greater contributor to perpetuating the game than Jaime Ortiz-Patino, but I took issue with this particular decision. Not forcing the Italians to forfeit will always to me represent gross unfairness and sadly I will always harbor bad feelings about the handling of the matter. And here we sit over thirty years later still facing the same challenges of foreign cultures trying to have their own way, regardless of the long-range effect on the game.

Many years have passed since that time in Bermuda. Looking back on it now, let me give you my *post bellum* assessment of what happened.

Both Keidan and Sheinwold tried to milk the scandal and gain personal credit and publicity. It is unfathomable to me (although I have never made the facts public until now) that Keidan has remained silent about who made him the hero of the scandal, and the fact that I put him on the dirt trail of the Vegetables, armed with the necessary information to dig up their secrets.

Some months before the Bermuda Incident, Sheinwold had written an article accusing Belladonna, Garozzo and Forquet of cheating. This had been much criticized by the world bridge press, and the Vegetables being let off essentially unpunished simply made Sheinwold look worse. However, Denis Howard's careful analysis gave the situation a whole new twist. His beautifully presented article, entitled 'Anatomy of a Scandal', first appeared in *Australian Bridge* and was reprinted in the official WBF book of the 1975 Bermuda Bowl. Howard, a lawyer by profession, was still unhappy with Sheinwold's article since he saw no evidence to support that specific accusation. However, in a careful re-examination of the accounts of what took place in Bermuda, he came to the conclusion that there was no doubt that Facchini and Zuchelli were cheating. He stated that 'any objective analysis of the evidence and of the surrounding circumstances will lead all but the willfully self-deceptive to the same determination'.

Later, it was also announced that Sheinwold's column had replaced our 'Aces On Bridge' in the *Denver Post*. As it happened, Sheinwold was at the time working with Len Smith, an old timer who wrote local bridge news for the *Denver Post*, and to whom Sheinwold had given an early lead on the Bermuda Bowl incident. Ira Corn was furious with me, but I was totally a victim of circumstances. A combination of factors (which I can only guess at), coupled with the scoop the *Denver Post* received, made me think it was not such an accident or coincidence that our column was replaced by Sheinwold's.

Another distressing situation occurred the last day of the Bermuda Bowl. Henry Francis, who was both Executive Editor of the ACBL *Bridge Bulletin* and Editor for the Bermuda Bowl daily press release, highlighted the USA-Italy confrontation in the final Sunday *Daily Bulletin*. Our team was 44 IMPs ahead with 32 boards to go. Francis' coverage seemed to be about The Ugly Americans and how most everyone was pulling for the Italians. Remember, not only had the Foot Soldiers been accused and convicted of touching each other's toes during the bidding and before the opening lead, but shockingly they had been allowed to play on. Eventually, Facchini and Zuchelli were benched, but only because they were playing miserably (their style being cramped by screens and footboards) — not for any moral reason.

I was shocked by Henry's stance and that he would write such a thing — but he did, and perhaps it influenced the crowd's reaction. When Bob and I entered the Vugraph room after playing the final sixteen boards in the Closed Room, the fateful 7♣ hand was up on the screen. The whole crowd, *which included at least ten Americans I could count*, was on its feet wildly cheering as Belladonna and Garozzo bid to a miserable 7♣ (which needed Kx onside in front of the doubleton AQ). What an absolutely disgusting feeling to witness the audience pulling for the Italians and turning a victory into a vile loss — especially in light of the foot-tapping exhibition! The pro-Italian sentiment was possibly even more painful than the incredible misfortune of such a poor grand slam being fulfilled.

The Closing Banquet took place with about 150 of the 200 Italian supporters in attendance. They had traveled all the way to Bermuda to cheer their team on. As Sheinwold was giving his losing captain's speech, the Italians cheering section charged the podium calling Sheinwold an 'American pig' for accusing their beloved team of cheating. Sheinwold, who certainly was no angel, was actually delivering a polite concession speech — replete with a request to put the name-calling behind us and go on from there.

As if the *Daily Bulletin* Editor's article that Sunday had not been distasteful enough, witness this Editorial (from Henry Francis again), entitled 'The Ugly American', which appeared in the April 1975 ACBL *Bridge Bulletin*.

No doubt about it — America's image was not heightened in any way by what happened at the recent Bermuda Bowl competition in Bermuda. Our representatives played well, and they did nothing for which they were reprimanded. Nevertheless, the Italians were cheered to the rafters when they came from behind and defeated our team. Why?

Because the Ugly American emerged. It was an Italian pair that was reprimanded for improper conduct. In fact, at least four witnesses testified that something strange was happening when Gianfranco Facchini and Sergio Zuchelli were playing (see WBF President Julius Rosenblum's report on page 23).

But the American captain and his team were not willing to accept the decision of the WBF Appeals Committee. They threatened to pull out of the competition, finally agreeing to play only when ordered to do so by the ACBL representatives on hand. Three other teams were even more affected by any 'unusual' actions on the part of the Italian pair — Indonesia, France and Brazil all had played Italy before the accusations were made public, but North America had not. But these teams accepted the WBF verdict without recriminations — at least in public.

Much was made of the fact that the Italian pair could continue to play, but the thorough investigation planned by the WBF was thwarted by the premature breaking of the news — by American journalists. Another session of observation could easily have convinced the Appeals Committee one way or the other about Facchini and Zuchelli. As a result, the committee felt something was wrong, but the evidence compiled was considered to be too skimpy for action more severe than the reprimand for improper conduct.

The Americans had egg on their face again on the final day when they once more refused to play. Again the ACBL representatives had to order them to take their places, but everyone knew the Americans were doing so under duress.

As a result, almost everyone forgot the Italian pair was under suspicion. Instead they remembered that the Americans were behaving like poor sports.

We had an exceptional opportunity to enhance our image in world bridge. But, we blew it.

Thirty years have elapsed and I still cannot fathom what could have prompted such a despicable article — its author clearly failing to understand the helplessness and pain we felt, the abuse we were forced to endure, and how our team had been victimized by a politically motivated decision. We ended up as losers of a world championship which we rightfully should have won — all because we were the prey of foot-tapping cheats. How could Henry have been so insensitive to our plight? *We* were the victims. It was *the writer* who blew it!

The ongoing ACBL and WBF practice of keeping bridge scandals as low key as possible by merely asking partners to not play together in the future goes a long way toward avoiding lawsuits. However, it does nothing less than nurture cheating. This ostrich-like tactic may be an extremely sound measure to keep the organizations afloat financially, but it offers little consolation to the cheaters' victims — and even worse, it recognizes, celebrates, honors and rewards the culprits for achieving victory in an insidious manner.

Once again, cheating allegations against a European pair had been swept under the carpet. In French, this kind of rerun is known as *déjà vu*; I don't know the corresponding phrase in Italian.

CHAPTER 10

THE COLOSSUS OF RHODES *REVISITED!*

CRUSADING FOR WHAT I BELIEVE is good for bridge is no easy task and doing so antagonizes those whom I am running up against. I'm sure that, when I was dropped from the Nickell team, many people who have crossed swords with me over the years felt a glow of satisfaction at the thought that I had been knocked down a peg. Don't think I'm feeling sorry for myself, though. Far from it! And don't believe for one second that I wouldn't take many of the same actions again in similar situations. I'm no hero, and I'm not trying to portray myself as a martyr. I simply believe that bridge is too great a game for me to sit idly by when I see something unjust or inequitable taking place or about to happen.

Yes, I've been wrong on occasion. Who hasn't? I haven't always handled situations in the best possible manner. Who has? I've never claimed to be perfect, but my heart is in the right place. No doubt you're asking yourself, what the hell is this guy talking about? I suppose a couple of examples of the Lone Wolff in action could help you understand where I'm coming from — where I've always come from. You might not agree with me, but I hope you will understand my motivation as well as my disappointment when those around me don't seem to have the same goals in mind.

Two cases that come to mind immediately occurred during the World Bridge Olympiad in 1996, which I attended as Chairman of Appeals, among other responsibilities. It is strictly coincidental that they are 'monumental', but it is worthy of note that both of these incredible bridge irregularities, for lack of a stronger word, actually occurred in Rhodes, historically the site of the Colossus, one of the Seven Wonders of the Ancient World.

The 10th Olympiad was the largest ever, with seventy-one teams in the Open event and forty-three in the Women's. With so many teams in the Open, the field was divided into two sections, one of thirty-five teams, the other with thirty-six. The qualifying segment took place over a number of days. The contestants in each group played a complete round robin — that is, each team played every other team. At the conclusion of round-robin play, the top four teams in each group would advance to the quarterfinal round. The rankings were done by converting the IMP scores from each match to Victory Points on a scale which awarded a maximum of 25 VPs to the winners and as few as zero to the losers (that would be considered a real blowout, but not an impossibility).

In such a large field, the standard of play will vary from very high to nearly hopeless. That might seem like a surprisingly cruel assessment for a world championship, but in the Olympiad, every country is entitled to a representative team, no matter what! Some nations have a fine assemblage of true experts. Others might have trouble fielding a squad that would finish average at a typical ACBL Regional or Sectional. In Rhodes, there were several weak teams in the field in both Open groups. When you're playing in a round robin with wide variance in the skills of the competitors, it is important to crush the weaker teams. Are you following me here? The weak teams are probably getting creamed in most of their other matches, so if you don't beat up on them by a lot, it's tantamount to a loss. A contending team might get away with playing two or three soft matches — particularly out of a total of thirty-five — but the competition in these world events is so stiff that any letup, at any time, can be fatal to your chances of making the top four in your group — and if you don't make the top four, you're out. Qualification for the knockout phase is your primary objective from the outset. That's how the story of the match between Russia and Cyprus came to my attention.

Russia had a fine young team, including Andrei Gromov and Alexander Petrunin. These two, playing four-handed with two Polish champions — Adam Zmudzinski and Cezary Balicki — won the Vanderbilt Knockout Teams in Kansas City in 2001. That's no easy feat, I assure you, especially going the iron-man route with only four on your team. Anyway, in Rhodes the Russians were considered serious candidates to make the quarterfinal round. For one thing, some of the perennial contenders weren't fielding their usual strong teams. This was especially true of the United States, which had sent a group from Chicago — all very good players but with almost no international experience. They had won the Team Trials in San Francisco, however, so they were the US representatives, perforce. As an aside, the inexperience of the Americans showed early on, and although they made a late run, they finished ninth in their group, far from a qualifying spot.

The Russians, meanwhile, had mixed success early. They were hanging around close to the qualifying spots, but had not yet climbed higher than fifth. In fact, the Russians were in fifth when they met Cyprus, the doormat of round robin Group B, in the nineteenth round. There's no way to sugarcoat it. The six-member Cyprus team was simply bad in comparison to the other powerful lineups entered. Of thirty-five matches in the round robin, they won three. They averaged fewer than 8 Victory Points (out of a possible 25) for each match. They were last in the field by a considerable margin. In my dealings with them after the controversy arose, I found the team members, including a lovely husband-wife pair, to be fine people. They simply were nowhere near the same level in terms of bridge expertise as most of the teams they played. They were completely outclassed, especially in the subject match with the Russians.

However, despite the disparity in skill and experience levels, Russia only defeated Cyprus by the surprising margin of a paltry 5 IMPs (50-45). That translated to 16 VPs for Russia. Considering that Cyprus was being manhandled by nearly every other above-average team, this very definitely equated to a loss for Russia and a moral victory for Cyprus. But — sit tight! A strange thing happened on the way back from the Kremlin!

On one deal, the couple from Cyprus bid to a grand slam in diamonds holding six to the A-J in trumps in one hand and three to the king in the other. As it happened, the long diamonds were in dummy and Gromov was 'in front' of the diamond length — that is, if dummy was West, Gromov was South, and he held three low diamonds. In the play, it turned out Gromov's partner had the singleton queen (declarer played the king first from hand, dropping the queen). The vulnerable grand slam was cold, and Gromov and his partner knew their teammates would never bid a grand missing four trumps to the queen. This was clearly a loss of at least 12 IMPs. (Indeed, the Russians at the other table bid only 6NT.)

However, in the minds of the Russians, this hand was not a done deal! Shortly after the match, the Russians sought out TD Bill Schoder, known to most people as 'Kojak' because of his resemblance to the late Telly Savalas. (Not only is he bald but his facial features are reminiscent of Savalas as well.) The Russians told Kojak that after thinking about the deal they had realized that the dummy had fourteen cards and the South hand — Gromov's — had only twelve. The boards had already been taken to a storage room, so Kojak went to conduct an inspection. Sure enough, the hand that had been dummy had fourteen cards. Gromov's had twelve. Instead of six diamonds to the A-J, dummy had seven.

The rules say that a board fouled in that manner should be thrown out. Something told Kojak it wasn't that simple, however, so he sought me out. He felt he had to throw out the board, but he wanted my advice (and perhaps my blessing). Throwing out the board would give the Russians a 50-32 victory and 19 VPs instead of 16 — and if you don't think that's important, consider that Russia didn't qualify for the quarterfinal until the final match of the round robin, edging out Israel by 1.5 VPs. In fact, Russia had never been higher than fifth in the round-robin standings until they scored 25 VPs against Kenya (another of the weaker teams) in the final round to move into fourth while Israel (fourth before the final round) was defeating Great Britain by only a small margin and dropping to fifth.

Meanwhile, the 'fouled' board had a rotten smell to me. Most people are not familiar with high-level bridge, but I can assure you that it is impossible — and I mean *absolutely* impossible — that a player of Gromov's ability, savvy and experience would defend a grand slam in a world championship and not notice that his hand had only twelve cards while dummy had fourteen. It wouldn't happen once in a million deals. It also turned out, by the way, that after the match was concluded the Cypriots who had played against Gromov and Petrunin had left the table while the Russians stayed behind.

My next move, therefore, was to talk to the Cypriots. I located the husband and wife who bid the grand slam and asked them about the distribution of the diamond suit. They assured me dummy had AJxxxx and declarer held Kxx. I advised them to appeal the ruling. They were an older couple — very nice people. Their first reaction was one of horror. Oh, no, they protested, they couldn't do that — no matter what! Cyprus was going to lose the match anyway and it mattered little to them whether they got another 3 VPs. Furthermore, they didn't want to cause anyone grief or appear to be accusing their opponents of anything bordering on cheating. I'm not sure they fully grasped the import of what I was suggesting. I told the pair that it was their duty to appeal the decision — that they owed it to the sanctity of the tournament and all of their fellow-competitors not to let this ruling go unchallenged. I guess you could say that I intimidated them.

At that time, of course, I was in a much stronger position than I am today. I had been President of the World Bridge Federation only a couple of years earlier, I had all those world championships, I was on one of the best bridge teams in the world — I could go on, but you understand what I'm saying. It's not that I think I'm great because I had that kind of status. I enjoyed being in that position because it allowed me to get things done more easily. Permit me a brief digression here. Over the years I have infuriated many people who object to my approach, which some liken to a sledgehammer, but I have found it's the only way to get some things done. One of my staunchest supporters, although not necessarily publicly, has been Jose Damiani, who has been President of the World Bridge Federation since I stepped down in 1994. Jose has been a good friend and, although I have made some decisions that negatively affected teams he favored, he has been on my side. A lot of what I have accomplished would not have been achieved without Jose's support and his belief in my dedication to what is best for the game.

Meanwhile, back at the Colossus, a committee was assembled to hear the appeal by the Cypriots. To their credit, they handled themselves well, recounting the deal and insisting that dummy had contained six diamonds, not seven. In fact, the woman told the committee that when she played the king, and the queen fell offside, she had to stop and count to make sure all her diamonds were good. Despite that, there were members of the committee who wanted to uphold the ruling and have the board tossed out.

It must have been clear to everyone what had happened, but no one wanted to face the issue. If the committee overturned Kojak's decision to throw out the board, it could be for one reason and one reason only — and no one wanted to be associated with even such an oblique statement as that. Even now, as I'm sure you have noted, I have not just come right out and said what I believed happened. But is that really necessary? If a man comes home late, smelling of another woman's perfume, with lipstick on his collar and mussed-up hair, do we have to write it down to understand what he has been up to?

I did not, of course, have any proof of what in my heart I *knew* had happened, and there's no delicate way to handle this kind of situation. Unfortunately for the Russians, I did not then, nor do I now, care if something I do makes people angry. There is no perfect solution in cases such as this. Some feathers are going to be ruffled, but the bottom line (and the only thing important) is that right is done and justice prevails — regardless of the consequences to the evil offenders. It wasn't right to have that board thrown out. I can't prove anything because I wasn't there, but I know the cast of characters involved, and I know with 100% certainty that a player of Gromov's caliber would have noticed long before the end of play the number of cards in his hand and the dummy!

As the appeal case began to wind down, we finally heard from the non-playing captain of the Russian team — a dark, bearded man by the name of Michael Rosenblum. "Well," he said, directing his comments to me, obviously hoping to put me on the spot, "how do you think that card got from the South hand to West?"

My reply: "Looking at the situation, I guess a great big Russian bird came swooping down and transported it."

Deafening silence descended upon the room. Rosenblum glared at me. I glared back. His face was — shall we say, Borscht Red? Finally, the Russians, including their captain, got up and left. To the great relief of many, the appeal by Cyprus was upheld. The board was not thrown out and the 12-IMP gain for Cyprus stood. They still lost the match — and it's worth noting that Russia qualified anyway.

The aftermath of the incident was more criticism of me. Sure, they said, there's Wolff on his self-serving mission again. My response: What did I have to gain? I had no ties to six inexperienced players from Cyprus. I didn't even know them. I had nothing against the Russians, and I wasn't even playing in the Olympiad. Remember, the Nickell team did not qualify to play in Rhodes. I challenge anyone to suggest I stood to gain anything. What was at stake was right, pure and simple. Once Kojak filled me in on the case, I knew it would be wrong to let this slide — and I didn't think twice about taking action. Does this make me a saint? No. But I don't understand why people are reluctant to do something when they see wrong being perpetrated.

Did I bend the rules to see that justice was done? I don't think so. I used the power of my status and reputation to make sure that Cyprus appealed, and I was forceful in dealing with the Russians. Nobody's perfect — certainly not I! Scrutiny of my track record will verify that. However, I just can't stand to see something wrong happening when I or others are in a position to prevent it. In some eyes, it is a shortcoming and perhaps a flaw of character. I look at it differently. In all good conscience, I can't sit by idly when I have the power to change it.

I asserted myself in another incident involving a deal which took place one round before the Russia-Cyprus incident, in a match between Indonesia and Argentina. What I did in that case created even more hard feelings toward me during the Rhodes tournament. Unlike the Russia-Cyprus case, which did not get much public exposure, this one was written up in the *Daily Bulletin* at the tournament, with commentary from me. This is what happened on Board 30, near the end of the match in question.

I will explain first the mechanics of play at high-level events. The screen cuts diagonally across each card table (and these days it goes all the way to the floor so that players cannot touch feet under the table!). There is a small door at the bottom of the part of the screen that goes across the top of the table. This allows a tray to be moved back and forth through the screen as players put cards from a bidding box on the tray. That is how the auction proceeds.

The way the screen bisects the table, West and South are screen-mates, as are East and North. In a game with no screens, an Alert (meant to give the opponents a heads-up about a bid that doesn't mean what it seems to) is made by the partner of the person who makes the bid. Using screens, both players make an Alert, each to his own screen-mate — and they do so silently, usually by a hand signal. If you make an alert and your screen-mate wants to know what the bid means, you have a pencil and a notepad so that you can explain in silence. Therefore, if West makes an alert, he will signal to South, who can ask if he wishes. You never see your partner in games with screens, and you likewise don't hear or see his explanations of any alertable bids that come up. Keep that background in mind as you read on. Remember, this is Indonesia versus Argentina.

Dealer: East
Vul.: Neither

                    ♠ A Q 6
                    ♡ A Q 10 8 6 5 2
                    ◇ 10 4
                    ♣ 8

    ♠ 9 8 5 2   ♠ 7 4
    ♡ 9 4   N   ♡ J 7
    ◇ J 9 6 3   W   E   ◇ Q 8 7 5 2
    ♣ 9 3 2   S   ♣ A J 10 4

                    ♠ K J 10 3
                    ♡ K 3
                    ◇ A K
                    ♣ K Q 7 6 5

West	North	East	South
Manoppo	Mooney	Lasut	Monsegur
		pass	1♣[1]
1♡[2]	2♡	3♣[3]	dbl
3◇[4]	4♡	all pass	

1. Strong, artificial and forcing.
2. Alerted and explained by West to South: spades and diamonds or hearts and clubs. Alerted and explained by East to North: two suits of the same color (spades and clubs or hearts and diamonds).
3. Directing West to pass if he has the black suits or correct if he has the reds.
4. West confirming to South: spades and diamonds. East confirming to North: hearts and diamonds.

As you can see, there is no defense to a small slam in hearts for North-South — or for that matter 6NT — but at the table, the Argentinians stopped in game. East did not lead the ♣A, so North-South made all the tricks for plus 510.

When the deal was completed and it was clear that they had been screwed, Mooney and Monsegur called a tournament director to complain. All of the facts in the bidding as presented here were confirmed by all players who were at the table. East's explanations to North were found to be correct in terms of their agreements. West's explanations to South were wrong, but he had indicated his real holding: spades and diamonds. North complained that if he and his partner had both been given the correct information, they could have reached the slam. Despite that argument, the tournament director allowed the result to stand.

Argentina appealed the ruling. During the hearing, my suspicions were aroused. Manoppo claimed that he thought he had bid 1◇ and not 1♡, and thus the explanation he gave to South was in accordance with the 1◇ bid. He claimed that he had not noticed his wrong bid at all during or at the conclusion of the auction and consequently had not altered his explanation.

North admitted that he had made no slam try because he thought he was bidding opposite a void in hearts (or a singleton at most) in his partner's hand. He could have made a slam try, but he didn't because he thought his right-hand opponent had a bunch of hearts. That's not unreasonable.

The committee, of which I was the Chairman, determined that East had given North the correct explanation. Thus the action taken by North could not be altered, as the Laws state that you may bid wrongly but not explain wrongly. South, on the other hand, had the wrong explanation.

The vote was not unanimous, and I had to dominate the group to see that justice was done, but in the end the committee determined that North-South would enjoy the full benefit of any doubt. The result was changed to 6♡ by North, plus 1010 (we still didn't think East would lead the ♣A).

As to West's explanation, the committee found it self-serving; it was hard to imagine that West had never noticed that the bidding card he actually put on the tray was not the one he had intended to put there. We also decided that West, when he entered the auction with one jack in that balanced hand, could have been aware that the bid he made could damage the opponents and be to his advantage.

Consider also that East knew he had a great fit for one of his partner's suits. If West had the red suits, East had five-card support for him.

If it was the black suits, East had four-card support, including three honors. And what did East do? He bid only 3♣. That might not seem too strange, but in the context of the event and considering how aggressive modern bidders are, that smells a lot like a rat to me. Normal pairs would try to put maximum pressure on the opponents by bidding at least 4♣ with the East hand (directing partner to correct to diamonds if he had the red two-suiter), and many would bid 5♣.

So why does this bidding stink? Well, obviously East knew that his partner might have a hand every bit as lousy as it was. He wasn't going to go jumping around and risk a huge penalty. The trouble is, East-West didn't disclose this to the opponents as they are *required* to do. When West knows his partner won't be jumping the bidding, he can enter the auction on practically nothing and incur very little risk. Quoting the committee report: 'Such bids are damaging not only to the other side in this case, but also to bridge in general. Furthermore, there was not one single high-card point reference on East-West's convention card that could denote that the bid of 1♡ could be made on such a balanced distribution and almost no high cards. The committee therefore regarded the 1♡ bid as a psychic bid, and did not at all take it kindly that the psychic was magnified through incorrect explanation.'

What brought on more grumbling about me was that I argued long and hard to add on a procedural penalty of 4 VPs against the Indonesians for their lack of full disclosure, the misleading description on the convention card and the failure to explain a psychic bid correctly. To me, it was mighty convenient for Manoppo to pull the 'wrong' card out of the bidding box and also mighty convenient that he 'didn't notice' through the entire auction that he had pulled out the 'wrong' card. Bear in mind that when the auction was over he had to pick up the 1♡ bid from the tray and return it to its proper place in the box. I was not buying the statement that he thought he had bid 1◇.

When the smoke cleared, Indonesia accepted the penalty and went about their business, qualifying easily for the knockout phase of the tournament. And to this day Eddie Manoppo and Henky Lasut, as well as the whole Indonesian team and Captain, greet me especially cordially, as if to say, "Thanks for keeping the game safe for all of us despite our having to pay the price for it." Yes, cultures sure are different around the world!

I got a lot of flak, however, because I more or less made the committee go along with me on the penalty. This was how it was written up:

> Our committee realizes that the procedural penalty of 4 VPs is a substantial one and could be looked upon as harsh. We based our

decision on the particular offenses committed. Pairs are allowed to play 'destructive' defense conventions. In return for their privilege, we must and do require the following special ethical responsibilities:

1. *Never* allow 'careless' misbidding which, if intentional, usually results in the favor of the misbidders.
2. *Never* allow incorrect explanations on either side of the table.
3. *Never* allow less than full disclosure at the table concerning the details of the convention or the tendencies of the players.
4. *Never* allow less than comprehensive disclosure on the convention card.

If ever *any one* of these requirements is not fulfilled, the opponents (particularly naïve or inexperienced opponents) are at too much of a disadvantage. Here, all four of these caveats were violated.

Remember, we on the appeals committee, particularly in anything but a straight knockout event, represent the whole field, not just the opponents. Allowing a team to psychologically intimidate another is unfair to all teams in particular and to bridge in general.

Our responsibility is to have a level playing field so that our teams have an equal chance for the result to be decided by bidding, play and defense, which are the cornerstones of our game.

I am proud to have been instrumental in righting the wrong that was attempted to be perpetrated in each of these 'colossal' landmark cases in modern Rhodes in 1996.

CHAPTER 11

THE ACBL... FLIRTING WITH DISASTER!

ONE OF THE EERIEST EPISODES in my bridge career involved an enigmatic character named Bob Nargassans. To many at ACBL headquarters in Memphis, the name Nargassans will live in infamy. There is no question that the ACBL had a close call in its brief encounter with the so-called promoter from Massachusetts.

It all started at the 1996 Fall NABC in San Francisco. During that tournament, I was approached by Paul Marston, a well-known, highly regarded internationalist from Australia by way of New Zealand. Marston had good credentials. Besides playing for his homeland in international competition, he had devised a player-rating system for use in bridge clubs in Australia that, at least at one time, was very popular and almost universally used.

Marston asked for a few minutes of my time so that he could tell me about a man he had met while this gentleman had been promoting a rock concert in Australia. His name was Bob Nargassans, and according to Marston, he was a philanthropist who was enamored of bridge and wanted to spend some money to help the game grow and prosper. The man, Marston told me, wanted to 'throw ten to fifteen million at bridge'.

I take a back seat to no one when it comes to love for bridge and a desire to see it increase in popularity, so naturally I was interested in hearing more about this unlikely would-be benefactor to the game. It wasn't long before I came face to face with him. Less than two months after the San Francisco tournament — in January of 1997 — Nargassans and Marston flew to Dallas to give me the word on his grand plans for bridge and the ACBL. I was all ears.

I picked Nargassans and Marston up at the airport, and it was difficult not to be impressed by this dapper, white-haired man with an expensive suit and a genteel manner. The urbane Nargassans appeared to be in his early fifties. He was impeccably dressed and very well spoken. Nargassans and Marston stayed only a couple of days, but they promised to return to Dallas for the meetings of the ACBL Board of Directors prior to the 1997 Spring NABC.

While Nargassans was in town, he gave me a preview of his plans. The first step was to be the formation of a company — Grand Slam Bridge, Inc. — which Nargassans and Marston said would produce a television show about bridge, create professional bridge tours and market a player-rating system designed for club players.

My role in the deal, according to Nargassans, was for Marston and me to be in charge of a circuit of professional players who would go on tour, much like the tennis or golf stars. I was to be a 'commissioner' of sorts for the pro tour, Nargassans said. My salary was to be $100,000 a year, and I was to have an office in New York. When I rejected the idea of living in New York, Nargassans said that would not be a problem. I would have a secretarial staff, and the office would be there when I needed to be in New York, which would be a maximum of two to three months a year. It all sounded too good to be true and, as is usually the case with things like this, it was.

Between Nargassans' first Dallas visit and his return for the ACBL Board meetings, he was on the phone to me several times each week. It is clear now that he recognized that although I was not myself a Board member at this time, I had influence with the powers that be in bridge. He was trying to solidify his position to assure favorable consideration by the ACBL Board of Directors.

When he returned to Dallas in March of that year, Nargassans was still the epitome of style and grace. On his arm was a very young woman whom he introduced as his wife. I was seeing someone at the time and one night my date and I were invited to dine with the Nargassans and Marston. We were chauffeured in a stretch limousine, with a full wet bar, to the most expensive restaurant in town, the one at the Mansion on Turtle Creek. Nargassans was really spending lavishly — although I learned later that he planned to recover all these expenses out of money that he expected to receive from the ACBL for the 'marketing' of bridge.

Nargassans was pushing his program, which he claimed would return bridge to household name status and raise public consciousness about the game. He was working the Board of Directors like an insurance salesman and name-dropping like crazy. Ivana Trump, according to Nargassans, was a dear friend, and he frequently visited Atlantic City to have breakfast with her. This was at a time when there was continuing media talk about Donald and Ivana Trump, who were having marital problems and were about to part ways, and Nargassans was telling everyone that Ivana often used his shoulder to cry on. He also hinted broadly that he was close to the Turners — Ted and Jane (Fonda) — and that his main business was the promotion of major concerts. He practically guaranteed that bridge would be a regular event on ESPN. At one point, Nargassans returned to Dallas solely to meet with Bob Hamman, whom he was trying to recruit to his side and planned to use in some capacity.

All of this sounded great, but there seemed to be a slight flaw. When we reviewed Nargassans' proposals, it was the ACBL that was putting up all the money — in the neighborhood of just under $2 million. Understand — the ACBL is not a poor organization. At the time, membership numbers had been in decline for some years, but thanks mainly to Roy G. Green, a banker who became Chief Executive Officer of the ACBL in 1992, the organization was on very sound financial footing. However, even with a healthy bottom line and a secure monetary structure, a $2 million hit to the ACBL would have been significant, even crippling. A question some were asking was, "What about the millions that the 'philanthropist' Nargassans was supposed to be interested in spending on bridge?" Unfortunately, many people were not astute enough to ask the question, and the Nargassans plan was gaining momentum and support from members of the ACBL Board of Directors — notably Howard Piltch, the representative for District 25, which includes Massachusetts. In fact, Piltch was one of Nargassans' strongest supporters and he did his best to convince the full board that the ACBL's 'salvation' lay in a pact with him. It seems appropriate to use the word 'pact' considering the cast of characters involved.

One aspect of the plan created near panic at ACBL headquarters, however. Marston and Nargassans were to take over in Memphis, making drastic reductions in staff. They had been told, possibly by Howard, that there was a lot of fat in Memphis and considerable room for trimming. As the Marston-Nargassans-Piltch steamroller moved inexorably forward, Roy Green was cautiously trying to figure out ways to make $2 million available without decimating the reserve fund. The only viable option was to reduce the staff drastically — an unattractive course after Green had worked very hard to upgrade service levels for ACBL members.

In May of that year, since I was a Pension Trustee for the ACBL, I had to go to New York for a meeting of the Trustees at Bear Stearns. Nargassans knew I was coming and he told me he wanted to get together to finalize our arrangements and present me with my first check as commissioner of the new pro circuit. I hadn't even come close to accepting the deal since I was somewhat dubious about the whole plan (although perhaps not as much as some others at that point), but I did agree to meet with him.

I don't know what inspired me to set up a meeting between Marston, Nargassans and Jimmy Cayne, but it turned out to be a fortuitous move that possibly saved the ACBL — at least from the standpoint of avoiding this particular landmine. Cayne, in case you don't know, has been a force in high-level bridge for some years. He has two second place finishes in world events and several national championships to his credit, and he is always in contention because of the caliber of teams that he hires. Unlike some sponsors, however, Cayne is a very good player. A wealthy man, he is the CEO of Bear Stearns, the Wall Street investment company. Cayne does not suffer fools gladly, and he can be unpleasant if you catch him on a bad day. Cayne's office is in New York, which must be what made me think of setting up the meeting. Nargassans, of course, was only too glad to meet another potential ally — and an important one at that. No doubt he was confident his charm and *savoir faire* would earn him another friend. Wrong! He underestimated Jimmy Cayne.

When the time came, I accompanied Marston and Nargassans to Cayne's office. Along for the ride was Don Moeller, a member of the ACBL Board of Directors at the time and another of the Pension Trustees. We made our way upstairs to the Bear Stearns offices on Park Avenue and were escorted by a security guard to Jimmy's offices. Surprisingly, considering Cayne's stature in the firm, his own office was, for the most part, ordinary. It was not especially big, nor was it lavishly appointed. But it wasn't the high-powered corporate setting that turned out to be interesting in this *tête-à-tête*. It was the bombshell that Cayne dropped on the hopeful prospectors!

From the moment we walked in the door, Cayne assumed an adversarial position with regard to Nargassans. Why, Cayne wanted to know, should you get all this money? Why do you deserve this? Who are you, anyway?

It took about three minutes for the whole scene to deteriorate into a virtual melée. Unfortunately for him, Nargassans took the bait and got into what might be described as a pissing match with Cayne — not a good move. Before long, Cayne was on the phone to his secretary, telling her in Nargassans' presence to have a background check done on him.

After some more back and forth exchanges that were decidedly not friendly, Marston and Nargassans both stood up and stormed out of Cayne's office in a huff. I was stunned. Moeller and I looked at each other as if to say, "What just happened?" Cayne merely watched them leave. As it turned out, he was quite serious about getting a background check on Nargassans. The results were frightening, as we learned later. For starters, Nargassans' close relationship with Ivana Trump was apparently a figment of his imagination. We were told that when asked about Nargassans, Trump said something, like, "I may have known him once — I can't remember." She didn't sound like a person who had only recently poured her heart out to him over the breakup of her marriage to The Donald.

I returned to my hotel room after the Cayne debacle and called Nargassans, who had planned to host a dinner party that night. I met Nargassans and Marston in the lobby of their hotel, the St. Moritz, and we sat down to talk. Nargassans wasted no time getting to the scene in Cayne's office.

"You set me up!" he accused. "Why did you set me up?"

"That wasn't my intention," I told him. "I thought the meeting might be useful."

The investigation Cayne had promised was also apparently on his mind, but I said, "All these things were going to come out anyway." Nargassans apparently didn't know, or pretended not to know, to what I was alluding. I glanced at Marston and said, "Paul told me you were a philanthropist who didn't want to make a penny on this deal." Marston blurted out, "I didn't say that," and he immediately got up from where we were sitting and hightailed it to another part of the hotel lobby.

The dinner plans included Jose Damiani, President of the World Bridge Federation. Jose had flown to New York expressly to listen to Nargassans' sales pitch. Nargassans sent limousines to pick everyone up for dinner. Besides myself and my date, the dinner entourage also consisted of Nargassans, his wife, Marston, Roy Green, and Howard and Barbara Piltch.

Piltch, the number one Nargassans cheerleader on the ACBL Board, can be very entertaining and at this meeting he was regaling the crowd with tales of his adventures on the debate team in college. Nargassans, meanwhile, was telling Jose that he had three well-heeled sponsors in Europe lined up, just waiting for the word to back any bridge tournament the WBF wanted to name. That sounded great, but as far as I know, nothing ever came of it — and knowing Jose's determination and unparalleled resourcefulness, he would never have missed the chance to secure a sponsor if there really was one. Something did not seem right and I was rapidly losing faith in bridge's potential savior.

At one point during dinner, Nargassans leaned over to me and whispered that he was having limos take the dinner guests back to their hotels, but he wanted me to talk to Marston before the night was through. I cornered Marston when I had the chance, and he admitted then that he had, indeed, told me initially that Nargassans was a rich man with money to throw around for the benefit of bridge. Marston sheepishly added that he was 'just selling' by stretching the truth. "I wanted to get your attention," he said, adding, "*I'm* bankrolling this. I've made all the money I ever want to make." Later I tried to verify this claim of affluence, but was unable to prove or disprove it.

Nevertheless, it appeared that it was the ACBL that was going to have to pony up the cash for this venture, and since Nargassans was planning to take the expensive meals, limousines and other outlandish expenses out of the initial payment from Memphis, the meter was already ticking. To their credit, many members of the ACBL Board were very suspicious of Nargassans and his grandiose plans. Others were justifiably concerned that he could not substantiate his claim that he had previously operated a successful enterprise similar in nature to the one he proposed for the ACBL. To the *responsible* Board members, this scheme looked like the wildest speculation. Still, there was enough support — led by Howard Piltch — to force a special meeting of the ACBL Board in Chicago. Many Board members wondered, why the rush? Why was it necessary to ratify an agreement with Nargassans in May instead of waiting to consider the proposal at the regular Board meeting in July, just a couple months later? That in itself was enough to scare some Board members and begin to raise more eyebrows.

After the dinner in New York, Howard Piltch, Roy Green and I met with Jose Damiani in his suite at the Pierre Hotel. Howard and I got into it right off the bat. I asked him what he knew about Nargassans and whether he had done any checking on him. He said that he had and I asked, "Where is it?"

"I don't know where it is," Howard said. I was astounded. At that point, Roy, whose job was most certainly on the line, also challenged Howard and his willingness, in Roy's view, to sell the ACBL down the river. If you think about it, Roy's view was quite reasonable. Howard was trying to convince the ACBL Board to hand over $2 million in cash to a man who, as far as anyone knew, had never done in another setting what he was proposing to do for the League. Was the ACBL buying a pig in a poke? If Nargassans had such great credentials, why were they not on view in writing for inspection instead of sheer supposition?

Leading up to the special meeting in Chicago, forces were rallying against the proposal. At one point, Hamman and I talked about Nargassans. I asked Bob what he thought, and Bob expressed the same doubts that many of the rest of us were feeling about the proposal. I asked Bob to write a letter to the ACBL Board expressing his concern.

A person with Bob's stature and clout surely could sway some votes, or at least get some of the pro-Nargassans Board members to think seriously about what they were doing. Bob wrote the letter all right, but it fell short of my expectations. He started off just fine, cautioning against the dangers of jumping into an alliance with an unknown, unproven entity. Unfortunately, the letter continued with what appeared to be a sales pitch on his own behalf. Bob added that he and Bob Blanchard (who runs the very successful Cavendish Invitational Tournament in Las Vegas) could do whatever Nargassans was proposing to do.

Suddenly, Bob's message had zero credibility. It had become personal in nature. Of course he would run down the upstart from Massachusetts. Why not? Nargassans was competition! Nothing ever came of the Hamman-Blanchard proposal, if indeed it was that, but I was disappointed because Bob's letter didn't have the impact I was hoping for at a time when it was critical to the future of the ACBL. Fortunately, by the time the Board met in Chicago, enough cool heads prevailed to put an end to the Nargassans-Marston master plan, and the Grand Slam Bridge proposal was defeated by a 15-10 vote. But note that *ten* board members were still willing to take the risk.

As with all things concerning the Board, however, there was political fallout. Many of the proponents of the Nargassans plan were bitter in their disappointment at the Board's refusal to go along with the program. One Board member who initially favored the deal but later changed his mind was Cecil Cook, of California. In the end, he lost his seat on the Board because he refused to gamble that Nargassans and Marston could do what they said they could. In the build-up to the Chicago meeting, Piltch had gained support from many prominent ACBL members, including Alan LeBendig, co-owner of one of the largest bridge clubs in Los Angeles and a former chairman of the ACBL Board of Governors. LeBendig was so strongly in favor of Nargassans that he told Cook that if Cook did not vote for the measure in Chicago, he (LeBendig) would oppose him for a seat on the Board in the next election. Cook wavered but admirably held fast and voted against the proposal. LeBendig kept his promise and unseated Cook.

Could Nargassans have done what he said and turned bridge into a household name? Could he have had bridge featured regularly on ESPN? The ACBL was not in a financial position to go out on a limb to chance it and we will never know. I have my own suspicions. No one has heard from Nargassans in over ten years since the Board rejected his proposal. If you try to find him with a search on the Internet, it produces exactly one reference: a report of the special meeting in Chicago, entitled 'Grand Slam Bridge Strikes Out In Chicago' and dated May 5,

1997, written by Board member Jonathan Steinberg, one of those in favor of the proposal. It makes interesting reading, naming the other nine who supported it and the remaining fifteen who voted 'No' and defeated the pending Grand Slam Bridge contract.

It is remotely possible that the man had some idea that would have hit the proverbial home run he was promising. It's more likely that the ACBL would have lost two million bucks, seen Headquarters gutted and the organization's future clouded for a long time. I can't claim credit for averting the impending disaster single-handedly, but whatever part I played in thwarting the plan, the fact that I did get involved affords me peace of mind.

CHAPTER 12

A TALE OF SURVIVORSHIP

I'M A LUCKY MAN. I've lived in relatively good health for over seventy-five years. I have been truly blessed to find a career revolving around bridge that has propelled me to the top of my profession — as a player, writer and administrator — and provided a good income for decades. Imagine waking up every morning loving what you do — and getting paid to do it. I also enjoy my contributions to the game through *pro bono* work. Yes, I am truly a lucky man! However, there is no denying that my destiny was shaped by three women...

Betsey Yuill's family had moved from Massachusetts to Texas in the early fifties. I met her five or six years later and we started playing together at Burt Gideon's bridge club whenever she commuted from Denton, where she was attending college. I also began partnering many other women — an easy way of getting to meet them. I was rather shy, so I needed all the help I could get. Playing with other gals was far more effective than I ever imagined, resulting in Betsey's taking an added interest in me. When we married, neither of us knew much about anything. We were eager, young, naïve, inexperienced and shared an immense passion for bridge. I was selling insurance but playing a considerable amount — a lot of the time with Betsey after my brother, Walter, quit the game. Betsey and I won frequently. However, her success was overshadowed by my being her partner.

Betsey had integrity, and that was one thing I learned from her. I recall one time playing with Betsey in a club championship in San Antonio in the early sixties. We were usually victorious when we played at the club and one particular night, playing with Betsey and sitting East-West, I was declarer in 3NT. The opponents scored it up as making four, but after reflecting upon it, I realized I had made only nine tricks. However, I didn't make any effort to correct the score.

A couple of rounds later, Betsey challenged me: "You do know you made only *nine* tricks on that hand, don't you?"

I asked, "What hand?"

"You know the one," she pressed on.

"I guess you're right," I reluctantly admitted. Betsey glared at me, inquiring pointedly, "Well, what are you going to do about it?"

"I guess I should go tell them, shouldn't I?"

"Right!" Betsey snapped.

I remember thinking to myself, "I hope this doesn't cost us winning."

I was rationalizing, of course, and telling myself that it didn't matter to the people who had the minus 430 instead of minus 400 — they were going to finish last no matter what I did.

That's a terribly poor excuse for such behavior, of course, and I'm not proud of that episode, but shamefully remembering it serves a purpose. The incident helps me comprehend what it is like when the shoe is on the other foot. It explains how the tremendous desire to win, at all costs, can motivate some people and why sometimes they act the way they do. I understand something now that I didn't understand then. Yes, I was just a kid at the time, but that's a copout! If your name is listed first on the final results sheet, but you didn't *really* win, it means nothing. You are only deluding yourself.

The chemistry between Betsey and me was never really great, but the marriage officially lasted seventeen long years. There were some stormy times, particularly involving Wendy, who was born in 1966. With all the financial insecurity, distractions and uncertainty in our lives, I suppose I didn't afford my daughter the attention a child deserves. The conflict between Betsey and me worsened, taking its toll on Wendy, who was only six when her mother and I separated. It was another four years before we got divorced and I remarried. In retrospect, it is clear we both should have moved on with our lives long before that, but that is history.

It wasn't anyone's fault that Betsey and I split up. When we were starting out, she was teaching school and actually making more money than I. At that time I was struggling trying to sell insurance and simultaneously attempting to make it in bridge. When I realized I had enough talent to earn a living at bridge, Betsey and I played less and less together. She liked bridge and wanted to play with me, but I was unavailable, because I was playing either with lesser players for money or with better players to improve my game and my standing in the bridge world. We seemed to grow further apart. My ambition and playing schedule didn't leave much room or time for Betsey — or Wendy, for that matter. Eventually, Betsey started playing with others and our lives took off in different directions. That was an eternity ago.

I first ran into Debby Polak in 1959 when I went to the Summer NABC in Chicago, where she lived. When she entered a room, people took notice. Debby was so lovely that she made an impression even on me back then. I later discovered she had attended Vassar. It was not until many years following my separation from Betsey that I had the opportunity to get to know Debby.

The year was 1975 and I had just finished playing in the International Team Trials in Palo Alto. I had been invited by Joan Dewitt to participate in a Charity Individual in Chicago. I originally declined, however, because Peter Pender had arranged for a special match with a sponsor in Palo Alto. The match fell through and I changed my plans and headed for Chicago. Debby was kibitzing at the Individual, and I saw her later at a cocktail party. I found out that her best friend, Gloria Turner Reysa, had married and moved to Dallas. Debby was planning to visit, so we made a date.

It was a whirlwind courtship — later, each of us claimed to have proposed — and we were married on April 9, 1976. Debby had a good job in Chicago as a supervisor for a big insurance company, but she packed up lock, stock and barrel and moved to Dallas with her young son, Michael. I couldn't believe the strength of the feelings I had for her and, even today, I realize how deeply in love I was. When Betsey and I got married, I'm not sure I knew what love was. By the time my path crossed Debby's, I had matured and understood a hundred times more about life than I had in the late fifties.

Debby had to make adjustments, of course. She hardly knew anyone in Dallas, but she had such a capacity for giving her all that she made new friends and even managed to penetrate *my* self-absorption (not an easy thing to do). Debby was so good for me that I know my accomplishments in bridge administration were due in large measure to her advice and support. She was my counselor, confessor and sounding board. She worried about my legacy to the game and fretted about my tendency to force my will upon people in certain situations. She wondered if my legacy would empower my successor to continue to wield power as I did — but with different motivation and very bad results. I was comfortable that I was working for the good of bridge, but Debby could envision a very different outcome if the wrong person fell heir to similar power and influence. Her insight proved to be frighteningly on target — and the situation is growing worse with every passing day with the new breed at the helm.

My life with Debby was as close to idyllic as a marriage can be. It came to an end abruptly because she couldn't stop smoking. Debby had tried to give it up for years, but she had no willpower. She was a five-time dropout from the Smoke Enders program. In the three years before the end, she became a closet smoker. She knew I detested the habit because it was so bad for her, so she never smoked in my presence, only surreptitiously — and we both pretended I didn't know.

Ironically, eight weeks before we got the worst news possible she put the first nicotine patch on her arm — but it was too late. I can still remember how it unfolded. I had been elected President of the World Bridge Federation, replacing Ernesto d'Orsi who had succeeded Denis Howard after the debacle in Geneva 1990 (see Chapter 13). In the middle of October Debby hosted a sixtieth birthday party for me at our house which was attended by all our close friends. Next Debby and I went to Memphis and ACBL headquarters for a visit with Robin and Denis Howard, whom I had recruited as interim CEO after Stephen Signaigo was fired. It was my first meeting with Denis' successor, Roy G. Green, and his charming wife, Mary. Then in early November, my dear friends Joe and Lucy Musumeci threw another bash for me at their home in Richardson, a Dallas suburb. I attended the party with Debby, Betsey and Becky Rogers, who was then running the WBF office I had opened in Dallas.

At the party, Debby looked unsteady. I didn't pay much attention to that, but a couple days later, Debby woke up in terrible pain. She thought it was pleurisy. I took her to the medical center, where unusual X-rays showed that she had walking pneumonia. The nurse knew how concerned we were but reassured us, saying, "Don't worry, it's certainly not cancer." We were supposed to go to Orlando for the Fall NABC, but Debby obviously couldn't travel. She had been given some strong antibiotics, which had not been very effective. "You go on to Orlando alone," she encouraged. "I'll catch up with you later." I still wasn't thinking much about what was going on or the potential seriousness of the situation. I suppose I was embracing the comfort of my own little cocoon and couldn't face even the possibility that there might be trouble on the horizon.

Debby never made it to Orlando — she just didn't feel up to traveling — but I talked to her two or three times a day. I was beginning to worry. I found out after I returned ten days later that Debby had been coughing up blood. She didn't tell me, but she confided in Becky Rogers, and I got the word from her. When I got back, I consulted Dr. John Fisher, an expert bridge player and a close, longtime friend. He took his own X-rays of Debby, and I journeyed to his office to talk to him about the situation. He knew Debby was following it up independently, and, as it turned out, he did not have the heart to be really straight with me about what was going on. He was trying to shield me from the worst.

Soon afterwards, Debby visited a pulmonary expert and a week later we learned the awful truth. It was almost certainly lung cancer. She underwent an operation to recover some tissue for a biopsy. When I met with the surgeon at the hospital after the procedure, tears welled in his eyes. It was lung cancer, and a particularly virulent form: small-cell carcinoma. It was also inoperable. He did toss us a bone, though — the form of cancer Debby had usually responds well to chemotherapy.

Her first treatment was in a doctor's office, followed by a ten-day wait to see whether it had worked. With the assault on her body by all those chemicals, Debby was very susceptible to fevers, and often she was freezing. When we visited the hospital the first time, the doctors were optimistic. I won't say Debby got rave reviews, but the doctor on duty thought the treatment might have knocked out the whole tumor. He brought us back to reality, however, by warning that cancer of this type often spreads, usually to the bones. While Debby was getting treatment and suffering, I was traversing the globe because of my official duties as President of the WBF. I canceled what meetings I could, but I couldn't stop everything — and Debby would not allow me to stay home with her. In fact, it was not a subject open for discussion. She was one of the most unselfish human beings God ever created. Even facing the stark reality of a fatal disease and imminent death, her primary concern was for me and my responsibilities to the world of bridge.

In the summer of 1993, I swung back through Dallas to collect Debby on one of my long trips. We traveled to Mauritius, a small island in the Indian Ocean, for the Asia and Middle East Championships, and then on to Menton, on the French Riviera, for the European Championships. Debby was doing pretty well on that trip. She had just had some radiation treatment, the cancer appeared to be in remission and Debby seemed to be handling her illness much better. She said she had never felt better.

Returning from abroad, we immediately drove from Dallas to Aspen, Colorado, where I had organized a WBF Management Committee meeting. After that, I went to the 1993 Summer NABC in Washington, D.C., and following that traveled to Arhus, Denmark for the World Junior Championships. Debby was fighting with every ounce of strength she possessed, but it was becoming increasingly difficult to keep up the hectic pace. She had intended to accompany me to Denmark, but decided it was in our joint interests for her to remain home and fortify herself for the trip to Santiago, Chile, where the World Championships were being held that Fall.

By the time I returned from Denmark, I was very tired. I remember opening the door to our home in Dallas, anxious to see Debby again. When I found her, I immediately sensed something was wrong. "I found another lump," she said. My heart sank and I wanted to cry. It gave me a chill when I realized that I wasn't sure Debby had the energy to continue waging her fight to live. We went to the doctor again, and the news was bad.

"There's only about a 67% chance that the cancer will respond to chemotherapy," he said, "and even if it clears it up, these cells routinely wait until you stop poisoning them and then resurrect themselves." This was three weeks before Santiago, and Debby wanted very much to go. However, she was afraid the chemotherapy would make her face swell, and she didn't want to look bad for the World Championships and have people whispering and feeling sorry for her. Santiago would be her swan song and she knew it.

Casting aside her vanity, Debby mustered up the strength for the trip to Santiago, but it was obvious to everyone how ill she was and she left after a week. I didn't tell anyone the truth except for Jose Damiani and Ernesto d'Orsi, but it didn't take a rocket scientist to figure out that her days were numbered. I stayed around a short time after Debby departed and then, at Jose's and Ernesto's insistence, I rushed back to Dallas to be with her. That was late 1993.

We made countless trips to the hospital so that Debby could get treatment. One doctor said she might be okay for a while, but three weeks after I got back from Chile, her dizziness began. At the hospital, we were told that the cancer had reached her brain. They attacked it with radiation, and it seemed to recede, but it left her unable to function normally. It was as though she had cerebral palsy. She couldn't even squeeze toothpaste from the tube. I cannot begin to impart to you my helplessness and frustration — I was feeling completely worthless as I witnessed my precious Debby waging a futile battle. I must have been numb, otherwise I would not have survived watching her slow downward spiral. This was the woman I loved, the woman who had been such an inspiration to me and the only person in my life who was capable of keeping me on the even keel that had eluded me for so long. I felt powerless and desperate. The thought of her death was devastating to me. I couldn't imagine life without her.

By early 1994 she was going to the hospital for daily radiation treatments, which sometimes worked and at other times were utter failures.

Some days she was half blind, but miraculously on Super Bowl Sunday in 1994 we were sitting in front of the television and suddenly her vision was totally restored. It was a nightmare not knowing from minute to minute what was coming next.

Before long the tumors showed up in other places. Once, after a doctor had taken some X-rays, she asked Debby if she had any pain. Debby said that there was none, and the doctor expressed surprise as she pointed out that the tumors had enlarged to such a degree that they were breaking her ribs. About twelve hours later, Debby started experiencing the pain the doctor had alluded to and had to have morphine administered to cope with the discomfort. Still, with all her grave problems, she would not entertain the thought of my canceling urgent WBF business and arranged for home care and someone to take her back and forth from the hospital. Her thoughts, even in this time of doom and gloom, were unselfishly always focused on others and making life easier for them — especially me!

Debby behaved incredibly courageously throughout the entire ordeal. When she came to grips with the fact that the end was very near, she began reading about the end of life. Debby died in a Dallas hospital on April 6, 1994 — just three days short of our eighteenth wedding anniversary. Nearing the end, besides myself, the only persons permitted to see her were her son, Michael, and a dear and attentive friend and neighbor, Charlotte Rock Anderson. She didn't want people to pity her and remember her the way she was after the cancer took over.

As word of her death started to circulate, I was overwhelmed and comforted by a monumental testimonial of love and respect for Debby as witnessed by the flood of notes, calls, cards and contributions in her memory from the four corners of the globe. However, I should not have been surprised as she was adored by everyone whose path she crossed. My heart was broken and it was painful for me to stand up at her funeral and talk about her, but I wanted to share with her mourners my memory of Debby.

My remarks were brief:

> Debby was fun, Debby was funny. Debby was real, Debby was love. Her smile could cheer up any group. She counseled me when I needed it, she was there for me whether or not I needed it. She cooked for me, she wrote for me, she loved for me, she loved with me. Debby was fiercely loyal, yet had understanding for everyone. Debby was born and educated a WASP, yet she was an anti-snob. She came into my life and made me whole. Debby was mine, and I am forever hers.

Someone asked me if I considered it fair that Debby died so young — she was only fifty-six. I don't know. I don't think anyone is qualified to judge what is fair or unfair. No one lives forever and sadly for all who knew her, it was 'her time' to go. In the grand scheme of things, we are all just specks. I suppose it is a callous way of looking at it, but death is the Puppeteer's way of controlling the population.

Yes, I said the Puppeteer. Everyone who knows me is aware that it is one of my pet theories — that there's a force driving us all, making us do the things we do, for good and for evil. Allah? Buddha? God? Jesus? Jehovah? The Puppeteer? You can name him (or her — I don't want Judy to accuse me again of being a male chauvinist!) whatever you like, but someone out there controls our destiny. Maybe it was the Puppeteer who made Debby start smoking, who made her desire for nicotine so uncontrollable that she just couldn't stop.

I will never have another Debby, and I pity those who are not fortunate enough to have a Debby even once. She had a very fast life. She was a beautiful girl. She had many suitors. I was lucky — my timing was right when we met. She had reached that period in her life where I could provide for her what she needed and in return she would love me and put up with my foibles — and make me the best I could be. What a tradeoff!

I have often said that whatever I've achieved was all due to her, but that's not totally accurate. I suppose my accomplishments were a combination of what I had to offer and Debby's refinement of those attributes, enabling me to put my best foot forward. I don't have any great insights about the very brief time Debby and I had together — eighteen years is like the blink of an eye when someone like Debby is involved. All I know is that there's not a day that goes by that I don't think of her. I don't know whether I believe in God or not, but I do pray to whomever is up there listening and I mention Debby every night. I suffered great pain and sadness when she died and I have tried not to feel sorry for myself over losing her. She would not have wanted that. However, I am so thankful that Debby was part of my life for as long as she was and she will always be with me in some way.

Let me digress a moment before moving on. I came into Debby's life when her young boy was just seven years of age. Raising a youngster as a single parent is no easy chore and she was concerned for his future welfare and security. Michael was Debby's son with her former husband, Chicago private investigator Gunther Polak, with whom I am still friendly. Michael, now thirty-nine years old, has taken an active part in his dad's business and plays an indispensable role in it. He is happily married to a very special gal named Karyn and they are the proud parents of two-year old Evan, all living in Morton Grove, Illinois. I burst with pride, witnessing the fruits of Debby's labors and dedication. All her dreams for Michael have come true.

And now to the third woman in my life, Judy Kay-Wolff. Her marvelous sense of humor allows her to refer to herself as 'Number Three'. Judy understands how I feel about Debby, because that's just the way she feels about Norman Kay, her own late husband. I knew Norman, of course, for many years — mostly as a worthy adversary. He and Edgar Kaplan formed one of the greatest partnerships North America has ever seen. In my mind, Norman was the epitome of class, both at and away from the bridge table. He also happened to be a sensational player. We shared two passions — bridge and sports. We would often seek each other out from across the room at a Nationals, discuss the current games and enjoy each other's predictions on season endings.

He was deeply affected by the events of October, 1987, when the stock market collapsed and he and others lost a great deal of money. One of those upon whom the crash took its toll was Edgar, and Norman blamed himself for allowing Edgar to be exposed to such risk. Edgar happened to be in Jamaica at the World Championships (as he usually was) during the market debacle, known at that time as Black Monday. As soon as he returned to New York, learning of the physical and emotional strain Norman was suffering, Edgar telephoned Judy, his partner-in-law (the pet name he coined for her), to ask if he could help, to which Judy replied, "He just needs time. His doctor is not in favor of visitors."

But Edgar's judgment was always superior to most and he begged to differ. He was not just 'any visitor' and he was soon aboard the next train to Philadelphia, where Judy met him at 30th Street Station. This gesture was really out of character for Edgar, who admitted to being a self-absorbed creature. He cherished his privacy and the comfort of his 94th Street surroundings and rarely ventured outside of Manhattan other than for major bridge tournaments or tennis matches. He was not one to go gadding about at the drop of a hat. Understandably, Edgar's impromptu visit to the Kay home brought a flood of tears to Norman's eyes, happy that Edgar was so concerned — but suffering overwhelming guilt that he hadn't had the foresight to prevent this from happening to Edgar. Prior to Black Monday, Edgar's account had been doing quite well and no one could have predicted the impending disaster.

From that moment on, the healing process began. Judy is certain Norman would never have made it through the ordeal without Edgar's visit and his gracious forgiveness of Norman's failure to protect his investments. As Judy points out, Edgar's intervention was not about the stock market, money or even bridge. It clearly highlighted the bonds of a mutually revered friendship and love affair that spanned nearly fifty years. They probably are still playing K-S in that big bridge game in the sky.

Norman eventually recovered from the trauma, regained his health and returned to the market successfully once again, but he never recovered from Edgar's death in September of 1997. Edgar waged a long, bitter battle with cancer, finally succumbing the week after Princess Di's death. The association with Diana's death reminds Judy of the final time she and Norman saw Edgar. Sidney Lazard, a close friend to both Edgar and Norman, had planned a trip to the Big Apple. He was pressed by the Kays to move up his flight from New Orleans and arrive a week earlier than scheduled as Edgar was sinking rapidly. Judy realized that time was very much of the essence. Sidney arrived in Philly on Friday and they all drove to New York on Saturday, joining Edgar in his bedroom to watch the media account of Diana's accident. Edgar lapsed in and out of consciousness; twenty-four hours later he was rushed to the hospital where he died a few days later.

Edgar's death had a devastating affect on Norman and from that day forward, he just wasn't the same. He had not only lost Edgar, but his zest for bridge as well. He played some, but never as seriously as when Edgar was alive. Sadly, bridge had lost its meaning. Unbeknownst to Norman or Judy, Norman himself had been harboring a slowly moving carcinoma which was not discovered until early 1999; its growth could be retarded by treatment but not cured. Their family doctor and the gastroenterologist (both close personal friends of Judy and Norman) made light of it, sparing them the sad truth that his years were numbered. The physicians made a joint decision to give it their 'all' by treating him with a highly successful, relatively new drug which actually added thirty-some months to his life after the fatal diagnosis. Norman enjoyed three wonderful, healthy, pain-free, productive years until the NABC in Vegas in November 2001, when the stealthy cancer surfaced once more and engulfed his body. Norman died at home on January 17, 2002. He was canonized and mourned by all who knew him.

Through the years, Norman's wife, Judy, and I had been more or less distant acquaintances. I can't really explain why I hadn't got to know her very well, but when Norman died, fate seemed to step in to bring us together, albeit not right away. Judy has repeatedly professed that after Norman died, she was certain there was absolutely no way she would ever marry again. She just didn't see how she could share her life with anyone other than this incredible human being who meant so much to her for almost forty years.

Perhaps it was because I regarded Norman so highly myself that after he died I called Judy to tell her how sorry I was that we had lost him. I learned later my condolence call was a complete shock to her as she claims I never said hello to her once during her forty-some years on the bridge scene, often kibitzing at Norman's side. She loves to recount her amazement when I announced myself on the other end of the phone and how she mused, "Could this be the same stuffy Bobby Wolff from Texas who played bridge with the Aces — who hasn't uttered a word to me in four decades? Unlikely!" She couldn't reconcile my indifference to her over the years with my sincere sadness at Norman's death. Yet she politely listened as I sang Norman's praises.

I suppose she must have forgiven my aloof nature as she later telephoned me in Dallas, inviting me to be one of the speakers at a memorial service she and her daughter Robin were organizing for Norman at the 2002 Spring NABC in Houston a couple of months later. It was a beautiful and fitting goodbye to someone so beloved by the entire bridge world, and I was quite flattered to make the impressive list of prominent speakers. Incidentally, although I may never have spoken to Judy, I did know Robin, whom I had met as a kibitzer at an invitational tournament in Southern Italy labeled 'The 1st Bridge Ryder Cup', back in the mid-nineties. We spent some brief time together and Robin made a lasting impression on me — cute, exuberant, perky and talented at the table, having inherited many of her dad's bridge genes to boot. Who would ever imagine back then that someday I would become, as she endearingly refers to me, her NOSD (Number One Step Dad).

I heard from Judy again slightly more than a year later, after my team had dumbfounded the bridge world by winning the second US slot in the Bermuda Bowl to be played in November of 2003 in Monaco. I was delightfully surprised when Judy sent an email to congratulate me. Her words: "What a marvelous triumph! Norman and Edgar would be proud of you..." My immediate reaction: what a touching message! Being exposed to top-echelon bridge for some four decades made the significance of our great surprise victory apparent to Judy, and she was genuinely excited that our underdog team had won the privilege of representing the country.

Not knowing Judy very well (or at all, according to her), I was impressed that she would go out of her way to exhibit such pride and pleasure in our success. I have alluded to the fact that she wasn't sure I knew that she existed all these years. (Imagine anyone not knowing about Judy!) I guess I was in the same boat when it came to her, which is why her email was totally unexpected (and perhaps unwarranted in light of my earlier blasé behavior). Anyway, I returned her email with a suggestion that we get together during the 2003 Summer NABC in Long Beach for a drink or maybe dinner. Her reply was succinct: "Cheers". I assumed that was a "Yes," and there was no further correspondence or contact until I saw her in California a week later.

The 'date' — I guess you could call it that — nearly didn't happen as Judy was playing and rooming with her dear friend of thirty years, Jane Segal, and had plans for the first few nights. Eventually we worked it out and dined with Dan Morse (my partner on the team bound for Monte Carlo) and his wife, Joan, two days before Judy departed for the East Coast. It was an enjoyable evening and I mentioned I would contact her when I got home.

We returned to our respective homes — I to Dallas and Judy to Philadelphia — and there was no contact between us until August 11th, when Judy heard I was under the weather. Upon my return from California, I had a vicious bout with vertigo and was not up to doing much of anything. I could hardly get out of bed, let alone get in touch with her as I had promised. Our mutual friend, Sidney Lazard, who had been checking in on Judy on a regular basis after Norman's death, called her that night and suggested she drop me an email. In retrospect, he had ulterior motives, but it all appeared so innocent at the time. A grin comes across my face every time I recall her opening lines: 'Sorry you are not well, but even if I lived in Dallas, I would not be much help!' Boasting of a virgin kitchen, she continued, 'I don't cook, I don't bake and even if I lived nearby, I would not be able to bring you homemade chicken soup or brownies.' I appreciated her self-deprecating sense of humor. Up until that point, I hadn't had much to smile about.

That started off a flood of emails. Can you imagine a self-absorbed individual like myself (immersed in bridge matters with round-the-clock TV sports happenings) carrying on the spontaneous courtship that resulted in our engagement? It all took about a week. Judy claims three days, and refers to it as our 'cartridge courtship' because all the wooing and banter was done via computer. Actually, I responded on August 12th and invited her to join me in Monaco for the World Championship. She casually checked her calendar, found the time not spoken for, nonchalantly accepted the invitation and after two more days of non-stop telephone calls and emails, on August 15th we agreed to get married. Yes, believe it or not, we had fallen in love on the internet. I had never held her hand — let alone anything else. It was as simple as that. Neither of us gave it a second thought. Honest! I am sure many questioned the advisability of such a spontaneous and seemingly precipitous decision, but luckily we were of age and did not need parental consent.

The ceremony took place at the Las Vegas MGM before immediate family on Sunday, December 7, 2003. Astute observers will recognize the date, December 7th, and notice that it is also the anniversary of Pearl Harbor; Judy has a pat retort — it's just another day that will live in infamy! That was the beginning — and we both agree it gets better and better every day. A real fairy-tale romance, if ever there was one… and over four years later, still going strong!

Our engagement was the talk of the bridge world — at the World Championship in Monte Carlo and later at the Fall NABC in New Orleans. Hosts of people were coming up and congratulating us — many whose names I did not even know. People were speaking to me who hadn't spoken to me in years. It was like the second coming of Bobby Wolff. Everyone loves a good love story, even heartless bridge players. I still marvel how the news of our union was received!

Shortly after news of our impending shotgun marriage spread, Judy called me, quite perplexed. She had received a call in Philadelphia from Edith Freilich (better known perhaps as Edith Kemp). Edith's pronouncement was, "Bobby Wolff finally got what he deserved." It sounded very accusatory until Judy learned Edith and I were old, old friends; she, like many other bridge greats in the late fifties, had recognized my unrefined talent by honoring me with an invitation to play. Both Judy's and my friendships with this legendary bridge giant go back over forty years and this was just Edith's unique manner of expressing her delight at our merger!

Judy has a refreshing way of making me feel special, telling everyone that she never thought she could ever find such happiness again and how fortunate she is to have lucked out a second time. "Some people don't get it right once," she brags, "but I defied the odds." Then she impishly adds, "And besides, I only marry Hall of Famers."

I feel equally blessed. Judy is loving, attentive, caring and takes great pride in my accomplishments and what I represent. We think very much alike. I can start a sentence and she finishes it! No one could be more perfect for me at this juncture in my life. The commonality we share in countless venues is mind-boggling. She is incredibly organized, bright, quick, creative, sensitive, energetic, a good sport and has learned to 'put up' with me. Life with Judy is never dull. As Robin jokingly warned me, "My mom's a handful!" and I can't argue with that.

Her attitude toward bridge further strengthens our bonds. She adores the game. Kibitzing or playing, local duplicate or world championship, it matters not. She welcomes a good challenge, is always prepared to rise to the occasion, steps up to the plate when called upon... and has the courage of her convictions, regardless of the consequences. Judy is highly principled. When she is wrong, she has no problem saying she's sorry. However, when she feels she is right, you *don't* want to be on the other side! Judy is very forthright. You never have to wonder what she is thinking, because she will never keep you in the dark. I suppose we are cut from the same cloth, but she is much more of a diplomat than I. I could not be happier and she professes the same contentment with me.

It's tough to express the gratitude I feel at the return of love, warmth and togetherness to my life. I had other relationships after Debby died, but they were short-lived, only temporarily fulfilling and they ended predictably. I suppose I was merely grasping at straws waiting for Judy to come along.

For ten years I floundered and I began to doubt that I would ever find another soulmate with whom I could share those proverbial golden years. The moment Judy Kay entered my world in the summer of 2003, I sensed my wanderings were about to cease. I was blessed with a feeling of inner peace, contentment, trust, serenity and love. The Puppeteer was at it again — looking out for Bobby Wolff. Timing, of course, is everything. Sometimes you're just in the right place at the right time. When that happens, there's nothing to do but seize the moment and go with the flow.

Judy will never forget Norman and the forty beautiful years they shared with their children, and I will never forget the time I had with my lovely Debby. Neither of us want to. With all certainty, we feel that Norman and Debby would have given our union a rousing thumbs up! So from now on — it's Judy and Bobby. Judy is certainly entitled to happiness, and I'd like to think that I am too.

CHAPTER 13

THE SPECIAL WORLD OF THE WBF

LONG BEFORE I MADE MY WAY to Geneva, Switzerland, for the 1990 World Bridge Championships, I foresaw the probability of much turmoil in that beautiful, historic city often referred to as the Center of Europe. My worst fears were realized. The expected upheaval had its beginnings four years earlier, and it pains me to admit that what triggered it was the undeniable fact that either Denis Howard did too good a job as President of the World Bridge Federation or the sudden change from one genius to another was too much for those involved. You need some background, of course, for that statement to make sense.

Denis Howard's predecessor as WBF President was Jaime Ortiz-Patino, known to intimates as 'Jimmy', a billionaire whose family owned most of the tin mines in Bolivia. He parlayed the family fortune into more billions with his own investments. At one time he lived in Switzerland, and in fact represented that nation in world bridge competition. When he is not traveling, he shuttles between London and Sotogrande, Spain, a resort north of Gibraltar on the Costa del Sol and the site of his famous Valderrama golf course (where the Ryder Cup was held in 1997). Valderrama was built to Jimmy's specifications and, not surprisingly, has been voted the most beautiful course in all of Europe. It was a breathtaking setting in which to hold meetings and during my WBF presidency, I attended a couple of management sessions there myself.

Patino *looks* like a billionaire — a distinguished grey-haired man always impeccably dressed, with a hint of a British accent despite his South American heritage. He has numerous personal assistants, including Albert Dormer, a respected bridge writer and journalist. For a long time in the period before the 1997 Ryder Cup, that event was his consuming interest. In the overall picture, however, bridge is still dominant in

Jimmy's life, and his contributions to the WBF and world bridge are absolutely unparalleled. He, more than any other individual, has shaped the destiny of universal bridge and is largely responsible for its survival. He is undisputedly Mr. WBF — and deservedly so!

Jimmy was active in bridge and the European Bridge League in the early days and was directly involved in the formation of the WBF in the fifties. He succeeded Julius Rosenblum as WBF President in 1976, a year after the infamous toe-tapping incident in the Bermuda Bowl, which had seen the US team lose out to Italy yet again. As described earlier, it was through Patino's efforts that screens were introduced in high-level competition despite opposition from those who felt that doing so would dehumanize the game of bridge.[1]

It is true that screens make it impossible for a player to see his partner, but each player does have contact with one of his opponents. As was explained earlier, if I'm playing East with my partner as West, I sit on the same side of the screen as North. My partner is on the other side with South. The player sitting on the same side of the screen as his or her opponent is known as a screenmate. I think the opposition to the screens was more of the human tendency to oppose change — and, of course, some elements had a vested interest in maintaining the status quo. It's much harder, as you can imagine, to exchange signals when your partner can't see your face or even your hands during the auction. There's no way to observe the tone of your voice or feel the tempo in which you produce your bids.

Be assured that screens do not obviate the possibility of signaling. Their employment merely serves as a deterrent and makes it more difficult to effectively communicate illegally. There are many accounts of attempts to cheat by subtle coughs, clicking of cigarette lighters, etc. You name it and they have thought of it. When it comes to taking the easy way to victory instead of earning it, there are many people out there with very fertile (and furtive) imaginations.

Screens are now commonplace in all major bridge competitions and accepted as the *only* way to play. The introduction of screens was just one of the ways in which Patino attempted to deal with certain unsavory characters who were threatening the very survival of bridge. Some people, in fact, viewed high-level bridge competition as a virtual cesspool when Patino ascended to the WBF throne. Thank heavens, Jimmy shared their perception, and he used a dictatorial style as WBF

---

1. Screens were of course used in that 1975 Bermuda Bowl, but they sat atop the table. After the Vegetables were caught touching their feet together during play, the need for modifications became evident and the screens were extended to the floor.

President to root out the bad guys and take major strides towards cleaning up the game.

At one point, he cast his net in the direction of the Italians, whose string of world championships was tainted by the rumors that some team members were gaining advantage in ways they shouldn't. Through the years, many different Italians made up the national team, including Benito Garozzo and Giorgio Belladonna, who were properly celebrated as truly great players. At one point after he took over, Patino simply told some of the suspect members of the Italian team that they needn't bother to show up for the world championships in the future. He didn't have to spell it out! Truth be known, many of them never played again after that edict. For good reason, people took Jimmy at his word. Jimmy's admonitions were accepted at face value. They were promises — not threats.

Yes, it sounds as though Jimmy was acting as judge, jury and executioner in deciding who should be barred. But at the time, such heavy-handed methods may have been the only way to achieve meaningful change. I'm certain that Jimmy saw it that way. Do I approve of that kind of action? My answer would depend on the particular case, but I've been in enough similar situations where it is necessary for someone in power to take the bull by the horns, lest the right thing doesn't happen. I salute Jimmy Patino for his daring pioneering in the controversial arena of ridding the game of undesirable tactics. World bridge would not be where it is today had it not been for him. In retrospect, perhaps I mustered up some of my own gumption from witnessing the success of Jaime Ortiz-Patino's fearless, undaunted, unilateral mandates issued in the name of fair play.

In my opinion, Patino did a tremendous amount of good, but his methods did not meet with the approval of everyone, including his dear friend Edgar Kaplan, who felt that due process was as important as rooting out the immoral elements that were a stain on the game of bridge. I must confess that, in Patino's shoes, I probably would have taken the same action, and I believe that few who know the history of the WBF and high-level bridge would question that what Patino did was necessary, if not perhaps mandatory.

This is an excerpt from Patino's biography in *The Official Encyclopedia of Bridge*:

> He attempted to do something about the destructive bidding systems that were invading international tournaments. He feels he was too late to stop the influx, but he helped design a complex convention card that makes it incumbent on all pairs to explain exactly

what their systems consist of, including follow-up bids. He also felt very strongly that international bridge should be on the highest possible ethical ground. He took major steps during his presidency to ensure the upgrading of ethics, and he was eminently successful.

All in all, Patino's presidency was extremely productive. I have known Jimmy for a long time, and I've seen him do a world of good, but he did take some actions of which I did not personally approve. In particular, the situation with Denis Howard saddened me.

Close to the end of his term in 1985, Patino summoned the WBF management team to Sotogrande. At one point during the proceedings, Patino advised four of the people in attendance that he planned to step down as WBF President. He suggested that the designated foursome adjourn to another room and decide amongst themselves which one of them wanted to be the next WBF President. Those four were Ernesto d'Orsi, a bright, likeable Brazilian and a wonderful gentleman; Jose Damiani, a true bridge lover dedicated to taking the game to untold heights, and the owner of a large and very successful public relations firm in Paris; Jim Zimmerman, a good player and strongly influential ACBL Board member who has since retired; and Denis Howard.

Zimmerman was not interested in becoming WBF President, but the others were. As the campaigning began, it was evident that none of the three had a clear majority. When and if the election was contested, it would necessitate a vote by the WBF Board. There were four ACBL representatives to the Board at the time: Ruth McConnell, George Retek, Jim Zimmerman and Ed Theus. By and large, the US contingent was supporting Ernesto. The European contingent, another four votes, would be in favor of Damiani, while Denis had the support of what we usually referred to facetiously as the Rest of the World, which constituted three votes.

It is ironic, of course, since Jimmy was the cause of Denis' downfall in the end, that it was Jimmy's throwing his support to Denis that made him president in the first place. Jimmy did this mainly because he felt the Australian attorney would bring a lot of dignity to the office of WBF President. The bottom line for Jimmy was always what was best for world bridge. Although he was stern and caustic at times, in my own opinion Denis Howard's presidency was as good as it gets. He was super-organized, and always negotiated with the welfare of bridge and the WBF in mind. He even learned to improve his French, an astonishing feat and a bow to the European contingent in the upper echelons of the WBF leadership. To top everything else off, Denis had an exceptionally charming, popular and gracious wife, Robin.

Denis negotiated a sponsorship deal with NEC, the giant Japanese electronics company. What an ideal sponsor they were, always coming through with money when needed — actually enough to fund the WBF all by itself — and their officers were absolutely delighted to be associated with tournament bridge and the WBF. Their company literature bragged about their sponsorship of high-level bridge. There have been few sponsors to equal NEC.

Denis was a class act and a special individual. In 1989, the world championships were in Perth, Australia. On our way to the tournament, Debby and I stopped in Sydney, where Denis lives. Denis and Robin were incredible. He arranged a luxurious hotel suite for Debby and me, paid for it himself, and invited us to dinner with Australian Tim Seres (who died recently), one of the all-time great players and one who always practiced active ethics. Denis made all the arrangements to assure our total comfort and enjoyment.

I hate to admit this, but I never did anything comparable for him when he visited Dallas. Whenever he and Robin came to town, I took care of them, but not in such an elegant fashion. When Denis got involved in something, he did it right. I recall that at the big ACBL tournament in St. Louis in 1987, Denis showed up with copies of an issue of *Australian Bridge* magazine. It featured an article about my having been voted the top player of the 1971 Bermuda Bowl in Taiwan when our team, the Aces, won our second world title. Denis had copies of that article laminated, and he gave one to each member of the ACBL Board of Directors. I was flabbergasted at his gesture. I had never met anyone like Denis Howard.

As good as Denis was, his meticulous habits and hard-line negotiating posture sometimes worked against him. The result, of course, was that Denis made enemies. He was not a favorite in Europe, for example. He once visited Brighton, England, where the locals were hoping to convince the WBF to stage a world championship. Denis insisted on being involved in site selection and in the details of the arrangements. This was probably going too far, and he made demands on the Brighton volunteers that turned them off. It wasn't long before they threw up their hands in despair and bowed out of the running for the tournament.

Denis might have had a smoother ride had he been willing to cater to and acknowledge Jimmy's genius. Jimmy, like most successful men, is deserving of praise, and he is fond of being told how great he is and reminded that he's the Father of the WBF — which no one could dispute. That isn't Denis's style, nor mine for that matter. I don't seek that kind of flattery for myself, so I don't think about handing it out even when it is deserved or would be to my benefit to do so. That has probably cost me over the years, but not as dearly as it did Denis.

I still say Denis had an intuitive nose (if there is such a thing) for what was good for the WBF and what wasn't, and he always worked for the good of the organization. What ultimately cost Denis the WBF presidency was that Jimmy was not in his corner. Perhaps one genius has to know how to handle another genius. There were some bumps in the road, but all in all Denis's WBF presidency was a highly successful one — he even made inroads in China, where millions and millions of bridge players reside. But it is human nature not to enjoy seeing one's own brilliant accomplishments equaled or outdone.

What brought everything to a head was an episode during the 1987 World Championships, played in Ocho Rios, Jamaica. At these events, there is always a lot of partying going on — entertaining players and bridge administrators, and there are always lots of both around. Just as the ACBL Board conducts meetings prior to each of the three annual NABCs, the WBF conducts its official business at the World Championships.

To my way of thinking, what helped provoke the rift between Jimmy and Denis was Jimmy's decision to go to Jamaica by yacht. Instead of flying in like most people, Patino arrived in his yacht, a ship that had once been owned by Henry Ford. The vessel, commissioned as the 'Sibilia' by the US Navy, was sold to Henry Ford, who renamed it the 'Yankee Clipper'.

However, there was much more to Patino's yachting to Jamaica than meets the eye. Much later, when Jimmy came to visit Judy and me in Dallas in the summer of 2005, we discussed the incident candidly. He explained that the host hotel in Jamaica had only one major luxury suite, the level of accommodation Jimmy would normally have taken. He thought the suite rightfully should be occupied by the WBF President, so to avoid the problem during the championship, he came over by boat so he could sleep and entertain there.

Denis probably thought it was Jimmy's prerogative to navigate over from Europe in the 'Yankee Clipper', but it didn't sit right with him that Patino had all the sophisticated bridge bigwigs out to his yacht every night entertaining them, while Denis was left on the island with a group of lesser lights, mostly players. He could hardly abandon his own suite to attend the festivities on the yacht. Denis did not understand Patino's reason for traveling by boat, and interpreted Jimmy's actions as a slight. His relationship with Patino deteriorated from there. Before it was over, the two had exchanged a series of vitriolic, angry letters. By the time the end came in Geneva, Denis had become a bitter man.

At the Los Angeles airport en route to the world championships in Perth in 1989, I had a planned meeting with Jimmy, who was not attending the tournament. I tried to make peace, but all I could manage was a short-lived truce. Jimmy had wanted to blow Denis out of the water in Perth, but I somehow managed to forestall the inevitable. Denis had already visited me in Dallas, telling me he was contemplating running for another term as WBF president — this time against Jose Damiani. I cautioned him against it because the friction between Jimmy and him was destructive and, ultimately, it would be the WBF which would suffer. Naturally, the WBF Board had split into factions. The Europeans would be siding with Jimmy (and therefore voting for Jose) while the four American representatives to the WBF Board would support Denis. There were by then (1990) five others, seemingly lining up in favor of Denis, but if it came to a vote, it would be a squeaker.

I didn't like what was going on and I thought it was a mistake for Denis to seek the presidency a second time, but I had made a commitment to him. I wasn't going to back down on my promise. I told him I thought he shouldn't run, but that if he did, he had my support. Despite my advice, Denis told me before he left Dallas that he was going to seek a second four-year term as WBF president.

I was playing on the Jimmy Cayne team with Bob Hamman, Chip Martel, Lew Stansby, Chuck Burger and Cayne, and as I prepared for the trip to Geneva, I did so with trepidation. I was not looking forward to what almost certainly was in store. All I could think about was what I might have said to influence Denis to change his mind about running again. I knew the meetings were going to be difficult.

My flight plans were to take a TWA jet from Dallas to New York and from there to Geneva. There was a storm on the East Coast, however, and my plane was forced to land in Philadelphia, where Debby and I had to stay the night. The delay was especially agonizing because I had a meeting set up with the European representatives to the WBF Board. They wanted to discuss what to do in the impending battle between Denis and Jose Damiani, who was opposing him for the presidency. When I arrived in Geneva a day late, I was surprised and pleased to learn that the WBF meetings had been held up until I got there. I did get a chance to meet with the European members of the WBF Board — Karl Rohan of Austria, David Bardok of Israel, Andre Boekhoerst of the Netherlands and Anna Maria Torlantano of Italy. Damiani was also a representative, of course.

The four I met with told me they were expecting to lose a close election — Howard appeared to have just enough votes lined up. The Europeans vowed, however, that they would walk out of the meeting and leave the WBF if Howard won. There was only one way they wouldn't do that — if Howard promised in writing that he would serve for only one year and then resign and allow Jose to take over. Denis, of course, wanted no part of that, so the two sides remained on a dangerous collision course.

The next day the fourteen members of the WBF Board assembled in a meeting room at the Holiday Inn in Geneva to conduct their business. The atmosphere was tense, although Denis maintained a civil tone with all, even his sworn enemies. When the vote was taken, Denis had prevailed, 7-6. I voted for him, as did my fellow ACBL representatives Dick Goldberg (proxy for Ruth McConnell), Jim Zimmerman and George Retek, plus Patrick Choy of China, John Wignall of New Zealand and Alberto Calvo of Panama. For Damiani were the Europeans plus Mazhar Jafri of Pakistan and Ernesto d'Orsi of Brazil.

When the result was made known, the Europeans, including Damiani, got up and walked out of the room. A hush fell over those who remained, just staring at each other in sheer bewilderment. Some of us had known it was coming, but it was still a stunning turn of events. We didn't know what to say. After what seemed like hours, although I'm sure it was only a minute or two, I said, "Let's get on with business." Denis was clearly shaken. "I don't know if we can do it," he said. "I don't know if we can survive without the Europeans."

I couldn't argue that it wouldn't matter if Europe dropped out of the WBF. There's no doubt it would have been a crippling blow to the organization. I was equally certain, however, that the Europeans were bluffing. "But can *they* survive without *us*?" I asked. "Do you think they're going to give up bridge?" Denis didn't answer me. Instead, we adjourned the meeting, planning to resume the next day. By the time the meeting resumed the next day, Denis had decided to agree to step down after one more year, but he said he wasn't going to do it if Damiani succeeded him, and he wasn't going to sign anything. He asked me to relay to the opposing faction on the WBF that 'if they leave it up to me I'll do the right thing'.

I didn't like what had happened, and I'm certain I would not have let anyone push me out of office if I thought I was in the right. In this case, however, I believe that what Denis did was in the best interests of all concerned. The final arrangement was for Denis to stay in office another six months, followed by Ernesto for a year and a half and me for the last two years. I ended up serving as WBF president for a bit more than two years because Ernesto actually left earlier than we had planned. Before peace was achieved, Jimmy and his European contingent wanted me to sign an agreement that I would not run for another term as WBF President once my time was up. It didn't take a great leap of logic for me to understand that this was an effort to pave the way for Jose to become WBF president. I had no desire to continue as WBF President after my pinch-hitting stint was completed, but I nevertheless refused to sign any restrictive agreement.

What distresses me about the whole episode is the way it unfolded and the reasons for Denis's demise. Throughout the dissension and struggles, never once did I hear Jimmy complain about anything Denis had done to harm the WBF. Denis could be difficult to deal with, but he was a good man. He worked very hard for bridge and for the WBF. When he finally left, it was under the pretext of having to spend more time with his law practice. It was a shame and indeed a sad day for world bridge.

Near the end of my two years or so as President — my farewell speech was delivered at the 1994 World Championships in Albuquerque — Denis sent me a letter. "After due consideration," he wrote, "I have decided you were not a good President of the WBF." He didn't say why he had formed that opinion, and we have never discussed it. I disagree, of course. I think I did a good job during an ultra-volatile period. Perhaps that was bitterness speaking, and Denis had valid reasons to be bitter. His criticism of my administration always stayed with me, but I was consoled by something another Australian, Dick Cummings, once said, though I don't remember the exact context in which the remark was made. He simply offered, "Denis is complicated."

Years later, I ran into Denis and Robin at the 2000 World Bridge Olympiad in Maastricht, Netherlands. He was non-playing captain of the Australian team at the tournament. It was a cordial meeting, but we didn't have a great deal to say to each other, mainly because we were both victimized by too many other responsibilities. I wish Denis Howard's chapter in the history of the WBF had turned out differently. Denis is a credit to the human race in so many areas and deserved better — much better!

My WBF term ended in 1994 and at the risk of sounding corny, much water has passed under the bridge since that time. With Jose Damiani at the helm, the game has grown beyond anyone's expectations: his indomitable drive and high standards have led to many positive changes. From his office in Paris he works unceasingly, never passing up an opportunity for the improvement of the game or the advancement of his dreams for the future. He is supported by a number of dedicated individuals from various WBF Zones who share his aspirations to make bridge a world-wide sport. He has great ambition for the game, as evidenced by the attempt to have it included in the

2002 Winter Olympics in Salt Lake City and the inclusion of bridge in the first World Mind Sports Games coming up in Beijing in 2008 (Jose is President of the International Mind Sport Association). Jose Damiani leaves no stone (or in this case — no card) unturned as he pursues the ultimate perpetuation and exposure of the game we share and love.

As I write this, Judy and I have just returned from the 2007 World Bridge Championship, where I served in a dual capacity as both Chairman Emeritus of the WBF Appeals Committee and a player on the Kasle team, capturing the Bronze in the Senior Bowl. It is perhaps worth describing what may well be my final World Championship appearance, to show you how far things have come.

The city of Shanghai has risen to great heights, literally — witnessed by the construction of mind-boggling numbers of buildings and skyscrapers. From our view at the Oriental Riverside Hotel, at all times of the day and night there was a steady, never-ending parade of freighters, ships, tour boats, cruisers, advertising schooners and more — on the Huang Po river, which separates the newer Pudong area from the rest of this immense city. The hotel rooms were spacious, and the morning buffet (in most cases included in the daily room rate) was popular, satisfying and well attended. There were many restaurants available, in all price ranges, within a five-minute walk.

The actual playing site, arranged in conjunction with the Chinese Bridge Federation, was unmatched. I have attended many world bridge events, but it is difficult to recall one better suited to our game. Adjoining the host hotel (but accessible from inside the building as well) was the Mandarin Hall which housed the carpeted Open and Closed rooms and included a third area where the contestants could gather to compare scores and relate bridge tales (both happy and sad). Video screens were also provided that gave live updates of the results in each match, citing how many boards had been played, the present IMP and VP score standing, etc.

At the same time, there was a large theatre-like Vugraph Room on the third floor with impressive, well-informed commentators (versed in different tongues) to discuss the play as it occurred, and compare the results of the contestants from the various events — the Bermuda Bowl, the Venice Cup and the Senior Bowl, and in the final week the Transnational Teams, a very popular event where players of different nationalities could combine in an open entry.

The third floor of the conference center housed the many adjuncts of the WBF, including the Press Room, WBF Secretariat, Appeals Committee, Directors, General Staff, the Bulletin Office, etc. The staff was extremely helpful and cooperative and the thousands of guests were accorded fabulous hospitality at the Opening Ceremony and an elegant dinner... and of course, similar arrangements for the Closing Ceremony banquet and official presentation of medals. The hospitality and amenities were provided by a host of corporate sponsors whom Mr. Damiani personally acknowledged and thanked at the Opening Ceremony before play commenced.

Most impressive were the actual playing conditions and the magnificent furniture. I am no connoisseur of woodwork, but the matching tables, chairs, table screens, foot boards and a pair of end tables to be shared by screenmates were made of a gorgeous light-colored wood — possibly ash. The décor was magnificent; the hall was colorfully adorned with the flags of all the participating nations, and included high marble panels with an excellent adjustable lighting system. Each table bore its own number and proudly displayed the names of the countries playing there with computerized flag images along with names and positions of the players. Security staff screened the kibitzers and both the Open and Closed Rooms were well policed. During the semifinals and finals, the contestants were moved to special private screened areas on the fifth floor to segregate them from the throngs playing in the Transnationals on the main level. An elegant forum for a world bridge championship — first class from start to finish!

Bridge has come a long, long, way since the early days of world gatherings and I commend the organizers and local hosts for their unparalleled efforts and all the pre-event insight reflected in the final presentation. It has been a long time in coming and everyone involved certainly rose to the occasion!

Judy and I regretted we were unable to attend the Closing Banquet at the Shanghai 2007 World Championship, but in retrospect, it seemed a blessing in disguise after I learned what transpired on the podium when the USA 1 Women's Venice Cup team were being presented with their gold medals. Shortly afterwards, photographs were displayed on the internet (courtesy of Swan Games) showing the captain, the six team members (and even one of the women's sons) holding up a placard vividly displaying their proud proclamation, "WE DID NOT VOTE FOR BUSH".

It is clearly written in the Conditions of Contest of World Championship events — as well as the prior qualifying events in the USA — that "... no political statement..." may be made by any country while the event is in progress or at the Awards Presentation. This incident occurred while the United States flag was displayed and our National Anthem was being sung. Since I played a small part in writing the WBF's policy that their competitions be totally non-political, it was especially distressful to witness my own country fall soundly from grace.

I, like many patriotic Americans, was aghast at the incident. When everyone returned to US soil, I went on record advising that the best way to put the matter behind us would be for each of the six players and the captain to write her own sincere letter of apology (not a very difficult assignment if they actually regretted their action). Such an apology was not immediately forthcoming. However, after initial fire and brimstone from the USBF via its capable legal representative, Allan Falk, suddenly and unexplainably the tiger lost its teeth. Then, out of a clear blue sky, the Venice Cup team and the USBF made nice-nice to each other, publicly regretting their joint handling of the situation and promising that things would get better in the future. Why the sudden change of heart? There is always the possibility of some veiled circumstance of which we are unaware.

Just another unsolved mystery related to the continued impotent nature of the USBF. The animals, who for my money have taken over the zoo, are probably just lying in wait for their next challenge. The zookeepers are an easy mark because of their reluctance to take a strong stance — even with overwhelming documentation to support their position. From my point of view the failure of the USBF to rise to the occasion appears to be their standard calling card. Unless in the future this organization is run by knowledgeable, fearless individuals who are experienced in world bridge situations and have the courage of their convictions, our international involvement is nothing short of doomed.

On the day the USBF announced the decision on its website, I sent the entire executive this email:

> You, as representatives of the USBF, have brought infinite sadness and disappointment to those who depended on you and trusted you to do the right thing.
>
> Whether the vote was 7–0 or 4–3 does not make an excuse for your ultimately cowardly decision.
>
> Respectfully,
> Bobby Wolff

14

CHAPTER

LOSING TEAM WINS!

BY THE TIME I WAS READY TO LEAVE Geneva in 1990, I had another reason to be saddened, angered and perplexed — and my feelings were shared by thousands of respected bridge players and observers around the world. I refer to the infamous case surrounding the Rosenblum Cup match between Germany and Canada. I warn you — if you have a weak stomach, you may want to skip this chapter. It is one of bridge's darkest moments!

The Geneva tournament, which started in late August and continued through the middle of September, was the largest-ever world championship up to that time. Attendance at the event had become gigantic because of the size of the venue, the modern, comfortable Palexpo — a massive convention center on the outskirts of Geneva near the airport. Having such a large facility meant that there was no need to place restrictions on the numbers of pairs or teams entered by each country.

The world championships of bridge do not have the same format every year. The Bermuda Bowl is held every other year, with the gaps alternately filled by the Olympiad (as in Rhodes) and a tournament consisting of both pairs and teams events, which was the case in Geneva. The premier event of these championships is the Open Teams, formally the World Knockout Teams Championship for the Rosenblum Cup, or the Rosenblum, for short. It has a prestige nearly equal to the Bermuda Bowl, the grandaddy of all championships.

The Rosenblum in Geneva started with 195 teams — a huge field. The first several days were occupied with a series of round-robin matches, followed by straight knockouts, that eventually reduced the field to four teams. One semifinal would feature two American squads, one led by the legendary George Rapee, the other by New Yorker Mike Moss.

In the other semifinal match, Canada (Boris Baran/Mark Molson, Eric Kokish/George Mittelman and Marty Kirr/Arno Hobart) took on Germany (Bernhard Ludewig/Jochen Bitschene and George Nippgen/Roland Rohowsky). It's worth noting that the Germans' methods included many strange treatments and unusual gadgets, such as the so-called canapé overcalls of minors, in which an initial overcall of a minor-suit opening typically shows a three-card holding with another suit of at least five cards.

One expert assessment of the two teams made the Canadians the slight favorites, partly because of their greater experience. In fact, the Canadians won the match; it just didn't turn out that way in the record books. Here is what actually transpired.

Canada had won the first set 49-42 and the second set 29-15, so were leading at the halfway point by a score of 78-57. The young German team took the lead 135-107 when they won a wild third quarter by a score of 78-29, thanks in part to Board 40.

Dealer: West
Vul: North-South

	♠ A Q 7 6 4 3	
	♡ 8	
	◇ K Q 8 5 2	
	♣ 5	
♠ 8		♠ 5 2
♡ J 10 7 5 4 2	N	♡ K 9 6
◇ J 4 3	W E	◇ 10 9
♣ 8 7 3	S	♣ A J 10 9 6 4
	♠ K J 10 9	
	♡ A Q 3	
	◇ A 7 6	
	♣ K Q 2	

Open Room

West	North	East	South
Kokish	Bitschene	Mittelman	Ludewig
2♠[1]	3♠	pass	4NT
pass	5◇	pass	6♠
all pass			

1. Weak three-bid in an unknown suit.

Closed Room

West	North	East	South
Rohowsky	Kirr	Nippgen	Hobart
2◊¹	2♠²	dbl³	redbl
3♡	3♠	4♣	4NT
5♣	dbl	all pass	

1. Weak in either hearts or spades.
2. Spades or takeout of hearts.
3. Instructing West to pass if he had spades.

In the Open Room, the Germans had no trouble with Kokish's gadget bid of 2♠, opting for Blackwood directly. Making plus 1430 was trivial for Ludewig.

At the other table, Rohowsky also had a gadget, the so-called Multi 2◊, showing a weak two-bid in one of the majors. Nippgen's double was a competitive effort — he liked his hand if partner's suit was hearts and he, of course, thought that his own bidding might interfere with North-South's assessment of their values.

Kirr's second bid confirmed that he had spades, and Nippgen was hoping his club bid might lead to a successful sacrifice. The Germans did have the advantage in the vulnerability. The double of 5♣ was meant to show one or four keycards (the aces and the trump king), but Hobart didn't read it, thinking it showed zero or three keycards, which was impossible since there are only five keycards for each suit and Hobart was looking at three of them (two aces and the trump king). Hobart, therefore, thought slam was impossible, so he passed to collect whatever penalty was forthcoming.

Hobart led the ♠K, which Kirr overtook with the ace to switch to his singleton heart. Kirr duly got a heart ruff with his singleton trump. Three rounds of diamonds followed. Nippgen ruffed and entered dummy with a spade ruff to lead a trump. When Kirr showed out, Nippgen conceded two more tricks for down six, which should have been minus 1400 and just 1 IMP to Germany.

What happened next is described in the official World Championship book edited by Tony Sowter:

> The play had been going very slowly and the players had been warned repeatedly by the director, who was again present to speed things up. There is some uncertainty about precisely what occurred at

this point, but someone (dummy, perhaps) called out "1100" and this is the score that the monitor recorded on the match record.

All the players entered '6' in the 'tricks taken' column (for declarer) although he won only five, and the next board was placed on the table. Beyond the time pressure, the Canadians were anxious to put this bad result (plus 1100 would be an 8-IMP loss against the almost-certain 1430) behind them and go on to the next deal. Hobart would recall much later that he quickly calculated the score as he picked up his cards for the fresh deal and arrived at 1100, but his mind had bizarrely fixed on the old scoring scale, under which six down was indeed 1100.

Canada won a thrilling final set 44-19, but they lost a close match 154-151.

It was a heart-breaking loss — Germany had actually won it on the last board — and at least some of the Canadians (Eric Kokish, for one) were preparing to go home. In the middle of the night, however, it came to Hobart that the score for Canada on Board 40 should have been plus 1400 instead of 1100. The question was whether there was anything that could be done about it.

Hobart frantically called Mark Stein, the team captain, and asked him to notify the tournament officials. There is normally only a short protest period to cover circumstances such as this one, but since the next match had not been started (after which it clearly would have been too late), I believe it was appropriate for the Canadians to have their say in trying to get credit for the victory they had actually achieved. Had the score been noted correctly, Canada would have lost 1 IMP instead of 8 on Board 40 and would have won the match 151-147.

A committee was convened the next morning, and both sides were there. The committee consisted of Jens Auken of Denmark, Jose Damiani, Edgar Kaplan, Ernesto d'Orsi of Brazil and Grattan Endicott of England. As Chief Director, Bill Schoder ('Kojak') also took part in the hearing.

A word or two about the makeup of the committee:

Auken, an attorney from Copenhagen, is an excellent player but perhaps is best known as the husband of Sabine Auken (formerly Zenkel), arguably Germany's best player (they were not married at the time of this tournament, and have since separated).

Damiani, a Frenchman, was at the time President of the European Bridge League. I love Jose because he has been a friend for a long time and has been of enormous help to me in some very difficult situations. He has given tremendous service to bridge and the WBF. Having said all that, with the human factor being unavoidably present, in my view it would have been extraordinarily difficult for him to remain unbiased at this hearing, which was essentially Europe versus North America. At the time, anti-USA feeling was very strong in Europe, and indeed exists to some extent today. Unfortunately for the Canadians, this often seems to rub off on them.

Edgar, of course, was American, and he spoke up for Canada. However, I somehow got the feeling that he was not unhappy to see the Canadians come out on the short end of the hearing. I seemed to be getting mixed signals as I knew for a fact that he served in WWII and made no secret of his anti-German feelings long after the war ended.

Ernesto is another great guy, but he is very close to the Europeans.

Schoder is American, and very talented in many fields (he is a concert pianist and linguist, as well as an airplane pilot) but he is wont to take sides, and in this case I don't doubt for a second that he supported the Germans. He has a long association with that country, and German is one of the many languages in which he is fluent. He has spent a lot of time there and was the chief tournament director at the annual ACBL Regional tournament in Wiesbaden, Germany. I was not part of the committee hearing — more on that shortly — but I was told Kojak argued for the Germans' position. As it happened, I didn't know the hearing was taking place, although I believe I should have been part of the committee. I'm convinced that I was excluded from the hearing because of my tendency to argue in favor of what's right. In this case, it is abundantly clear what was right, but that's not what turned out to be the majority's way of thinking.

I was told after everything had taken place that someone had been sent to fetch me but that I couldn't be found. If I was not in my room, where could I possibly be at that time of the morning? In fact, I was in the restaurant at the Holiday Inn across the street from the Palexpo (where just about everyone ate) having breakfast. It would have been logical to look for me there, but I was 'not found' — deemed Missing In Action. Why? Well, as you may have noted in reading other parts of this book, I can be persuasive when I feel right is on my side. I feel strongly that the correct ruling in the case of Canada versus Germany would have been to allow the score change and to declare Canada the winner. This statement was given to the bridge press after the hearing was concluded:

> At this morning's first appeals committee (Stein vs. Ludewig), the
> committee comprised Jens Auken, Jose Damiani, Edgar Kaplan,

Ernesto d'Orsi and myself. [Endicott wrote the statement.] The committee heard the two captains, the four players, the chief director (on the law) and Mr. d'Orsi spoke as to the regulations, their wording and intention. The decision handed down by the committee was reached unanimously. — Grattan Endicott, 10 September 1990.

The following comes from the ACBL *Bridge Bulletin*:

The committee heard all the testimony, including, according to the Canadian players, the statement by the Germans that they actually were set six tricks. The committee noted, however, that the scorecard said six tricks were made and the penalty was 1100. Since these figures are consistent with each other, the score was allowed to stand. Germany had the chance to win its first world championship, which it did (Germany defeated the Moss team in the anticlimactic final).

What is a 'manifestly incorrect' score? It could be the score of the match, perhaps the totals of the IMPs would be incorrectly added. Plus 420 on a vulnerable board would be manifestly incorrect. Down three vulnerable with a score of 1100 would be manifestly incorrect. In the case in question, the number of tricks and the score matched. That was the key to the committee's decision.

The feelings were strong throughout the Palexpo, site of the championships. "How can the team that lost at the table be declared the winner?" was the question that epitomized the feelings of the Canadian players. Most competitors who offered comment were aghast at the ruling, echoing the Canadian feeling that the team that wins at the table should be the winner.

Bill Schoder, Chief Tournament Director, said the committee really had no alternative. He said the laws of bridge dictated the ruling that had to be made.

The Germans, in a letter published in the *Daily Bulletin*, expressed their regrets and sympathy:

No one wins when a match is decided by a mis-scored deal. It is an impossible loss for the side that is declared the loser and there is no satisfaction or pleasure for the side that is declared the winner. We as bridge players, and bridge as a competitive sport, are all losers.

The letter went on:

> We as a team would have preferred to be eliminated early rather than gain a berth in the final as a result of the tragedy that took place.

Pardon me, but that statement makes me sick to my stomach. If the Germans were so distressed by the turn of events, and so regretful that they had been declared the winners when they had actually lost, why didn't they step forward and say that Canada should play in the final? Do they believe that the organizers of the tournament would have refused to let them make such a magnanimously sporting gesture?

In my view, the interpretation of the laws put forth by Schoder, who does not profess to be a bridge expert, was a technicality for the committee to hide behind — and a pretty thin one at that. A courageous panel would have interpreted the law in such a way as to have the team that won in fact be declared the winner. I would wager that had Germany been on the other side of the issue, had they been the ones who had scored up 1100 when it should have been 1400, that particular panel would have found a way to allow the change. These kinds of things are bad for bridge, and having it happen among the experts sends the wrong message to aspiring players.

It's not just bridge where you see this kind of hunger for victory *no matter what*. There is precedent in other sports for this kind of atrocity. I recall a college football game between the Colorado Buffalos and the Missouri Tigers in the nineties. With time running out in the game, Colorado was trailing by less than six points. The Buffalos had fourth down virtually on Missouri's goal line. They made one last effort to get the ball into the end zone and were stopped cold. Unfortunately for Missouri, the referees lost track of the downs, and Colorado got a fifth try for a touchdown. They made it and won the game on the game's last play as time ran out... but it wasn't until after the game was over that anyone noticed the extra down.

It was disturbing to me that Colorado didn't do the right thing and acknowledge that they had actually *lost* the game — perhaps even forfeit if necessary. I guess the stakes for college football programs are too high for one of them to give up a win, even when they didn't earn it. Also the alumni factor (and their financial support to the institution) may have been a consideration — if there was heavy wagering on the game, forfeiting would not have been looked upon with favor. Colorado wasn't coerced to give back the victory, but it left a bad taste in my mouth to know that they were willing to take something they hadn't earned. Undeserved triumphs are meaningless!

Eric Kokish's memories of the Geneva incident provide an even darker image of the scene. Eric says he recalls having rearranged his flights to leave the next day after his team lost the semifinal.

> Then Mark Stein, our non-playing captain, called me in the middle of the night to tell me that Arno Hobart had just contacted him with the news about the incorrect score. We agreed to hustle over to the (Palexpo) first thing in the morning.
>
> Mark Stein, a real character, comes across as extremely nervous when he's agitated and when he informed Kojak of the situation and received some unsatisfactory response, Mark was beside himself. However, we were permitted to appeal because the 'next stage of play' had not yet commenced. As Edgar and Ernesto d'Orsi were on the committee, we thought there was a chance that justice would prevail and the *right* result would emerge, but it was not to be, the whole thing hanging on a technicality, the subjective interpretation of a single word ('manifestly') in the conditions of contest, usually an Edgar forte.

Eric was later told that the European lobby had carried the day on the committee, but when the Canadian team got together they shared all sorts of stories they had heard about the whole incident, including one from the previous night in which the Germans were drinking and laughing about "those stupid Canadians not knowing the score", which meant that they knew the true result and didn't report it.

Eric told me, "We found it difficult to believe that an entire team, once they knew about the error, could agree to continue. Surely someone among them would realize that they had not won and insist that they concede the match. But no." At the closing ceremony, the Germans were cheered mightily. Eric was one of several players who felt an overwhelming sadness at the turn of events. "I felt the game was no longer worth playing," Eric told me, "that anyone who could honor a team that behaved that badly had to have a warped sense of values, but the truth was that the anti-American feeling at that time (which included Canadians, willy-nilly) was particularly high. The Europeans were simply demonstrating their solidarity."

I share Eric's feeling that the Geneva incident was a low point for bridge. It might be little consolation now, especially to the Canadians, but I have seen to it that from then on and continuing to this very day, in all North American Conditions of Contest, the following phrase was added: *When it possibly can be so interpreted, the winner at the table will be named the winner in fact.* Too little, too late... but a safeguard against another such travesty occurring.

As an epilogue, some people have compared this whole affair with Argentine golfer Roberto DiVicenzo being disqualified for signing an incorrect scorecard. Directly from Wikipedia: 'He is best remembered for his misfortune in the 1968 Masters, where he signed his scorecard for a score higher than his actual score on the 17th hole, signing for a par 4 when he actually made a birdie 3.' Had the score been correctly entered, he would have tied for first and been in a playoff the following day.

In my opinion, that happening was correctly decided since DiVicenzo's penalty was punitive in nature and not in the natural order of things. Since the penalty for signing an incorrect scorecard is clearly spelled out in the rules, not to mention necessary for the orderly running of the tournament, there was no justification in that instance for an overrule.

The young Bobby — below, during Army service years.

The original Aces in 1968. Back (left to right): Billy Eisenberg, Mike Lawrence, Bobby Wolff, Bobby Goldman. Front (left to right): Jim Jacoby, Ira Corn. (Photo from ACBL archive.)

The Aces in 1969. Back (left to right): Wolff, Jacoby, Corn, Bob Hamman, Lawrence; front (left to right): Eisenberg, Goldman, Joe Musumeci. (Photo from ACBL archive.)

DETROIT
The Detroit Hilton
February 19, 20, 21, 22

ITS PLAYERS AND PERFORMERS

Leon Yallouze: Is 50 years old, a consulting engineer in Paris, and is an extremely energetic and quick-witted man. As a bridge player, he is famous for both his stubbornness and astuteness. In the Circus he customarily is paired with Sharif or Delmouly. He has been playing bridge since 1944 and has won an impressive number of French and International Championships.

He does not play chess, but enjoys soccer and tennis. As the Circus' manager, he is extremely happy to bring the Circus to America.

Omar Sharif: Is 38 years old and a professional actor, who has lived in all corners of the world wherever film cameras (and bridge) take him. He has played bridge for about ten years now, at each available hour. In fact, one cannot be certain as to whether he actually played bridge in between the films for "Lawrence of Arabia," "Dr. Zhivago," and "Funny Girl," or whether he interrupted bridge in order to film. Along with his many other activities, Omar Sharif has mastered the "Blue Club" system and is able to be teamed with any member of his illustrious circus.

Giorgio Belladonna: Is 46 years old and is a civil servant in Rome. He started playing bridge in 1946. In the Blue Team he and Avarelli are partners. Belladonna had an active part in the designing of the Roman Club System. He is admired and feared for his technical skill, but more especially for his "flair" at the bridge table. It takes a lot of stamina if one is to hold out against Belladonna. He was Olympic champion in 1964 and has won no less than ten World Championships. He plays chess (in a small way) and likes tennis and soccer. He is, beyond any doubt, one of the world's great bridge players.

Michael Ledeen: The "baby" of the Circus, is 28 years old and Assistant Professor of History at Washington University in St. Louis. He is the author of one book and several articles dealing with the Fascist Movement in Europe, as well as one of America's promising young bridge players. He recently finished third in the Spingold Championships in Los Angeles. He is also the American manager of the Circus.

Benito Garozzo: Was born in Rome in 1929 and still carries on a jewelry business there. He started playing bridge 23 years ago. In the Blue Team he is the partner of Forquet. In 1964 he won the Bridge-Olympiad and is eight times world-champion.

He is a brilliant player with incredibly strong morale. Nothing ever shakes his nerve. He prefers the Blue Team Club System to the Roman Club. He must be a very modest man for, when asked who he thinks are easily the most impressive players, he mentions a whole list of names, among them those of Slavenburg and Kreyns.

Claude Delmouly: This forty-year-old Parisian is a professional teacher of bridge. He also likes swimming and a game of chess and tennis. He is a master in the theory of bridge and has written a great deal about his ideas. As a player, he is composure personified, and his play is incredibly stable and cool-headed. Nervous opponents will find Delmouly one of their most difficult challenges.

To the question who is his most formidable opponent, he usually without any hesitation: Belladonna.

Delmouly holds many French and International Championships and was Olympic champion in 1960.

Pietro Forquet: Is 44 years old and a bank manager in Napoli, Italy. He has been the Italian Bridge Champion 10 times and the World Bridge Champion 10 times. He has won two World Olympiad titles and has been European Champion 5 times. He has been the manager of the Blue Team since 1956. His main hobbies are tennis, football, and yachting.

Souvenir program from the Sharif Circus visit to Detroit in 1970.

Valkenburg, 1980 Olympiad, Silver Medal team. Left to right:
Paul Soloway, Mike Passell, Fred Hamilton, Ira Rubin, Wolff
(Hamman missing).

The second-last incarnation of the Aces, 1981. Back (left to right): Rubin,
Alan Sontag, Wolff; front (left to right): Peter Weichsel, Hamilton (Hamman and
npc Corn missing). (Photo from ACBL archive.)

1984 International Team Trials winners. Left to right: Soloway, Ron Andersen, Goldman, Hamman, Wolff (Malcolm Brachman missing). (Photo from ACBL archive.)

Venice, 1988 Olympiad Gold Medal team: the only time the USA has won this event. Left to right: Eric Rodwell, Jeff Meckstroth, Jacoby, Wolff, Hamman, Seymon Deutsch. (Photo from ACBL archive.)

Bermuda Bowl team 1987. Back (left to right): Hugh Ross, Peter Pender, Dan Morse (npc), Wolff, Hamman, Lew Stansby; front: Chip Martel. Pender dropped out due to illness and was replaced by Mike Lawrence. (Photo from ACBL archive.)

The legendary Nickell team. Back (left to right): Wolff, Meckstroth, Hamman. Front (left to right): Nick Nickell, Rodwell, Dick Freeman. (Photo courtesy Nick Nickell.)

Mr. Bridge USA! The Dutch Bridge Federation magazine, June 1989.

Press conference at the 1994 Albuquerque World Championship. Left to right: Jose Damiani, Wolff, Warren Buffett.

Bobby in play at the
Sunday Times *pairs in*
1980. The kibitzer is
Debby Wolff.

Engaged! Bobby and
Judy in Monaco, 2003.
(Photo by Ron Tacchi.)

CHAPTER 15 | LOOKING OUT FOR NUMBER ONE!

I've heard a lot of bellyaching over the years about professional players. Much of it is pure envy. Why wouldn't a person, if he or she had the money, seek expert help to improve at whatever the individual was trying to accomplish? People do it at golf and tennis all the time and you don't hear all this griping or criticism.

In my opinion, it's good to have pros at tournaments. There was a well-received event at the 2003 Spring Nationals in Philadelphia called 'One on One' (coincidentally organized and run by my then-future wife, Judy Kay) where rank and file players got to spend time and exchange small talk with the big shots such as Lisa and David Berkowitz, Larry Cohen, Eric Greco, Geoff Hampson, Eric Rodwell, Tobi Sokolow, Zia and a host of other bridge luminaries. At many Regionals, the pros give lectures to the new players and draw huge audiences. Professionalism serves bridge well in many capacities.

Another way of looking at it is that if these really good players did not have some way to earn their living from bridge and support their lifestyle, they probably wouldn't be playing — and the only people with a chance to go to the world championships would be the rich guys. It costs big bucks to jet across the oceans to participate in world championships. That's why just about every country nowadays is represented by a team that is sponsored in one way or another. The great team from Italy that won the Rosenblum Cup at the World Bridge Championships in Montreal in 2002 was sponsored by Lavazza, the coffee maker. Two recent Bermuda Bowl champions — the Rose Meltzer team in 2001 and the Nick Nickell team in 2003, both from the USA — are sponsored teams. Both sponsors, unlike Maria Teresa Lavazza, are playing members of their teams. For a long time, of course, I was a member of the Nickell team, and I still do play professionally.

There is a theory that if sponsors don't step up to the plate to keep the best players together on teams, our country will not have the best representatives at the world championships year after year. Perhaps that is a subjective evaluation. Many options and methods are available for selecting teams to represent the country, a topic which will be dealt with later.

You might ask why anyone other than the professionals themselves should care whether we field competitive teams in international competition. The answer is *patriotism*. Why should a club player in Kansas City care whether Jeff Meckstroth wins another world championship? How is the average player supposed to be able to relate to the champions of the game? Do the big shots care about the little people? These are all good questions, and I can assure you that the stars of the game care deeply. It's not bragging for me to say that I'm one of the extremely lucky ones who have been able to play at high levels with a fair amount of success. I care about bridge, regardless of the level of play. It's the greatest game in the world, and I want to be sure it's still around and prospering long after I'm gone.

This book was midway to completion during the 2004 Summer Olympic Games in Athens. I watched much of the competition on television and found myself rooting very hard for the Americans who represented their country in the Games. I'm well past any athletic competence I ever had, and, for some of the sports I watched, I couldn't begin to conceive of emulating the competitors' achievements. Yet I cheered them on, sharing their excitement when they conquered and their anguish when they were vanquished.

Bridge is no different. We should all root for the ACBL players, a label which encompasses Americans, Canadians, Bermudans and Mexicans, who have labored hard to make it to the world championships and are striving to represent you, as a bridge player, in competition. These men and women are more experienced and certainly much more accomplished than most, but they're bridge players the same as you and they deserve your support, whether they are professionals out to make a living or simply lovers of the greatest game on earth.

Professionals make many positive contributions to the game. That said, there are some dark sides to that scene, particularly at levels where the pressure to win seems overwhelming and success, at any cost, is the singular objective!

There have long been stories of pros meeting each other in restrooms during tournaments to exchange information. Player A has already played Boards 7 and 8, for example, and he knows that every card is lying right for a 25-point grand slam on Board 7. It's too late for

Player A, but not for Player B, who hasn't played Board 7 yet. Player B, meanwhile, knows that on another deal, a heart lead rather than the normal spade lead will defeat 3NT, so that information gets passed along. The matchpoints gained from these kinds of exchanges could be the difference between third in the section and first — or even several places in the overall standings. This is reprehensible, but some competitors will give in to the pressure to win, especially when they are playing with weak players, and they will look for whatever edge they can latch onto.

In the mid-nineties, I learned about another disgusting 'technique', a private, surreptitious arrangement between contending teams: deliberately reporting incorrect scores, resulting in massive tampering with Victory Points. For about a year or so, some of the professionals had been participating in a scheme amongst themselves, making deals that only the most devious of minds could have concocted. Here's how it was pulled off.

Let us say two teams play in the late stages of a Swiss event — not unlikely because the pros can be found at most tournaments during the year — and both are in contention to win. The top three or four teams, for example, might be bunched up within 3 or 4 Victory Points of each other, possibly a little more. With a 30-point VP scale (or even on the 20-point scale), there's a lot of room for movement on the final round and the standings can change radically between the penultimate and the last round, depending upon the margins of victory.

The expected scenario is that you are likely to be playing one of the top several teams in the event on the final round. You have to be pretty darned lucky to be still in contention if you aren't a tough team to start with.

Anyway, in the final stages of such an event, if two contending teams are playing each other, it probably won't help either side if the outcome is a close win by one of them. All it would take to knock them both out of contention would be to split the Victory Points. For example, on a 30-point scale, a tie results in 15 VPs for each side. If it's a two-point win, the split is 19-11 — still not great for either team if there are several contenders with a shot at the victory.

So the deal was this — whoever won when two 'friendly' teams played each other, *no matter what the margin*, the loser signed off on a score ticket that indicated a blitz. The next time, it might be the other team that won and got the benefit. What benefit, you might ask? You must be kidding! Well, if you're a pro, how much better is it going to be for you if you can help your client garner first place rather than fifth or sixth? Think about it. Won't your client be more inclined to hire you again if you win 35 or 40 gold points than if you win 6 or 7? That's all you would get if your team ended up way down on the overall list.

The unscrupulous creators of this ruse named it 'Double IMPs'. It was sickening to think about all the teams that were screwed — teams that were playing honestly. And who wouldn't be upset to find that their second-place finish really should have been first and that they were jobbed out of it by a phony blitz on the last round? I felt that the perpetrators should be in jail, but I also felt that I had an opportunity to nip this thing in the bud. I was less interested in punishing the criminals than I was in just ending the practice.

To this day, I don't know who started it, but I'm 99% sure it's not going on any more. I learned the names of some of the principal characters, and at the next NABC I looked up one of the players involved in the scheme and took him aside. "I know what's been going on with the Double IMPs," I said. "If this continues, I'm going to try to run you out of bridge." People who know me have no doubt about my sincerity and that I don't make idle promises or threats. I'm serious in matters of this sort, and the person I was talking to had every reason to believe I would follow up on my threat. Individuals with larceny in their souls will do as much as they feel they can get away with, but if the heat is turned up and their livelihoods are threatened, they'll toe the line. They may do it begrudgingly, but they will behave. The potential loss of earning can be a very cogent argument for conformance!

It would be interesting some day to perform a psychological case study on how the bridge mind works in devious ways to achieve something not necessarily deserved. I'm thinking now about a scheme from the fifties that wasn't exactly considered cricket, but at the same time there was no law against it or preventive measures taken to guard against its adoption. I might add it wasn't evil or crafty like the Double IMPs ploy described above. Also, when it came to light, I wasn't in any position to do anything about it. The loopholes were eventually plugged to assure that bridge would be conducted on a level playing field... but you will find the story amusing and worth noting for the record.

At one time, the rules for the Vanderbilt Knockout Teams were different from today as far as seeding goes. Back in the fifties, all teams entered four players initially, and the teams were seeded according to the average number of masterpoints held by those four. The tournament directors who did the seeding took the total masterpoints and divided by four. The team with the most masterpoints was the top seed and the one with the fewest was the bottom seed. In the days when teams could have only five players, you could then add one player to the initial roster. In later years, the conditions were amended so you could add two. In those days, by the way, the higher-seeded teams were practically guaranteed victory. The lower seeds were essentially hopeless. As with many events in which a large number of teams are entered, the competitors were divided up into brackets — and that's where the scheming became important.

I vividly remember the machinations of Tobias Stone (of Roth-Stone fame) known as the incomparable 'Stoney'. He was one of the leading players of his era and was inducted into the Hall of Fame in 2003 in Long Beach, California. Stoney, who has been retired for decades, was an actively ethical player, although his style against his opponents could be very intimidating. He enjoyed a longstanding, successful partnership with Alvin Roth. Stoney always had a contending team, and, in fact, won the Vanderbilt three times. He had a likeable and amusing personality with a lightning-fast mind and quick wit.

Stoney was one of the most colorful characters ever to grace a bridge table. He could often be found in the wee hours of the morning on 3rd Avenue in mid-Manhattan at P. J. Clarke's, hobnobbing with the stars and entertaining them with his repertoire of stories! He was great company, clever and resourceful... and always at least one step ahead of the game. After his retirement from bridge, he left the Big Apple and moved to Las Vegas where he still lives and enjoys the action.

Recently we had dinner with him here in Vegas and I am happy to report that Stoney, now in his mid-eighties, didn't miss a beat. Stoney played on teams with Judy's late husband, Norman, in the sixties, and the three remained close. Whenever visiting Vegas, it became a ritual to have dinner with him at The Diamond Horseshoe and reminisce about days gone by. Stoney has been blessed with good health, agility, a delightful sense of humor and a memory second to none. I wouldn't want to challenge his recall of sporting events, statistics, details of bridge or backgammon matches, the names of players and scores — and certainly anything to do with the movie industry. The years have been kind to him.

You are about to witness a prime example of his perfectly legitimate 'one-upmanship'. After many of the teams had submitted their Vanderbilt lineups to the directors, Stoney would go around and question the staff about who was playing for what team, getting the masterpoint information at the same time. What he was doing was checking to see which bracket his team would fall into depending on which four members of his team he listed initially. If putting in a starting four with more masterpoints meant he would have a higher seed and land in a tougher bracket, Stoney would submit a starting four which included a player who had fewer masterpoints. He didn't care about having a lower seed if the bracket was easier. Pride was not the issue — an easier path to victory was! If getting a higher seed put him in an easier bracket, that is the course he would pursue.

Stoney was my mentor in a way, and I watched his activity with interest. The tournament directors — Harry Goldwater, Al Sobel and Paul Marks — also observed Stoney in action, but they thought it was amusing. Actually, the rules allowed for this chicanery. Anyone could have figured this out. Stoney was just sharper, more resourceful and more intuitive than his peers and he discovered a way to advantage his team — and it was all perfectly legal, as witnessed by the directing staff. Presumably if someone else had been clever or astute enough to conjure up the same battle technique, that person would have had access to the identical information of which Stoney availed himself.

Seeding is done much differently today, and you don't add players after the fact, so it's not possible to manipulate the system as Stoney cleverly did back then.

CHAPTER 16

PAYING THE PIPER

LOOKING BACK, one of the most glaring indications that the Bobby Wolff/Bob Hamman partnership was in jeopardy occurred in London in January of 1998 at the Macallan Invitational Pairs. This tournament, for most of its history, was sponsored by the London *Sunday Times*.

The Macallan, which was cancelled after 1999, was staged at one of London's most elegant hotels. The dress was always formal. Men were clad in tuxedos and the few select women invited over the years donned evening gowns for the occasion. It was always a small, prestigious field, usually sixteen pairs; they were almost all world-class players, so it was very tough. The Macallan did not use screens like most big-time events nowadays, simply bidding boxes. There was a Vugraph presentation, but kibitzers could watch in person if they chose to, and it was not uncommon to see throngs of people clustered around a particular table. As you can imagine, Zia Mahmood and the redoubtable Omar Sharif were favorites of the kibitzers, as they remain today.

In 1998, Bob and I were doing pretty well in the Macallan, with a good chance for second. As it happened, Geir Helgemo and Tor Helness, two Norwegians, had practically lapped the field and would eventually win in a runaway, but second place in such a tough field is nothing to sneeze at. Actually, the incident at the Macallan, although significant in retrospect, was not the first ominous hint of trouble for my doomed partnership.

The previous fall, Bob and I and the rest of the Nick Nickell team had made it to the finals of the Bermuda Bowl in Hammamet, Tunisia, losing a disappointing match to a tough French team. Despite the outcome, I thought Bob and I had played very well. In fact, in the round-robin, the worst Bob and I had done was a tie with Italy, one of the top contenders in the field. We won every other match we played, but when the tournament was over, all Bob could talk about was one particular deal that came up in the final against France. In retrospect, he was nit-picking — but I was too naïve and unsuspecting of things to come.

Our side was vulnerable and the opponents were not, and Bob opened 1♣, which was strong and artificial in our methods. The next player jumped to 3♣, natural and weak. My hand was

♠ 3 ♡ Q 10 7 5 ◊ Q J 10 8 6 4 3 ♣ A

I bid 3◊, natural, and the next hand bid 5♣, doing his best to jam our auction. There are different ways to handle situations like this. Most expert pairs play that a pass by the opener in a bidding sequence like this is forcing, which means his partner cannot pass if the next player passes. Opener's partner must double or bid something, and double is often the choice. Some pairs play that 'pass and pull' — that is, opener first passes, then pulls partner's double — shows a better hand than just bidding directly over the interference. Bob and I, on the other hand, played that an immediate bid showed a better hand than a pass and pull action.

Anyway, Bob passed, so I rebid my seven-card diamond suit. Bob pulled that to 5♡, which improved my hand because of the shortness in spades and clubs. Those four good trumps I had for Bob might well produce tricks by ruffing. The textbook bid in this case was 6♣, showing first-round control in that suit. It was clearly the correct bid in this case, as you will see.

I had my reasons, however, for doing what I did, which was simply to bid 6♡. First of all, Bob's decision not to bid directly over 5♣ meant to me that he didn't have a great hand, at least according to our agreements. I didn't think 7♡ was a reasonable possibility on that basis, so I didn't want to cuebid the ♣A, which would certainly have been a grand slam try. Secondly, if I cuebid 6♣ and Bob bid 6♡, the opponents probably would understand that, as we had made a stab at the grand slam, we were most likely cold for the small slam, which would give them a strong incentive to save in 7♣ over 6♡. I wasn't sure what I would do over that, so rather than put myself in the position of having to guess, I decided to make a bid that produced a bit of doubt for the opponents as well. If they thought we were unsure about 6♡, they would be much less likely to save.

The upshot, of course, is that my decision turned out horribly. This was Bob's hand:

♠ A K J 6 2 ♡ A K J 8 4 3 2 ◊ — ♣ J

The grand slam for our side was frigid as you can see by examining the full deal:

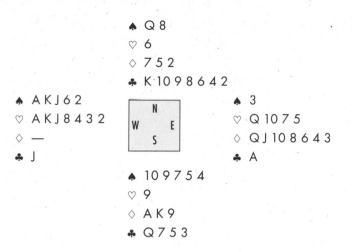

```
                    ♠ Q 8
                    ♡ 6
                    ◇ 7 5 2
                    ♣ K 10 9 8 6 4 2
♠ A K J 6 2                         ♠ 3
♡ A K J 8 4 3 2    ┌─────┐         ♡ Q 10 7 5
◇ —                │  N  │         ◇ Q J 10 8 6 4 3
♣ J                │W   E│         ♣ A
                   │  S  │
                   └─────┘
                    ♠ 10 9 7 5 4
                    ♡ 9
                    ◇ A K 9
                    ♣ Q 7 5 3
```

This was our bidding against Michel Perron and Paul Chemla:

West	North	East	South
Hamman	Perron	Wolff	Chemla
			pass
1♣	3♣	3◇	5♣
pass	pass	5◇	pass
5♡	pass	6♡	all pass

At the other table, Jeff Meckstroth and Eric Rodwell opposed Alain Levy and Christian Mari.

West	North	East	South
Levy	Meckstroth	Mari	Rodwell
			pass
1♡	1NT	2NT	3◇
3♠	4♣	4♡	5♣
5◇	pass	6♡	7♣
7♡	all pass		

Some explanations are necessary. Jeff's 1NT overcall showed either a balanced hand with 1NT opening strength or a weak hand with a long suit. Mari's 2NT showed a good hand with at least four-card support for hearts. Rodwell's 3◇ showed where his strength lay and, in the end, helped Levy bid the grand slam because he felt that even if the defenders had a club to cash, he was going to get a diamond lead. What that means, of course, is that Mari made the same decision I made — he could just as easily have cuebid the ♣A but he chose not to. You could say that Rodwell's 7♣ bid pushed the opponents to the grand slam, but his bid is certainly not out of line. For all he knew, his side had a diamond trick coming, meaning that if the opponents went to seven on speculation and went down, it would be a huge swing for our team.

Another point to be made here is that this board came in the ninth set out of ten (16-board segments) and was the 130th we played. At the start of the set, we were down 51 IMPs. Yes, we dropped 13 IMPs because I failed to cuebid, but it's not as if this deal all by itself cost us the match. Do I wish I could do it over? Of course, but I usually stand by my judgment — and there are plenty of cases where I have taken similar actions that resulted in big gains for our side, something I felt was overlooked on the subject hand. I was crucified by Bob for taking a position which appeared justified at the time in light of his bidding.

There was another case in the round-robin against a team we blitzed that seemed to annoy Bob more than usual. We were playing one of the weaker teams in the field, really drilling them, when we had an auction where one of the opponents had shown a two-suiter over something we bid. I ended up taking a conservative course in the auction, failing to cuebid when I might have, and we missed a slam. It didn't matter, of course, because we blitzed the team anyway, but Bob seemed much more critical of my failure to cuebid than he normally was. It didn't strike me then as significant, but in retrospect, it was.

Back to the Macallan in London. Bob and I were pretty deep into the tournament — the eleventh round out of fifteen — when we came up against Jeff Meckstroth and Tony Forrester. In fact, we were doing pretty well at that point. We had won four matches in a row, including a 50-10 pasting of Canadians Dianna Gordon and George Mittelman (former World Mixed Pairs champions) in round nine.

Meckstroth was playing with Forrester because the tournament had invoked severe restrictions on allowable conventions, pretty much eliminating the Rodwell-Meckstroth Precision system, which has many artificial and complicated sequences. The organizers, it seemed, wanted to present a show to the public that was comprehensible — that is, if someone bid hearts it meant he had hearts, not something else. Rodwell, the principal architect of the system, didn't want to participate if he had to play something akin to standard bridge. It is worth noting, of course, that Jeff and Eric had won the tournament two years in a row, in 1995 and 1996, without any system restrictions. Anyway, Bob and I came up against Forrester, one of England's top players, and Meckstroth, our teammate on the Nickell team.

On one deal, Meckstroth opened 1♡ on my right as dealer. I held

♠ Q 10 4 ♡ K 9 8 6 3 ◊ — ♣ A K J 8 5

I bid 2♣ and Forrester passed. Bob bid 2♠ and Meckstroth passed. I thought his bid improved my hand, so I jumped to 4♠, which was followed by a long hesitation by Forrester — at least forty-five seconds to a minute. Bob passed and Jeff said, "Well, I'm going to do what I would have done anyway," meaning he had planned to double. Jeff's hand was

♠ A K 5 2 ♡ A Q J 5 2 ◊ J 9 7 3 ♣ —

In my experience, there are a lot of misguided ideas regarding the onus and moral obligation that rests squarely upon the player whose partner hesitates for a long time before passing. When that happens, especially in a game with expert players, there is *always* information passed. This is information to which the partner of the hesitator is not entitled. In this case, Forrester's hesitation clearly indicated he had some values because he was considering making a bid. It turns out he was thinking about bidding diamonds, for this was his hand:

♠ 6 ♡ — ◊ Q 10 8 5 2 ♣ Q 10 9 7 6 3 2

Of course, 5◊ doubled would not have fared well because Bob held

♠ J 9 8 7 3 ♡ 10 7 4 ◊ A K 6 4 ♣ 4

Bob certainly would have started with a top diamond, then followed with another and a third trump, cutting dummy's ruffing chances down to one. So 5◊ would not have produced a good result for them, but that was never an option under the circumstances.

At any rate, in my opinion, Meckstroth was completely out of line to take action after his partner's long break in tempo. Bob, of course, went down two doubled for minus 500 and a very poor score on the board. When the deal was over, it was clear I was disturbed by what had happened. Meckstroth, picking up on my sullen demeanor, asked me, "Do you think I shouldn't have doubled?" My reply was that I didn't think there was another player in the event who would have doubled after his partner hesitated so long before passing. Meckstroth shrugged and made no more comments, but, looking back, I can now remember that Bob seemed displeased with me for challenging Jeff as I did. I recall now having a distinct feeling that he was not on my side in this situation.

To try to articulate what was going on at that time, I guess I would compare it to a couple who have been together a long time, but one becomes disenchanted with the other. At that point, every little thing that comes up seems much more annoying than it ever did before. In many ways, of course, a bridge partnership *is* like a marriage. There will be many times when things don't go right, and it's important for the partners, as it is for a husband and wife, to think long term and to remember all the pluses.

At that point in our twenty-six years as partners, I don't think Bob was able to remember all the good that had come of our playing together. On the other hand, I don't think the change in his attitude was all his own doing. I believe there were strong outside influences. In all fairness, I cannot blame Nick, who I don't believe initiated my firing, but I believe he would have gone along with the wishes of the majority of his players to preserve harmony and team spirit.

If you have followed this book closely, you must be aware that my stance on various issues, along with my lack of political acumen (not kissing asses or buttering people up) and my stubbornness in standing up for what I believe in, all contributes to antagonizing people and recruiting enemies. There were lots of people who wanted to see me knocked from my perch. I suspect that two of the people who were happy at the prospect of my being fired by Bob were my teammates, Jeff and Eric.

Don't get me wrong. I believe they are two of the best players in the world, certainly one of the top partnerships ever. I have no complaints at all, at this point in time, about their ethics. That said, there have been clashes with them over the years, even when we were teammates. One that overwhelmingly stands out in my mind occurred at the 1995 Fall NABC in Atlanta.

Bob and I were playing in the Open Board-a-Match teams, which takes place the first weekend of the tournament. Now there are two ways to run a BAM. One is with a mirror Mitchell, in which a team's East-West pair goes to a different section when the game starts. As the game progresses, for example, when North-South Pair 9 are playing against East-West Pair 6 in one section, their teammates (East-West 9) are playing against North-South 6, and so on throughout the session.

The other way is with what is known as an 'internal' movement, which is almost always used for one of the two sessions on the second day of this three-day event. In that setup, when the game starts, East-West Pair 9 simply moves to another table in the same section. In that alignment, you aren't playing the boards at the same time as your teammates. They play half the set in the first part of the session while you play the other half of the set, and it's the reverse in the second half.

Anyway, at one point during the set, Donna Rodwell, Eric's wife, sat down at our table to kibitz. We happened to be playing a good pair from Michigan, Steve Landen and Pratap Rajadhyaksha, who were later to become my teammates in some successful ventures, including finishing third in the 2003 Bermuda Bowl. When the round was over, Donna got up and left, and Steve asked contentiously, "What is Donna doing at this table? She was just watching Eric a few minutes ago."

This caused Bob to get as close to irate as I've ever seen him and he immediately challenged me to do something about it, egging me on saying, "I thought this is what you believed in." If the significance of this is not readily apparent, you should understand that if she watched some boards that Bob and I played in one round, then went and watched Eric and Jeff play them later, she would have information to impart about what happened. I'm not suggesting that she would do such a thing or that in fact she did, but if Landen noticed her kibitzing both tables of our team, others probably did, too. *Even the appearance of impropriety is something to be avoided at all costs.* Why give anyone food for thought? The longer we sat there, the more agitated Landen became. "You should say something," he said. "Somebody's got to say something."

Bob designated me as the messenger — so I went out to look for Donna. When I found her, I told her she could not kibitz us. "I'm not cheating," was her response. I insisted, however, that what she was doing didn't look good for our team. "Nobody's going to stop me from doing what I want to do," she defiantly remarked as she turned away from me. Later in the evening, an indignant Eric confronted me, admonishing, "You can't talk to Donna that way." I attempted to explain where I was coming from, but Eric was unappeased. I stood my ground, of course, and since it was I, not Bob, who had talked to Donna, I was the whipping boy and the object of the flak. But I have strong shoulders and the deed had to be done. However, it did nothing to improve my standing with Eric and Jeff.

There was another time, at the 1995 Spring NABC in Phoenix, when I got a knock on my door late at night to find Eric and Jeff in the entryway wanting to know about a rumor that had been circulating. It seemed that one of the top professional players was spreading tales that an investigation had broken the 'code' allegedly employed by Jeff and Eric to communicate with each other when they were behind screens. They inquired what I knew about the story. Clearly they suspected that I was in some way responsible.

First of all, I would never have believed that Jeff and Eric would do such a thing. Second, I knew nothing about any such investigation.

The first I had heard of the rumor was when they came to my room. It was clear they were upset, and I'm not sure if they believed me when I proclaimed my total innocence. As far as I know, nothing ever came of the story, but it amounted to another black mark against me with the two of them. My dossier seemed to be bulging at the seams!

Looking back on 1997, I can recall several incidents that seemed to drive me further and further from Bob and the team. At the Team Trials in New Orleans that summer, there was a notorious incident involving Jeff and Eric. The two of them were playing against Sam Lev and Brian Glubok. At the time, Jeff had the habit of getting up and going out of the playing area to smoke whenever he was dummy. That routine also entailed passing by and having a look at Eric's hand on his way out. He also had the opportunity to see at least one of his opponents' hands.

In the case in question, Jeff performed his usual ritual, and a few minutes later, while he was still in the middle of declaring the hand, Eric excused himself to go to the restroom. Not coincidentally, Glubok got up from the table as well and went to the restroom, where he saw Jeff and Eric side by side at a pair of urinals. It has never been established that they exchanged any information, and there is no evidence that Jeff told Eric anything about the opponents' hands. Eric did succeed in making his contract, adopting the only reasonable line of play there was — but it looks very bad when something like that happens. Such behavior places you in a no-win situation. In fact, it's customary for a player to ask a monitor to accompany him whenever he wants to leave the playing area. *No one should consider himself above the law.*

There was a furor over the so-called 'bathroom incident', of which I was totally unaware — until I got home to Dallas after the Trials. We had won and the team had all gone out to dinner afterwards, receiving congratulations from various people we encountered. I was completely oblivious to the uproar, but by the time I had flown over to Italy a short time later for a meeting of the management team of the World Bridge Federation, the story was on everyone's lips. Gossip spreads fast in the bridge world, especially when the stars are involved!

People questioned what was going to happen to Jeff and Eric and whether we would keep them on the team. In fact, Nick Nickell, Bob and I had a conference call after I learned about it, and Bob and I entertained various courses of action: resigning from the team ourselves, kicking them off or some other alternative. Talk reached me that some of the players who were in New Orleans were calling me a hypocrite if I didn't resign from the team after all the preaching I had done about ethics and proper behavior. It occurred to me, of course, but in the end nothing was done, and, in fact, Eric and Jeff received only a slap on the wrist. I am not able to judge objectively whether the actual penalty given for the bathroom incident was fair or not. Self-interest is a tremendous driving force and I don't even trust myself, much less others, to be a fair judge. As you can see, however, once again I ended up right in the middle of the action even though this time I was really nothing but an innocent bystander.

A digression from my personal tribulations at this time seems entirely fitting as the game of bridge is not the only hobby or sport associated with so-called bathroom incidents. Very recently a scandal was flushed out during a major chess tournament. The press had a field day with the story. Under the guise of going to the bathroom on routine business, a player was accused, while in the facility, of using a communications device linked to computers for determining the best strategy once he returned to the table. To my knowledge, up to this point the chess brouhaha has been mere speculation and nothing concrete has yet been proven.

Interestingly, there are parallel overtones relating to bridge players taking a break and departing the table during a session. Records reflect that on more than one isolated instance a visit to the restroom, or the dire need to use a telephone in the middle of a session, resulted in untoward actions. "What untoward actions?" an innocent reader may inquire. Well, in one instance, information was known to have been transmitted from a kibitzer who had witnessed the board in play earlier, reporting what the result should be on a specific deal yet to be played by the person who had strayed from the table.

Obviously any player (even the most ethical) runs the risk of finger-pointing simply by leaving the playing site before the completion and comparison of the boards played. During the International Team Trials and other major events, security measures are in place to make the bathrooms and other environment totally safe from any hanky-panky and off limits to all bridge intercourse. Ideally, monitors should be available to accompany players leaving the playing site for any reason whatsoever. No one should be placed in a position where they might be accused of communicating or receiving information or be observed in a compromising situation of any kind.

The contagion spreads.

There has recently been an expansion in live internet coverage of major tournaments from the four corners of the globe. However, the marvel of relaying up-to-date information to an audience thousands of miles away — including deals and scores — allows for the leaking of crucial information to parties with vested interests. What (or who), without cautious monitoring, is going to prevent a person from leaving the playing room and contacting a friend or spouse with access to a computer — who may have already witnessed the on-line results in another room where a specific deal has already been played? Suffice it to say, even Wells Fargo, the FBI and the CIA would have their hands full policing cyberspace bridge.

Without such monitoring protection, a certain amount of doubt is inevitable. What happens if, upon returning to the table, a player plays or defends a hand in an unusual manner (successfully, of course) as if he or she knew where certain cards were. Or, during the bidding, suppose he or she arrives in a very lucky aggressive contract that just so happens (because of the lie of the cards) to be cold. The combination of extracurricular meandering away from the site with extraordinary luck in reaching a fortuitous contract or the amazingly good fortune of 'guessing' the cards right outweighs the element of coincidence and realistically points to unauthorized information.

The enforcement of more rigid regulations regarding freedom of movement during a live contest should be mandatory. At the recent Open Team Trials in White Plains, the fire alarm sounded during play and the building was evacuated. The Directors in Charge had no alternative but to throw out the last three boards; they had not been played by the entire group and he could not take the chance of a security breach. That necessitated abandoning the original results, good or bad, and tacking three extra boards on to the final session to replace those discarded from the previous one. That forced a comparison of an abbreviated number of boards in one set and a distortion of the original conditions of contest as a result of the three additional boards in the final quarter. It may not seem fair to some because undoubtedly the outcomes of certain matches, through no fault of any of the players, were affected by the elimination of the results on the disallowed boards, but *protecting the integrity of the game at any cost* should be the sole objective of those in command.

Getting back to the 1997 Team Trials in New Orleans... There was a case that I can now cite as another indication that things were continuing on a downhill course for Bob and me. We were playing against Ralph Katz and Howard Weinstein, two top players then living in the Chicago area, and Bob and I had the following auction, with the opponents silent:

West	North	East	South
Wolff	Weinstein	Hamman	Katz
1♣	pass	1♦	pass
1♡	pass	1♠	pass
2♦	pass	2NT	pass
3NT	all pass		

My 1♣ was strong and artificial, 1♢ was positive (1♡ would have been negative), and 1♡ by me showed a minimum 1♣ opener (17-19) with a five-plus card suit in diamonds, hearts or spades. Bob's 1♠ showed a five-card suit in spades, hearts or diamonds with 6-10 points. I bid 2♢, a natural suit, and Bob bid 2NT. I raised to game. The above treatment was designed to keep the bidding as low as possible after a 1♣ opening bid.

When Katz, who was on lead, asked for an explanation of the bidding, I told him Bob's bidding seemed to indicate that he had a diamond suit (he would have bid 2♡ or 2♠ had he had five of either of those, and his 1♠ bid had denied five clubs), but that looking at my hand, I didn't think he actually did have five diamonds. I told Katz it was possible Bob had a very weak five-card major suit he didn't want to bid, but I didn't state that as a certainty.

Perhaps I was being overly ethical — if there is such a thing. Actually, I volunteered more information than I needed to, but Katz, who was trying to decide whether to lead a spade (he had QJ9x) or a club (he had Q10xx) finally decided on a club, which was wrong because Bob actually did have a five-card club suit. He had forgotten the system — and it was *his* treatment within the system! He, not I, had devised it.

It turned out a spade lead would have defeated the contract, while the club lead made it easy. Not unexpectedly, there was a protest, and Bob reacted angrily to my statement that he might have bypassed a weak five-card major, which was curious to me considering that it was *he* who forgot what we were playing. The case fell to Richard Colker, who waffled back and forth but finally decided to give Katz the spade lead to defeat our contract. He made the announcement of his decision while we were on a break in the hospitality suite, and it annoyed me so much that I caused a scene in front of everyone. It was another nail in the coffin of my partnership with Bob.

That brings me again all the way back to the Macallan, where the game with Bob, although it started very well, seemed to fall flat toward the end. We were lifeless and ineffective, finishing in a disappointing eighth place after being in contention well past the halfway point of the event. Upon my return from London, I headed directly for the Bermuda Regional. Bob went on back to Dallas, but when I got home on Sunday night from Bermuda, I had a message to call him. I did, and he asked me to drop by his office the next day. I told him it had to be in the morning because I was driving to the Houston Regional at noon.

Bob and I did business together occasionally, so I didn't attach any significance to the fact that he wanted to have a meeting in his office. I was stunned when he told me I was being fired from the Nickell team.

Bob had been designated as the hatchet man — not Nick. Part of what surprised me was the suddenness. About five years earlier, Bob and I had discussed some rumors that had been floating around that he was trying to find a new partner. When we talked about it then, I told him that if he ever did consider changing partners, I would appreciate some notice so I could make other arrangements as well. He told me at that time that he was considering no such move, but that if he ever did (and it was not at all likely), he would give me plenty of notice.

He was giving me almost no notice at all as we spoke that Monday in his office, and it was later confirmed he had been scouting around for a new partner for some time. Apparently, his plans were no secret (except to me) as word had spread like wildfire that year at the Hilton Head Regional in South Carolina that a change was in the works. I felt like the proverbial 'wronged wife' — the last to know.

I told Bob this was a big blow to me, and I asked him if there wasn't some way to salvage the partnership. I offered to make compromises on the system, to meet with him regularly to go over our agreements. I pointed out that things were going pretty well for us on the Nickell team. We had won all four Spingolds from 1993 to 1996 and had three straight wins in the Reisinger in the same period. We had just finished second in the Bermuda Bowl after having won it in 1995. Our partnership went back twenty-six years. I wasn't ready for this shattering divorce, and it came at a tragic time in my personal life when I was still suffering the pain and loss of Debby's death.

I asked Bob what could be done and made several suggestions. Bob seemed to think my ideas had merit, and he told me he needed to check with Nick, passing the buck. He promised to call me on Wednesday in Houston. I left his office with the impression that things could be worked out. When he didn't call me by Wednesday, I called him. He said he still hadn't talked to Nick. That seemed hard to believe as so much was hanging in the balance — especially for me. When I finally got through to him that Friday, he said he was going to follow through with the plans — meaning I was fired. *Sayonara*!

We were, however, to go ahead and play together in the Vanderbilt that spring in Reno. Predictably, it was a disaster. We lost early, and Bob played about as poorly as I ever saw him play — not that it would have mattered if we had won. I would still have been dumped. I was very disappointed to learn (directly from the horse's mouth) that minutes after I had left the meeting with Bob that Monday in his office, Paul Soloway received a call from Bob confirming their arrangement to play. Despite Bob's assurance he would reconsider his original decision, he never meant to think seriously about keeping our partnership intact and my remaining on the Nickell team. They were merely empty words.

I still think Bob is a good guy. He has a lot of character, and he is a great player. He is highly ethical and a credit to the game. In my mind, in the area of deal analysis, he is one of the two best in the world, right up there with Benito Garozzo. He tried to take sole responsibility for the decision to cast me adrift, but I believe he was influenced by a number of people. There's no doubt I could have helped myself with the Nickell team along the way, but I've never been good at nurturing relationships, and the thought of being disingenuous makes my blood run cold.

At the Bermuda Bowl in Beijing in 1995, Dick Freeman was feeling bad about his game, and Bob took him aside and gave him a pep talk. I should have done the same, but I didn't. I am simply not a people person. At the Fall NABC in Atlanta that year, Freeman invited members of the team to his home, but my date didn't want to go, so I didn't go either. That was another mistake. These kinds of things add up, and the bottom line for me was gradual alienation.

Nick, to his credit, was more than fair in settling with me monetarily, and he wrote a very touching letter of thanks for all my contributions. In a three-page hand-penned note, he expressed gratitude to me for making him "a better bridge player", adding, "More importantly, the time we spent together has, I'm sure, made me a better person, in many ways." In the case of Frank T. Nickell, it is difficult to imagine room for improvement. For a long time he has stood in a class by himself.

To this day, I'm not sure that Bob realizes how much losing my spot on the team affected me. It wasn't necessarily because of the money and prestige attached to being part of a winning team, but because of the loss of the clout that had helped me accomplish much that was good for the game I revere.

After the Houston tournament, I went to San Antonio to visit my brother, Walter. As I noted before, he is a guru of sorts to me, and I value his opinion. He advised me not to contemplate suing anyone (you know how litigious our society is) or to think about quitting bridge — not that either thought ever, even fleetingly, crossed my mind.

It's been much tougher for me since I was fired, but my demotion has not changed my commitment to what I think is right for bridge, and, lo and behold, I *have* managed to more than just survive without Bob and the Nickell team. Since then, I have won the World Senior Bowl in 2000 in Maastricht, Holland representing the USA with John Mohan, Dan Morse, Steve Robinson, John Sutherlin and Kit Woolsey; won the 2002 Reisinger (my eighth) in Phoenix. I then won the Open Team trials with the same team of Doug Doub, Steve Landen, Dan Morse, Pratap Rajadhyaksha and Adam Wildavsky — a victory that allowed us to represent the USA in the Bermuda Bowl held in Monte Carlo in 2003. Our team, though as inexperienced as any USA team has ever been (none of my teammates ever having participated in the Bermuda Bowl before) went on to finish third, bringing home the bronze medal. It reduced my Bermuda Bowl record to seven wins, four seconds and now one third, but in many ways that third could be the most shining accomplishment in my career. All I can do is thank my partner, Dan, and my teammates for rising to the occasion in the face of strong odds.

In October of 2001, together with Fred Hamilton, Dan Morse, Steve Robinson, John Sutherlin and Kit Woolsey, I won the Senior Trials and played as USA 1 in Paris (that was the event that was moved at the last minute from Bali because of the 9/11 attacks). We led the qualifying but lost our semifinal match to USA 2 which went on to win the World Championship (Grant Baze, Gene Freed, Gary Hayden, Joe Kivel, Chris Larsen and John Onstott). However, the more noteworthy accomplishment for Dan and me was that we led the Butler scores (a measure of each individual pair's performance). Our score of more than 1 IMP per board against the entire field of pairs sitting in the same direction, at that time, is said to have set the record for the highest plus score ever since the Butler results came into existence.

Late last year in Bethesda, Maryland, my Senior Team won the right to be USA 1 in the 2007 World Senior Bowl to be held in Shanghai, China. The odds against us (Dan Gerstman, Gaylor Kasle, Dan Morse, Ron Smith, John Sutherlin and me) were high, but that did not deter us from making every effort to represent our country well and with dignity. We took home the bronze medals, in what was probably my final hurrah on the international stage.

Life continues to be good to me! I could not be more content. Judy and I savor the daily routine of our relaxed (well sort of) life in Summerlin where we recently bought a home. It lies in a gated suburban community twenty minutes northwest of the famous Las Vegas Strip and offers every convenience anyone could want.

We are trying to curtail our up-until-now vigorous international travel schedule as we delight in our daily routines on home turf. When leisure time permits we play in a nearby duplicate twice a week. For a while I was giving impromptu *pro bono* lectures at the start of games and enjoying them considerably, because of the overwhelming positive response of the players. Our home is within five minutes of two rather large local hotels and casinos which Judy and I visit for short sessions of blackjack, drawn to the '21' tables by the proximity of the sinful eateries that most (including yours truly) find irresistible. It is a misconception that gambling is dangerous. Not so! Let the truth be known — the real danger lurks in the calories from the fabulous buffets.

Some would consider it a decadent life, but we keep it in its proper perspective. I am still devoting much time to bridge writing and viewing (not to mention betting on) my beloved sports. As ever, participating in the furtherance of bridge ideals consumes much of my time. I hope my contributions will continue to strengthen and perpetuate the game and I will maintain the high esteem in which I am held by the administrators of the World Bridge Federation. I believe my opinion still carries the proper weight in the right quarters. Of course, life cannot be the same after leaving the Nickell team, but I am who I am and will never cease trying to do what I know is best for the game I love. I never tire of doing battle with those whose agendas do not match up well with the best interests of both the playing and the administration of the game itself.

CHAPTER 17

WEAPONS OF MASS DESTRUCTION AND LESSER ATROCITIES

IF YOU PLAY ANY BRIDGE AT ALL, you have seen this happen many times. Someone opens, say, 1NT and the next player bids something, maybe 2♣, which is alerted. Third hand asks and is told 2♣ shows the majors. From that point on, everything goes to hell in a handbasket because it turns out that 2♣ actually showed a one-suited hand, not the majors. Because of the wrong explanation, the opening 1NT bidder misses out on a cold major-suit game, and ends up going down in 3NT. The victims of the misbid (or if you will, the misexplanation) might seek some redress from the director, but they're usually told that it's the rub of the green — no adjustment. So sorry! If you think this kind of incident is confined to your local duplicate or the newcomer games, think again. It's prevalent even at the highest levels of bridge. That makes it even worse. It's bad for the game, and it's time we did something about it.

Bear in mind that my concern is directed *primarily* at the high-level games, not at the local bridge club or even tournament play, although it wouldn't be such a terrible thing if the act could be cleaned up there as well. Local authorities, such as club directors, club owners, etc., can determine the severity of the penalty, if any. Misinformation at this level (with few exceptions) is usually unintentional or accidental, at worst, with no ulterior motives. It is in the major events at the big tournaments, such as the NABCs and the Team Trials, that change is mightily needed.

Hammering down on the higher echelons and not the lower levels is perhaps unfair and somewhat of a concession for me, but I put it forward with the hope that discipline at the higher levels will eventually reach the lower ones and prevail. My proposals are not popular because many of the players who conveniently 'forget' an agreement or 'haven't discussed' some convention are the ones who benefit from the uncertainty that results. They want to maintain the status quo, and some of them are in a position to keep things the way they are. That doesn't make it right.

The following example involves my wife, Judy. She was playing in the Mixed Board-a-Match Teams at the Summer NABC in New York in 2004 with a top Philadelphia player, Howie Cohen (with whom Judy had been playing before our marriage and her move to Dallas). In case you aren't familiar with board-a-match scoring, there are three possible scores: 1 for winning the board; 1/2 for tying it; and zero for losing it. The actual score at each table is irrelevant, just which of the two is greater. Each board is a match, as the name of the game indicates. I sat down to kibitz, and this deal arose.

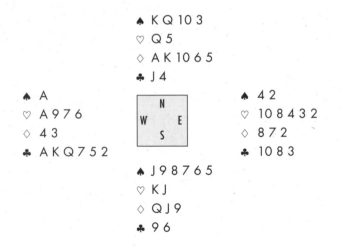

♠ K Q 10 3
♥ Q 5
♦ A K 10 6 5
♣ J 4

♠ A
♥ A 9 7 6
♦ 4 3
♣ A K Q 7 5 2

♠ 4 2
♥ 10 8 4 3 2
♦ 8 7 2
♣ 10 8 3

♠ J 9 8 7 6 5
♥ K J
♦ Q J 9
♣ 9 6

Judy was South, and West opened 1♣, a strong, artificial bid. Her partner overcalled 1◊, which according to their agreement showed diamonds and hearts (a treatment devised by Alan Truscott). Judy alerted and explained, according to her understanding, what they were playing. You can see, of course, that after that explanation, there was no earthly way East-West could reach their cold heart game, one which was admittedly lucky to make because of the fortuitous trump division. Nevertheless, it would have made had they bid it. The actual final contract was 3◊ by North, making three, for plus 110. It was a clear loss on the board for East-West, who under normal circumstances would probably land in some number of hearts, possibly even 4♡ — or they might have defended a 4♠ save (North-South were not vulnerable, East-West were). At least East-West would have had a plus score then.

The director was called after the deal, and the ruling was that it was clearly a misbid by North-South and that the result would stand. Judy's team won the board since their teammates doubled their opponents in 4♠ and set it one for +100. If I had had anything to say about this case, Judy and Howie would have received a big fat zero and East-West half of a board. Luckily for them I bit my tongue, as kibitzers are nothing more than silent observers.

You might think the punishment I favor is harsh, but forgetting obscure conventions, particularly by what usually turns out to be the side with the weaker holdings, often causes an undue and impossible-to-solve hardship for the innocent side. We must resolve this problem by requiring the conventioneers to know their conventions — not an unreasonable expectation.

Howie didn't recall what they were playing and thought he was overcalling in diamonds. There was nothing out of order going on there. Judy and Howie hadn't played together in six months, and they are both highly ethical. He just 'plain forgot' — but that doesn't help the injured parties. People have no right to employ conventions they may forget.

My contention is that many of the 'forgets' and misexplanations by experts are much too convenient. It has been my strong objective for years to change the rules to assess penalties for pairs who forget their homemade systems (whether conveniently or otherwise). Another option would be that if you forget what you are playing or give an inaccurate description of it to the opponents, it comes off the convention card. In other words, you are barred from playing that convention for the session — or perhaps longer, for chronic offenders.

There's more to the issue than just the problem of screwed-up conventions and inaccurately explained agreements where the transgression may be purely accidental. I take issue with inequities resulting from methods that are deliberately preconceived, practiced and executed with intent to defraud. I am alluding to what I call the poison gas laboratories, a much more serious problem. It's one thing to use a convention such as a 2◊ opener to show a limited hand with both majors, something like:

♠ K J 8 7 6 ♡ Q J 7 3 2 ◊ 5 ♣ J 4

It's another thing when for some this convention has evolved to include a hand with four spades to the jack and four hearts to the ten when not vulnerable — and it's tough to double them with any certainty that you will profit from it. Bidding of that kind has only one purpose — to foul up the opponents' auctions. It is intentionally destructive, plain and simple.

There are many more conventions just like that and plenty of players willing to wield them to gain any advantage they can. For example, the Multi 2◇ provides lots of room for, shall we say, artful subterfuge. Let's say you open a Multi, showing a weak two-bid in one of the majors. The next player passes and your partner bids 2♠ (this usually means that if your suit is spades, that's as high as he wants to get, but he's willing to go to the three-level or higher if your suit is hearts). Fourth seat then enters the bidding with 3♣. You pass and your left-hand opponent asks about your partner's 2♠ bid.

Players have been known to respond to such a question with a statement that the 2♠ bid or your pass haven't been discussed. That's total BS; if you really haven't discussed 2♠, you should be penalized severely or be prohibited from playing Multi 2◇. But the real twist is what your pass means. It should show that your long suit is spades since your partner with his 2♠ bid has asked you to correct if your suit is hearts, and has shown himself prepared to compete at least to the three-level if that is the case. Partner's hand may be great for hearts but terrible for spades, e.g.

♠ 3 ♡ K Q 10 4 ◇ K Q 9 5 4 2 ♣ A 8

However, *if you haven't discussed it* and you pass, now all anyone knows is that the hand probably belongs to the opponents. Meanwhile, you have deprived them of an important cuebid, leaving them further out to sea in their attempt to find the best contract.

This is the kind of injustice I'm talking about — and it happens. It's unacceptable for anyone to say they 'haven't discussed' some aspect of a convention like the Multi. You shouldn't be allowed to play it if you don't know the responses and the nuances.

If you don't think it's tough to make progress in this area, I'll describe a well-attended meeting I had with many knowledgeable players and administrators at the World Championships in Venice, Italy, in 1988. We were discussing how to deal with the multitude of different systems players encounter at world championships. Some of them have been dubbed 'brown sticker' conventions, a term originated by Edgar Kaplan. You don't have to be a rocket scientist to figure out why the color brown was chosen.

Anyway, I was pushing for a requirement that if a pair was using complex and unfamiliar conventions or agreements, they had to provide written defenses to their methods. Further, these defenses were to be available to the opponents at the table. This is practical because there is no way to remember defenses to all the different systems, and believe me, you would be blown away by some of the stuff these various pairs are playing. Almost no one in the audience at this meeting (some 200 in number) was on my side. The majority were in favor of allowing whatever the traffic would bear!

At one point, we were discussing so-called 'fert' bids — short for 'fertilizer', another descriptive reference. P.O. Sundelin, a world-class player from Sweden, was arguing that 'ferts', usually some nonsense bid such as 2♣ showing a very weak hand that might contain a diamond suit, were descriptive. I challenged P.O. or anyone else in the audience to give me an example of a 'fert' getting a pair to the right contract. My challenge was greeted with silence. It seemed that I was making progress.

However, one of the people attending the meeting was Doug Drew, a Canadian who at the time was a member of the ACBL Board of Directors and an ACBL representative to the World Bridge Federation. Just as I thought I was mustering the support of the WBF Executive Council, Drew launched into a harangue about players who had traveled to Italy expecting to play their systems. Drew is one of those people who tend to favor the underdog — and, unfortunately, the teams Canada had been sending to the world championships through those years were not uniformly stellar, though there were exceptions, of course. It was easy to see where he was coming from! Drew's position was that the lesser teams should be allowed to gain *any* advantage they could, including using unusual conventions. He even told the Executive Council that my proposal was against the rules. Surprisingly, I lost a close vote. It was very frustrating.

Despite Drew and those who took his side, I prevailed, thanks to Edgar Kaplan. He pointed out that while it might not be within the rules to be able to refer to your own notes about how to defend against the opponents' methods, it is within the rules to be able to refer to the opponents' convention cards. Therefore, all pairs using non-standard conventions were required to include adequate defenses to their systems on their cards. It is worth noting that few play 'fert' bids any more because there is little advantage to them. That doesn't mean there aren't hordes of weird systems and agreements to cope with, however. There are still many brown sticker conventions, but their use is usually restricted to the knockout phases of the world championships. Edgar's brilliance and all-consuming dedication to the sanctity of the game were his legacies to bridge. However, no less memorable was his marvelous sense of humor, and it always brings a smile to my lips when I recall another of his labeling gems — 'Particularly Unusual Systems' or PUS, a beautifully descriptive acronym! He certainly had a delightful way with words.

You might be wondering how bridge has reached this state, where players are continually manufacturing oddball systems that give them an advantage for no other reason than unfamiliarity. The answer is not simple, but it has a lot to do with the rules of the game. As you may know, contract bridge evolved from auction bridge, a vastly inferior game. In auction bridge — nearly extinct now — it took 30 points to make a game, and the scoring went as follows: if you bid 1NT and made it, your score would be 10. If you happened to make two, your score was 20. For making nine tricks — even if you didn't bid 3NT — you got 30, and so forth. Spades were worth 9, hearts 8, diamonds 7 and clubs 6. However, if you failed to make your bid, you lost 50 points per undertrick, a huge difference. The concept of vulnerability didn't exist, but with the great disparity between the score for making a contract and the minus for going down, there was no sacrificing. Your aim was obviously to stay as low as possible. Accurate bidding was pretty much a non-factor because you got credit for however many tricks you took regardless of where the bidding stopped.

When Harold Vanderbilt conceived the idea of contract bridge in 1927, bidding became much more important. To earn the game bonus, you had to bid the game, not simply take the requisite tricks. It was an innovation that revolutionized bridge and made it much more interesting. Contract bridge replaced auction bridge practically overnight. Unfortunately, except for introducing the concept of vulnerability, Vanderbilt did not change the penalty for failing to make your contract. In auction bridge, the penalty for failing to make your contract was much greater than the score for making it. At contract, the penalty for going down is considerably less than the typical partscore (when the 50-point bonus for making your contract is factored in).

I believe it would be in the best interests of bridge to increase undertrick scores to something like minus 90 for non-vulnerable undertricks and possibly minus 160 for each vulnerable undertrick. It's easy to foresee objections to this, of course, the main one being that people would have to learn a whole new set of numbers. When it comes to change, many people resist on principle alone. Why clutter your mind with more things to remember?

In contrast to other sports, bridge has seen relatively few changes in its rules, although there have been a couple of minor changes to the scoring, including one for which Jeff Meckstroth is single-handedly responsible. In the Bermuda Bowl in 1981, Meckstroth heard the vulnerable opponents bid to 7♡. He was not vulnerable, and holding six spades to the queen and no other values in his hand, bid 7♠ out of the blue. He was doubled and went down nine tricks, so he was minus only 1700 (he should have been down ten tricks for 1900, but the defenders erred) — compared to the 2210 the opponents would have earned for making their grand slam. Meckstroth's mistake was he did this while Edgar Kaplan was watching, and Edgar soon pushed through a change in the scoring to make down nine doubled, not vulnerable, worth minus 2300. There has also been a change to provide a bonus of 100 instead of 50 for making a redoubled contract. Other than those two adjustments, however, the scoring is pretty much as it was in 1927. The Meckstroth occurrence, of course, represents a precedent for changes in the scoring — just as changes in other sports reflect developments in their games.

In fact, there are few sports that have not implemented rule changes, changes which have usually been for the better. In the NBA, for example, the rule against zone defenses was recently eliminated, possibly because it was so difficult to enforce fairly. The placement of the line for three-point shots has been changed a couple of times since it was introduced. At one time, there was some discussion of a rule change in tennis allowing for only one serve — a reaction to the big servers like Roscoe Tanner and Kevin Curren. That change didn't come about, but the point is that it was considered, as being potentially beneficial. Other changes included limiting, for example, the size of a tennis racquet, the curvature of a hockey stick and the dimples on a golf ball. The idea is that the winner should be determined by the player who displays the greatest skill — not the one with the technological edge. The ruling bodies want a level playing field. And that's exactly why the gentleman's game of bridge, which should involve the highest possible level of ethics and deportment, requires full disclosure of methods. We want the winners to be the players who, along with the usual amount of luck, play with the greatest skill and the sharpest judgment.

But in the end I am a practical person. While I strongly believe that something like increasing undertrick scores would be good for bridge, I don't think it will ever occur — and perhaps the disruption such a change would cause makes it not worth pursuing.

At any rate, this refusal to make changes to the structure of the game is where the 'scientists' in the poison gas labs come in. They exploit all the loopholes in the rules and take advantage of them. There is a famous deal from the world championships in Santiago, Chile, in which a Dutch player opened 2♣ to show any hand (possibly including a five-card diamond suit) with something like 0-5 high card points. Could anyone argue that this bid has a constructive purpose? I think not. The deal is famous, of course, because the 2♣ opening accomplished its purpose and the opponents ended up with a bidding disaster created mainly because of their unfamiliarity with the convention. We must not allow the poison gas labs to produce destructive conventions wielded by opponents with no regard for how the game should be played. Those who love the game agree with me. Those whose only goal is to win using any means often take another view.

In my opinion, there *should* be changes in the laws of bridge — and I would like to see the establishment of the position of Bridge Commissioner. This would be someone with broad powers whose responsibility is strictly to zero in on the spirit and equity of the game and whose charge is to keep the game up to date and make sure the playing field is level.

My brother, Walter, is a fine attorney. He is a beacon of common sense. I have learned from him that a good judge hears the facts of a case, knows the applicable laws and interprets those laws to arrive at a fair ruling. A *great* judge, Walter says, knows the law and the subject, and interprets the law, if at all possible, to see that *equity* is served. I have often argued with my friend and former ACBL Recorder, Richard Colker, whom I like and respect but who is blindly adherent to the laws. I also note that many bridge-playing attorneys tenaciously cling to that position, not allowing for the protection of the innocent as they feel nothing can supersede the law. Rich and I will discuss a case, and Rich will say, "I agree with you, Bobby, but that's not how the law is written." In my view, Rich has it backwards. When it's clear that an injustice is about to be perpetrated, he should be saying, "This is not how the law is written, but this is how I'm ruling." Better yet, let us see what can be done to rewrite the law to reflect equity... starting with the case in point. Why keep compounding error upon error upon error?

If we had a Bridge Commissioner, I would like to train that person to help see that it is the *game* that is always served by the rulings — not individual players or political interests. Yes, it has been sad to witness — but the fact remains that many rulings are made on the basis of the individuals involved rather than the issues. Make no mistake — *it is the game that is important, and only the game!*

There will be people who oppose this point of view, but as long as there is strict accountability, naming names, and enough pertinent publicity on the matter, we are safe to interpret the laws to favor what is fair and what should be done immediately. To me, at the stage where bridge is today, it is not enough merely to say, "You were right, but the law says differently."

We need to exercise more initiative in bridge rulings. I have been able to witness the achievement of equity in many cases at the top level as Chairman of Appeals at World Bridge Federation championships. The way I got cases resolved was not always popular. I have learned to live with the fact that my viewpoint is often unpopular — but equity is what I always strive for, and I believe I have accomplished it in most of the cases I have influenced. I'm happy with that and I can live with myself! Also, this type of 'cowboy' behavior serves to stir the lethargy that seems to work against law changes. Perhaps my Texas heritage has inspired me to take the bull by the horns!

18

CHAPTER

PROFESSIONALISM, PERSONAL AGENDAS AND RECUSALS

IN 2003, I PLAYED IN THE UNITED STATES Bridge Championship in Memphis with Dan Morse, Steve Landen, Pratap Rajadhyaksha, Doug Doub and Adam Wildavsky. Because we had won the Reisinger Board-a-Match Teams at the Fall NABC the previous year, we had a good seed in the event, which would determine who would represent the country at the Bermuda Bowl in Monte Carlo in 2003. In somewhat of a surprise ending, we emerged victorious. Our chances were enhanced because we had to win only three matches to capture the berth in the world championships. We beat the Gaylor Kasle and Jimmy Cayne teams to reach the final and then defeated a four-man Roy Welland squad to earn the right to go to Monaco.

One very significant aspect of our victory is that, as plans were in the works to arrange our flight to Monte Carlo, we were aware that we were one of the few truly 'amateur' teams to represent the USA in a very long time. In bridge jargon, the term 'amateur' does not suggest new or inexperienced. It simply means there is no sponsor, which translates to no additional remuneration for either our travel expenses (at that time partially subsidized by the ACBL) or our bridge prowess.

The Nickell team, by contrast, is a highly paid group, particularly Jeff Meckstroth and Eric Rodwell, unquestionably the linchpins of the squad. If Nickell wasn't forking over the dough for this team, most of the members would be playing for someone else. I certainly am not saying it's wrong, just that's how it is. I play professionally as well and I am not knocking it. In a sense, bridge resembles any other sport. You can't blame Alex Rodriguez, for example, for accepting a contract offer of $275 million for ten years from the New York Yankees, even if you feel it's ridiculous to pay a baseball player $27 million a year.

Similarly, you can't blame Meckstroth and Rodwell, or Bob Hamman and Paul Soloway, the other pros on the Nickell team, for agreeing to be paid handsomely to play on one of the best teams in the world. I'm not judging or casting aspersions on players for wanting to exploit their skills to make a living.

Many people in the bridge world were unaware that Charles Goren was the original sponsor in the early days. It should be noted that bridge is very different than other team sports since, to the naked eye, there is no way to determine who is the weak sister (or sisters) on a team without some painstaking (and not often done) analysis. In all other team sports there are comprehensive statistics to evaluate player contributions — but they are not so readily available in bridge.

Goren was making good money off the game and it was in his best interests to have a strong team. No one knew he was probably the weakest member of his teams. It was one of bridge's best kept secrets to which the rank and file was not privy. Imagine — the Father of Modern Bridge being a *sponsor*! Being a sponsor is no disgrace and should carry no stigma. In fact, it is a popular trend among the wealthy players of today. It is not so unusual when one considers that through the years there has been, on more than one occasion, a moneyed top-level player footing the financial burden in order to have his pick of the litter as teammates. Admittedly, the concept is much more prevalent today and is accepted world-wide. And why not?

As noted in earlier chapters of this book, I was instrumental in introducing professional bridge to Texas, playing at clubs for $5 and $10 a session and later earning money at tournaments. I still play for pay today, although not as regularly as I once did. Players in the early days of professional bridge had to do a lot more than they do now. Mary Jane Farrell, of California, is a good example. When she was starting out, she was probably playing fourteen times a week to earn her pay. She was attractive, well-mannered, a good player and in demand, but earning meager pay by today's standards. In comparison to current fees those of yesterday seem ridiculously low, but professional bridge has come of age.

Nowadays, there is a plethora of professional players, but maybe only three or four handfuls are really thriving — and it's so much better for them if they can hook up with an affluent sponsor who will hire them, especially on a continuing basis. When I say 'affluent sponsor', I'm talking about people like the late Malcolm Brachman, Jimmy Cayne, Russ Ekeblad, Mark Gordon, Bob Hollman, George Jacobs, Carolyn Lynch (Peter Lynch's wife), Jim Mahaffey, Rose Meltzer, Nick Nickell, Lou Ann O'Rourke, George Rosenkranz, Richie Schwartz, Rita Shugart, Roy Welland and others.

Some of these sponsors have relieved themselves of the nitty-gritty work by hiring managers or agents to tend to laborious details (like contract negotiations with pros), lineups, matchups, paperwork and other cumbersome arrangements. Professionalism in bridge has become Big Business! Some agents or managers require the professionals to sign a restrictive covenant or non-compete agreement, as is common in normal business practices. This precludes the pros from approaching the sponsors directly for a predetermined designated number of years. I don't think the legality of these documents has been challenged at this point, but I am sure the time will come. When I came upon the scene over a half century ago, the beauty of the game and the thrill of winning were the sole attractions, but now, for some at least, serious money is involved.

A new facet of event organization has recently come into play for the convenience of the sponsors. The sponsor (or someone acting on their behalf) arranges to 'buy' a site where a Team Trials will be held. That means money is offered and accepted, steering the selection committee to gear their efforts to searching out and firming up contracts with a hotel situated conveniently to the sponsor — and 'making the site work'. It matters not that it is inconvenient for the other participants or that additional expenditures and issues are involved (including the need for car rental or an ungodly travel distance from the nearest airport). Those in charge accept the 'offers' with their eyes wide open, as the treasuries of the Trials organizers are not bursting at the seams. It is obvious that this is accepted practice and considered a legal form of bribe as we are so desperate for subsidization. There has to be a better way — but it has yet to be implemented. A tournament site should have three unalterable prerequisites: (1) it should be near to a major airport; (2) the facility should accommodate the players and the playing space at reasonable rates; and (3) there should be decent eateries on the premises or within a very short walk, obviating the need for car rentals.

There are many top-flight bridge professionals who have devoted their lives to improving their own skills (as players and teachers) and learning how to handle their clients to extract the most from them. They not only teach these sponsors conventions and techniques, but instill in them confidence, composure and much more. Being a good player is not enough. There are a number of qualities one must master to become a successful pro. Although many pros are educated and often are college graduates, all of them became addicted to the game at an early age. Many of these talented individuals have no other livelihood to fall back upon. It has become the only means of survival for some and, regrettably, has forced them into a competitive dog-eat-dog existence.

I recall an amusing story about the former Philadelphia basketball player, Wilt Chamberlain, who (unbeknownst to many) played a lot of bridge in his later years. At one point in his career, a couple of weeks prior to the season opener, Wilt was a 'holdout' — refusing to sign a new contract. Dave Zincoff, popular radio announcer for the team, was asked, "Do you think Wilt will sign?" It was a titillating question for Dave. He impishly grinned and replied, "If not, he will become the world's tallest elevator operator."

The analogy to bridge professionals comes to mind, although not to such an extreme. They are good at what they do, but it is a lazy life, and many are not trained to do much else. Playing pro is not always a piece of cake. You must have nerves of steel, be able to restrain yourself and bite your tongue, show no disappointment, anger or disgust when partner commits an egregious error, be on the road a great part of the year, give up a normal home life if you are lucky enough to have one, and live out of the proverbial trunk like the vaudevillians of old. Being a pro is not easy, but if you get lucky, it can be very rewarding. It beats a real job, and besides, very little else is as exhilarating as playing bridge!

Pros who have contracts to play on the top sponsored teams, for a pre-arranged number of tournaments or on a calendar basis, are on easy street compared to the rest. The unlucky ones have to schlep around to Regionals week after week (if they even have dates lined up) to try to drag inexperienced sponsors — some call them 'clients' — into the overalls in Pairs games, Swiss Teams and/or Knockouts. The players who are fortunate enough to sign on with sponsored teams get to play with other pros for the most part in the Trials, the big Team events at NABCs or the top brackets of Knockouts at Regionals. The really fortunate ones are Meckstroth, Rodwell, Bob Hamman and Paul Soloway on the Nickell team. Nick plays with Dick Freeman and, since they are both good players, the other two pairs don't have to cope with unfamiliar partnerships. Contrast that with the case of the late Malcolm Brachman, who always played with one of the pros on his team. It's not as though Brachman and Mike Passell didn't have a partnership, but it is safe to say that Passell would really have preferred playing with one of his regular pro partners as part of the deal. Just imagine, playing with your favorite partner and getting paid to do it. Like dying and going to heaven. It doesn't get much better than that.

It's not all beer and skittles even for these top-level pros, but their lives are much less stressful and more lucrative than those of their counterparts at the lower levels. It should not shock you to learn that many of the top-flight professionals start with healthy six-figure annual earnings which are enhanced by bonuses for winning. Again, this is not to say anyone is doing anything wrong. It's a free market economy, and these top experts have extraordinary skills that are worth paying for in the judgment of a significant number of wealthy people. That's what makes America so wonderful.

There's a major flaw in the system, however, when the players who are making so much money off the game wind up in administrative decision-making positions influencing significant bridge issues (especially where their personal interests are involved). In case you're wondering, I'm not singling out Jeff and Eric, my former teammates. In fact, if anything, they are less active politically than most of the pros I'm talking about. However, there are many players (both pros and sponsors) who are in responsible positions despite the fact that they usually have a vested interest in maintaining the status quo.

Here's a case in point. A week after the world championships in Monte Carlo concluded, I went to a meeting of the International Team Trials Committee during the Fall NABC in New Orleans. Mike Becker was chairing the meeting, and I asked to address the group, an assemblage of about forty people. Perhaps the reason for wanting to be heard had to do with the fact I pride myself on being the founder of the International Team Trials Committee, breaking it away from the control of the ACBL and bringing about improvements such as better conditions of contest and site venues as well as player amenities and, most importantly, player input. I had been responsible for the Committee's inception and felt I had the right to the floor.

I had just read in the newspaper about the bombing of a synagogue in Istanbul, Turkey, the spot where the World Bridge Federation planned to hold the 2004 World Championships, including the Open and Women's Olympiad Teams. This had significance, of course, because the entire world changed after the events of September 11, 2001. There was a hubbub brewing about the safety factor. People had become a lot more apprehensive about visiting countries where the environment is significantly different than the United States. Europe, of course, is okay for the most part, but places where there are large Muslim populations tend to frighten some people because of the obvious connection to terrorism.

In 2001, the Bermuda Bowl and Venice Cup were scheduled for Bali, Indonesia, and after terrorist attacks in New York, Washington and Pennsylvania, significant numbers of players refused to go to Bali. The island of Bali itself is predominantly Hindu, but Indonesia is the world's most populous Muslim-majority country and many Americans simply did not feel safe traveling there. When some other countries began to express concern also, the event was moved to Paris at an extraordinarily high cost to the WBF. As a footnote, our concerns were certainly underlined when a major terrorist attack took place in Bali almost exactly a year later.

Now, as plans were being made to take the 2004 tournament to another Muslim country, Turkey, a terrorist act had taken place there (and there would be some others later). I was thinking ahead that there was sure to be a chain reaction to the events in Istanbul. In fact, early in 2004 our State Department issued an advisory (later rescinded) telling Americans they should defer non-essential travel to Turkey because of the unrest and uncertainty and therefore the danger.

I stood up before the ITT meeting at the Marriott Hotel in New Orleans and told them that while the WBF was determined to have the tournament in Istanbul, there might still be time for the venue to be changed if there was a good reason to do so. If, for example, the ITT took a vote and indicated to Jose Damiani, President of the WBF, that Americans did not want to go to Turkey because of recent developments and the potential danger, he might take notice. If the ITT felt strongly about the venue, positive action had to be taken *at that meeting*. There was no guarantee that Damiani would change his mind, of course, but he is a reasonable man and it was certainly worth the effort. However, time was the enemy of site change and if too much of it elapsed, the WBF would be locked into Istanbul. They would not be able to pull their money out and the chances that the tournament might move to another location would be reduced to zero.

As Chairman of the meeting, Mike Becker was impatient with me, pointing out that there were many other items on the agenda. Although no one said it in so many words, the message I received was, "Why should we listen to you? You no longer have any official present-day status. Let's not waste our time." However, the anti-Istanbul sentiment was very apparent. One of the exceptions was Zia, who passionately and cogently spoke out in favor of going. But it was obvious that the general feeling of a majority of the high-profile experts was that if there was, indeed, a world championship in Istanbul, they were not going to put their lives in jeopardy and therefore (for selfish, personal reasons) felt the USA should not participate.

Now, let me make my views on that position crystal clear. It is perfectly acceptable for you, as an individual, to decline to play in an event, either personally or on behalf of your team (especially if you are a sponsor). Freedom of choice is your cherished privilege as an American. However, you do *not* have the right to decline for anyone else who may be qualified and eager to play on the US team and proudly and fearlessly represent his or her country. Reading between the lines was the ugly part... if they chose not to go, it was perfectly obvious they didn't want anyone else to go in their place.

Interestingly, I was accused later of blindly taking Damiani's side, assuring that the tournament ended up in Istanbul. In fact I was trying to help the ITT propose a viable and practical solution to enable and encourage the WBF to change its venue so that the USA would attend and present its best team.

No vote was actually taken, so no message could be sent to the WBF. It was like a wolf howling at the wind. Six weeks later (early in January) Damiani, in good conscience, returned to Istanbul and designated that city as the WBF's official choice for the world championships. There was a lot of subsequent hand wringing and finger pointing. At first, the USBF decided that the USA would not send any teams to Turkey. It was not until I, and a few other outraged players, vehemently challenged such a dictatorial edict that they reluctantly relented and allowed US participation — with the conciliatory proviso that the Trials winners could defer their world championship appearance for one year if they wished.

In the aftermath of the Trials, the winners of the United States Bridge Championship (the Nickell team) and the winners of the Senior Team Trials (the Meltzer squad) chose to exercise that option and use their qualifications for the 2005 World Championships in Portugal instead of going to Istanbul.

I salute the triumphant Women's team (Carlyn Steiner, Marinesa Letizia, Jill Meyers, Randi Montin, Janice Seamon-Molson and Tobi Sokolow) who entered their Trials determined to go to Istanbul if they won and never flinched in following through. Incidentally, they were in contention in the Olympiad all the way and were nosed out by the Russian women in the final, bringing home the silver medals.

You might be asking yourself, what's wrong with the way things came out? After all, although the safety of the Istanbul venue was the subject of much concern, the USA eventually did send teams and the tournament went off without incident. Well, for starters, the ITT is made up of players, many of whom who are paid by sponsors (or who have familial ties to sponsors) and whose teams take up slots in the trials. It's in the players' interest, since they are usually paid each time they play, to make sure there are plenty of opportunities for them to earn their fees. In essence, the animals are running the zoo, and the zookeepers don't even realize what's happening. At the ITT meeting in New Orleans, I could almost see the wheels spinning in the heads of the players with these inherent conflicts. Instead of thinking about what was best for the game of bridge, many, if not most of them, were considering how any proposed action would affect their own personal situations and pocketbooks.

There's another element to this situation that bothers me. I believe it's wrong for teams to enter the Trials *with no intention of going if they win*. In essence, they have disenfranchised and displaced at least one team for the following year. What happened at the USBC in Memphis was that the Nickell team won, then (as expected) announced they weren't going to Istanbul, leaving the second place team — Roy Welland, Bjorn Fallenius, Zia Mahmood and Michael Rosenberg — with the option to replace them if they were willing to go. All of them were anxious to win a world championship, particularly Zia, and apparently without trepidation they agreed to go. They invited Bobby Levin and Steve Weinstein to join the team, and together with their wives, they eagerly headed for Istanbul. The incongruity was that the Welland team didn't win the Trials, but they got to represent the country anyway. And since they had lost in the final of a knockout event, there was no assurance that they were in fact the second-best team.

The following year, in 2005, Trials were held to select the Bermuda Bowl team. The normal rules would have dictated that the winner would have a berth in the world championship, along with the winner of a playoff between the losing finalist and the winner of a match between the losing semifinalists. However, because Nickell's group was allowed to move their qualification to 2005, only one team emerged from the 2005 Trials. This is a total bastardization of the Trials. By contrast, in the 2005 Women's Trials, two teams earned qualification to the Venice Cup in Portugal. I tried to talk to Chris Compton, then President of the USBF, about this many times, but to no avail. He always seemed to be changing the subject. I've known Chris a long time. He's a good guy and a good player but this administrative gig is not his long suit. He also plays professionally, which undeniably presents a conflict of interest. It is very difficult to detach oneself when personal interests are involved. I know I'm not always right, but I think it's simply evil to make decisions and take actions just for the sake of money, when they may be against the best interests of bridge.

In the Spring of 2004, Compton went to Paris to talk to Damiani about whether relocation of the world championships from Istanbul had a chance. It was *rumored* that Chris was offering money — $300,000 to $400,000 — to defray the costs of moving the venue out of Turkey, possibly to the USA or some other, in his opinion, less tumultuous spot. Some may consider that a bribe, but, in my opinion, it was a rather well-intended effort (though one launched considerably too late) to change the venue to satisfy US concerns and at the same time ante up for some of the enormous loss of deposits and additional expenses that would be incurred if the WBF moved the event out of Istanbul. It was alleged that the money was being coughed up by certain American sources and that the trip to Paris was being made to deliver it to the WBF. In fact, Houston was on a short list of potential sites, as was Seattle, which had hosted the Olympiad Teams in 1984.

Whether or not money was offered is not known, but Chris was told in no uncertain terms by Damiani that the tournament was staying in Istanbul. Furthermore, he was advised that many Europeans were more concerned about traveling to the USA than they were about going to Istanbul. There were also passport and visa problems for visitors to the USA that no one was taking into account. I personally saw many emails backing up that statement.

It is of interest to note that the United States was the only country in the world which did not send their best teams to Istanbul (or at least the teams that had earned the right) — with the exception of the Women's team! One must not deny the hard and cold fact that the world championship is a WBF event, and it is not geared to cater to the safety and euphoria of the Americans. *It is not about the USA alone.* We are not their focal point. Certainly, it would add more integrity and pizzazz to the event if we had representation, although there is some conjecture that no one would have lost any sleep over our absence. Over seventy other nations stood ready and eager to participate and had we not been among them (the original plan of the USBF), we would have been the only country to assume such a cowardly stance.

As it turned out, it was much ado about nothing. Turkey was one of the loveliest tournament sites ever. The safety factor was never an issue once we touched down in Istanbul. Those of us who attended the event lived to tell about it. Throngs of players left the hotel every evening to enjoy the marvelous cuisine and the evening skyline, while those not playing found many fascinating places to visit in the historic city every day. The big attraction for the women was the preponderance of shops nearby. The latter took its toll on my bank account as Judy frequented the Grand Bazaar, a world-famous indoor shopping site. Haggling was the order of the day and the bargains were so irresistible, she could have opened her own jewelry store upon her return to Dallas.

I'm not saying that everyone — or even anyone — on the ITT or USBF is corrupt, but it cannot be a good situation for the players who are making the money to be making the decisions as well. It's just that many of them simply have a vested interest in keeping things the way they are. And as always, a lot of people dislike me because I go all out to be candidly objective and not allow them to pursue personal agendas that are counterproductive to the game and what it stands for.

A classic example of my throwing a monkey wrench into something I found to be reprehensible involves the Canadian national team. The way the WBF Zonal qualifying works, it was (and is) fairly routine for Canada to qualify to send a team to the world championships each year. But it seemed to me that Canada was sending one dreadful team after another to the WBF tournaments. Indeed, in one stretch Canada finished last or next to last in the round-robin phases of various tournaments — six Bermuda Bowls running. Besides these results being disconcerting, surely the powers that be owe it to their nation to field the best teams available. We know Canada can send good teams if no one interferes with a fair selection process. Just look at the silver medal squad the Nickell team beat in the 1995 Bermuda Bowl final, or the team that was robbed in the 1990 Rosenblum incident that I discussed in Chapter 14.

I went to Canada one time to talk to the Canadian Bridge Federation, an organization that seemed to prefer politics to top bridge teams. I wanted to talk about the embarrassment of the parade of bad Canadian teams going to world championships, but they weren't interested in making any changes. The politicians liked the setup — and why not? Some of them had got to play in a world championship on those 'embarrassing' Canadian teams.

Anyway, I got sick of seeing all those terrible Canadian teams in world championships, so in 1994, when I was President of the WBF, I pushed through a change in the rules: *In order for a country to be eligible to send a team to the Bermuda Bowl, that country's entry in the previous Olympiad had to finish in the top one-third of the field.* This was later watered down, not surprisingly, thanks to ACBL Board member and former WBF Treasurer George Retek, who is from Montreal, to lower it from 'top third' to 'top half' of the field, but I had accomplished my goal. George, who I like and respect, probably promised the other Canadians that he could use his influence with the WBF to prevent my restriction going through at all, and he was furious when he wasn't able to do it.

I have no doubt that this Canadian teams issue had a direct bearing on the infamous 'Oh, shit' case, when my team was shamelessly raped by an Appeals Committee of which the president of the CBF, Doug Heron, was Co-chairman. That decision, as you will see in Chapter 22, has clearly won the distinction as the *worst* ruling ever handed down by any Appeals Committee. It incurred the wrath and indignation of the entire worldwide expert community. People still shudder in horror at the travesty of justice. It was an embarrassment to bridge and once again strengthens my position that people with personal agendas or previous involvements should not be in decision-making positions. It *should have been mandatory for Heron to recuse himself from serving on that Committee.* But more on that later.

In the summer of 2004, I was involved in a crucial decision involving professionalism which had a direct bearing on Senior Team representation in the world championship in Istanbul. Earlier in the year, in Las Vegas, the Senior Team Trials produced the winning team of Rose Meltzer and company — who had never planned to go to Istanbul to play in the Seniors Cup. The second-place Senior Team fell heir to the throne: John Onstott, Jim Robison, John Schermer, Neil Chambers, Marshall Miles and Leo Bell.

My team also entered that event but thanks to the randomness of the matchups, we played the Meltzer team in the semifinal round, losing to them. Had we been in the other bracket, we might well have survived to challenge Meltzer in the final — *which would have been like drawing a bye into the world championships.* Of course, at this point, everything is speculation, but it was the compromised Conditions of Contest that allowed such a farce to materialize.

It is the responsibility of the Trials administrators to ensure that 'randomness' is eliminated to make it equitable for all. However, when a team which never intends to play in the upcoming world championship is permitted to compete, randomness is introduced. Anyone unfortunate enough to be in their bracket is disadvantaged — because whoever comes through the other bracket and faces them in the final still gets to represent the country, even if they lose! This was the result of a terribly flawed Condition of Contest approved by the organizers. A forthright way to solve the problem is to require that any team entering the event commit to participating in the world championship should they win. Deferment should not be an option. What evil motivation caused the USBF to consent and approve that Condition? Very simply, the professional lobby — they got themselves another payday by playing in an event with something major at stake for their sponsors.

The point I am making is that the Meltzer team's abstention created an automatic entry into the Senior World Championship for a losing team — in this case Onstott. The decision of the Meltzer group not to play in Istanbul unilaterally transformed a loser into a winner. As it turned out, the story had a happy ending — but a lot transpired before the final composition of the team was determined.

Onstott, a likeable, successful businessman from Louisiana and a frequent sponsor, had thrown his Senior team together at the last minute. In assessing the team after the tournament, it was no secret that Onstott didn't like his chances in the Seniors Cup in Istanbul with Miles and Bell on the team. When Miles and Bell refused to jump ship, Onstott said he was no longer interested in traveling to Istanbul. His wife had already been putting pressure on him not to go, so this was the perfect excuse for him to bow out. The big question was, who would replace Onstott on the team? I became involved as a member of the ITT Credentials Committee, whose charge is to see to it that the USA fields the best teams for world championships — keeping in mind that the right of the winners to go is paramount. The objective is etched in stone: *get the best replacement qualified and available*! I was on the Credentials Committee with several expert players, including Paul Soloway, and ACBL representative Gary Blaiss, a former Chief Tournament Director for the ACBL, who has an administrative position in Memphis.

It seemed that the team wanted to replace Onstott with Gene Freed, a popular, wealthy ear doctor from Los Angeles, who also served as a sponsor. The team was already receiving a subsidy from the ACBL's International Fund to travel to Istanbul, but without a rich sponsor, the pros on the team weren't going to be paid for their services. If Freed was added to the team, they would be 'taken care of'. Simple as that.

I was invited to participate in a conference call in late July to discuss the situation. In the conference call, I didn't need to lobby for 'the best possible replacement' as I was immediately gratified to note that four committee members, Cherie Bjerkan, Marty Fleisher, Mike Kamil and Beth Palmer, all expressed and supported my feelings, although at that time they had no way of knowing what those feelings actually were. Blaiss and Soloway did not. Soloway, as I expected, was sympathetic to the pros having the opportunity for another pay date. In fact, he expressed his views and then bowed off the Committee regarding the Freed issue as he did not want to get involved further. The name of Grant Baze, a top professional, was suggested by the Committee as a possible replacement for Onstott, and I would have rubber-stamped that choice in a New York minute, but that was not to be. Grant would certainly have obliged — he was known to have said something to the effect of, "Just find me five other fellas and I'll be delighted to go!" However, replacing Onstott (or Freed) with Baze would have presented a problem — namely, *the removal of the sponsorship element for the hired guns*.

Paul was not the only one who was in favor of adding Freed to the team: Gary Blaiss spoke up for him as well. I think Gary Blaiss is a great guy, but he and I are not of like mind. He noted that Freed had won a world Senior event previously and that, in any case, who were we (the Credentials Committee) to judge that he wasn't the best replacement? My response — who *better* than we (a panel of experts chosen for this very purpose) to make that judgment? That is precisely what we were charged with doing — not allowing someone to be added simply because he was willing to pay the pros and keep them happy. I think a very hard look should be directed at the purpose of a Credentials Committee. If the members are worthy of appointment, then their opinion and final decision should be respected and honored — not challenged. Perhaps the composition of the Credentials Committee should be better defined with regard to qualifications, responsibilities and the finality of such decisions, but that is a different discussion.

Just for the record, Gary and Charlotte Blaiss were good friends with Gene Freed and his late wife, Louise. Louise Childs Freed was a beautiful, wonderful, popular lady loved by all who was taken from us in the prime of life. Perhaps this is a touchy subject, but should not have Gary recused himself from any involvement whatsoever in the Freed case, assigning someone impartial from the League office to fill in for him on this issue? Similarly, Bob Hamman, whose wife, Petra, was another close friend of Louise Freed, sent a letter of indignation when Gene Freed was not welcomed by the Credentials Committee with open arms. People with personal ties (either prejudice or bias) should detach themselves from the situation as it is impossible to be impartial... one way or the other.

There was no formal vote on the issue. It wasn't necessary and it never came down to a show of hands. It was clear that if there had been a vote, it would have been against allowing Freed to join the team as a substitute. When plans were finalized, Freed was not approved to join the team as a player, but came along as the non-playing captain. Onstott reconsidered, decided to remain on the team and actually played and helped bring home the gold medal. The results at the table are a moot point. However, the issue of augmentation and the need for better and more specific parameters has been brought to the attention of the USBF, along with recommendations to delineate their guidelines better!

It may be shocking for some readers to learn that the persons in charge recently reorganized the USBF Credentials Committee and I was the *only* current member not to be reappointed. I have chaired the WBF Credentials Committee for twenty plus years and have been a major, respected force in US involvement as well. Since my own qualifications and experience could not have been challenged, it must be difficult for some of these power wielders to look themselves squarely in the mirror and see what they have become. It is disgusting to recognize the depths to which these individuals have sunk and yet they show no shame or remorse for their actions. Personal egos and the craving for self-importance have, in many instances, supplanted what should be the Committee's primary focus — what is best for the game.

In reflecting upon the present state of the union, I can't help thinking back to the bridge teams I knew as recently as fifteen years ago. I can recall the old days when Chip Martel and Lew Stansby, one of the world's top partnerships (who recently played professionally on the Meltzer team until their release in 2005), declined offers to play for money, preferring to line up with their friends, internationally celebrated players like themselves. The winning Bermuda Bowl team in 1985 in Sao Paulo was Martel/Stansby, Pender/Ross and Hamman/Wolff, with Freddy Sheinwold as captain. In 1987 in Jamaica, the winning team was Hamman/Wolff, Stansby/Martel and Ross/Lawrence, captained by Dan Morse — and not one of us was paid. The first time Stansby and Martel played for pay was with us on a Jimmy Cayne squad in 1990.

For a long time one of the top sponsorless teams was Kit Woolsey, Eddie Manfield (replaced by Fred Stewart after Eddie's untimely death), Steve Robinson and Peter Boyd, but change is in the wind. In the bridge world of today, groups like these are an anomaly, just as our 2003 Bermuda Bowl team was. It was similar to the impressive all-expert teams of the sixties and seventies with Kaplan/Kay, Murray/Kehela and Root/Roth (and later Pavlicek replacing Roth). Few sponsored teams were on the horizon at that time — unlike the glut of them today.

It's a valid argument that without sponsors many of the best players would not have the chance to play in world championships. So perhaps we should consider doing it the way it's done in other countries. As mentioned previously, the current great Italian team is sponsored by Lavazza, the Italian coffee company. The owner, Maria Teresa Lavazza, provides the funds for the team but does not play. She simply enjoys the honor and sits in the stands cheering for the team bearing her name. It's true that finding such corporate sponsors and signing them up is easier said than done, but if we never look for alternatives, we will be stuck with the system now in place. That is unacceptable as I see it!

CHAPTER 19

EVEN IDOLS HAVE CLAY FEET

ALL SPORTS HAVE THEIR HEROES. My home state of Texas proudly claimed Oswald Jacoby and Johnny Gerber in bridge. However, when I broke in, the real hotbed of the game could be found on the East Coast, with the likes of B. J. Becker, Johnny Crawford, George Rapee, Alvin Roth, Howard Schenken, Sidney Silodor and Tobias Stone. These men were the true gods of the fifties and sixties, but there were many new stars on the horizon. One of those was Edgar Kaplan, whose contributions to the world of bridge proved to be unparalleled. Undisputedly, he was our Man for All Seasons!

I first met Edgar Kaplan in the sixties. We were acquaintances rather than good friends. It was not until he took over as Editor and Publisher of *The Bridge World* magazine around the middle sixties that we became close. I had been recruited to the magazine's Master Solvers Panel by former Editor/Owner Sonny Moyse in about 1964, and I became the Master Solvers Director with the longest tenure. I held that position from the late seventies until 1993 and still serve on their staff and as a panelist.

I didn't know much about Edgar at the time except that he and Norman Kay were a formidable pair. I probably lost more to them than to any other twosome in my early years before the Aces. They employed the bidding system that Edgar had created with Alfred Sheinwold, appropriately named Kaplan-Sheinwold. Though it did not suit my particular style of play, it sure worked for them. (I am constantly reminded of its advantages by one of Edgar's present-day disciples, namely, one Judy Kay-Wolff. In fact, she even has me playing weak notrumps non-vulnerable with her — quite a concession for me.)

I remember playing with Dan Morse against Edgar and Norman in the 1967 Spingold. Together with Al Roth and Bill Root, they slaughtered us in the final. We also played against them in the Pairs Trials to select the international team at the time when the ACBL used that format. Kaplan and Kay were among the leading pairs in North America, and their teams were usually in contention for the major events — until the Aces came along. In 1971, when the Aces won their second world championship, Kaplan's team (Kaplan, Kay, Lew Mathe, Don Krauss, John Swanson and Dick Walsh) also played in the Bermuda Bowl in Taipei but, out of the six teams competing, they trailed the pack when the final standings were posted.

In a way, that was the story of Edgar's bridge life. Many people in the bridge world consider Kaplan/Kay and Kehela/Murray the best two pairs never to have won a world championship — and the shame of it is that they almost certainly would have if the famous Italian Blue Team had not been around. Yes, I use the word *shame* advisedly. In the 1967 Bermuda Bowl, Kaplan-Kay (playing with Sami Kehela/Eric Murray and Bill Root/Alvin Roth) lost to Italy in the final. The next year, Edgar and Norman, playing with Arthur Robinson/Robert Jordan and Root/Roth again lost to the Blue Team in the final of the World Bridge Olympiad, but in the opinion of knowledgeable sources, this time it was merely tit-for-tat.

The partnership was forever caught up in the 'always a bridesmaid never a bride' syndrome — *but not necessarily because they were the weaker team*. If what the Burgay Tapes suggested was true, victory against the Blue Team was decidedly out of Edgar's team's control, something that has gnawed at Judy for all these years. If you have never heard of the Burgay Tapes, you may be surprised by what follows here. Even if you have, I doubt whether you know the whole story. This is the tale Jimmy Patino himself related to me.

In 1976, Leandro Burgay taped telephone conversations with Benito Bianchi, who was Pietro Forquet's partner for a long time (including the Bermuda Bowls in 1973 and 1974). The tapes detailed the way many of the combinations of leading Italian partnerships were exchanging illegal signals. Many of their scams involved using cigarette placements. According to Burgay, the crooks included the whole Blue Team, with no exceptions. The exposé was triggered by the refusal of the Blue Team to allow Burgay and his partner to play, in spite of their high finishes in the Italian trials. He was disliked and was not considered to be a top class player by the Italian administration.

The tapes were delivered to the WBF Executive Council in 1976 before the Bermuda Bowl in Monte Carlo. In order to avoid an immediate scandal, the WBF allowed the Italians to play in both the Bermuda Bowl and the World Team Olympiad in Monte Carlo (the one and only time the two major championships were ever held together and consecutively). However, after reading an English transcription of the tapes Jimmy Ortiz-Patino, with the unanimous vote and blessing of the WBF Executive Council after the 1976 championships, barred for life every player implicated. Jimmy later relented, making exceptions for two of their leading stars, allowing them to play as a partnership for Italy in the 1979 Bermuda Bowl in Rio de Janeiro, Brazil and the 1983 Bermuda Bowl in Stockholm, Sweden. It is interesting to note that both times they lost to an American team in the finals (the only two occasions when those players ever lost as a partnership, in contrast to their fourteen World Championship winning performances). In 2005, two of their leading players (also among the same barred group) were allowed to play in the Senior Championships in Estoril, Portugal. They did not finish well, losing before the medal round.

Sadly for Edgar, the revelations of the Burgay Tapes and the ensuing sanctions came far too long after the fact to afford Edgar's teams of the sixties and early seventies a fairer shot at some world championships. Just one of many disappointments that punctuated his life.

Another occurred in 1963, when Albert Morehead was retiring as Bridge Editor of *The New York Times*, considered by the *hoi polloi* as the most prestigious bridge job in the world — and a good-paying position at that. Morehead, another legendary figure on the bridge scene, and Edgar were fast friends and fellow intellectuals. Morehead had arranged for Edgar to take over the *Times* bridge column, but before the appointment was finalized, Edgar made a major mistake. He wrote something in *The Bridge World* that was uncomplimentary to Sam Stayman, another famous bridge personality who was very cunning but not quite as talented as his cohorts. Stayman, credited with the convention bearing his name (which was actually devised by George Rapee), also had a massive ego, and he wasn't going to take the insult lying down.

As it happened, Stayman managed an investment fund that did very well — and one of his best customers just happened to be the President of *The New York Times*. Using his influence, Stayman made sure that Edgar was passed over for the Bridge Editor's position at the newspaper. At the 1963 Spring NABC in St. Louis, Alan Truscott (who had just immigrated to America from England) was announced as the choice to succeed Morehead. Edgar was crushed, although he and Alan became and remained very close personal friends, enjoying much in common, including their annual outings to the tennis matches in Forest Hills right up until the time of Edgar's death in 1997.

He took another devastating blow in 1985 when Betty, his wife of 22 years, died of cancer, the disease that would eventually claim his own life. Edgar, a bachelor, was well into his forties when he and the former Elizabeth Sheinwold took their vows. Their union raised some eyebrows and provided juicy gossip for the bridge world since Betty was wed to Edgar's partner and close associate, Alfred Sheinwold, when she and Edgar first met. Betty was a part-owner in a neighborhood music school and it was Edgar's love of music that drew them together. Betty actually gave Edgar musical instruction and under her tutelage he became an accomplished flutist — adding to his long list of other talents. The Kaplans' marriage was simply perfect for both of them as they absolutely idolized and adored each other. Edgar had found his true soulmate. I remember being at the world championships in Sao Paolo, Brazil, in 1985. It was a pathetic scene; Betty had just died after a lingering illness, and there was Edgar, totally alone and lost.

As I have recounted earlier, another major setback occurred two years later on that fateful day in October 1987 when the stock market suffered one of its biggest one-day percentage losses in history. Before that, Edgar had lived quite comfortably though most of his wealth was inherited. He never made much money from *The Bridge World*; it was his passion and a proverbial labor of love. After the crash he was just about wiped out, but his devoted friend, Jimmy Patino, graciously came to his aid and made Edgar whole again.

After Betty died, Edgar devoted much of his time to *The Bridge World* magazine, and his close association with his business partner, Jeff Rubens, was very satisfying. Edgar enjoyed his solitude — welcoming only a select few to his private portals. He continued to play in the Nationals with Norman even after he was diagnosed with cancer in the mid-nineties. Despite many physical problems and pain, he never lost his unique sense of humor. Everyone recalls his famous retort to Norman when, after a crucial match they won, Norman complimented Edgar on a brilliant defense. Smugly, Edgar replied, "Norman, I have cancer of the liver — not the brain." That was Edgar!

On December 7, 1997, he lost the toughest match of his life. Some months later an incredibly beautiful memorial service and luncheon was held at the Honors club in Manhattan, hosted by Joan Gerard, Gail Greenberg, Sylvia Kaplan (Edgar's sister-in-law) and Judy Kay. Over a hundred and fifty friends and fans gathered from near and far to pay tribute to one of the game's most respected gurus of all time. Jeff Rubens presided as Master of Ceremonies and adoring friends of

Edgar's ascended the podium one after another — each with warm, touching stories. Following the tributes from those present and the reading of messages sent by many world famous dignitaries who could not attend, an elegant buffet was served. Edgar received a sendoff he so richly deserved, having devoted his entire being to the good of the game — locally, nationally and the world over.

Through all his trials and tribulations, Edgar Kaplan remained a proud man with a wry sense of humor. Edgar, often paired with the late Ron Andersen, was absolutely brilliant at the commentators' table when there was a Vugraph show. No one ever sat through a Vugraph show with Edgar on the podium without being impressed by his wit and knowledge of the game. With all he accomplished as a player, writer, teacher and businessman, however, I would wager he was most proud of his status and reputation as *the* authority on the laws of bridge. Such was his power and persuasiveness that he could convince anyone of anything when it came to the laws. His admirers boasted that if you gave Edgar all the details of an appeal, he could win it for either side. Such confidence underlined the respect Edgar commanded in that realm of the game. Edgar was the absolute guru of the Appeals process. Everyone relied on him, and he enjoyed wearing the crown!

Edgar also had a sympathetic, poignant human side, as was evidenced in 1993 in the World Championships in Santiago, Chile. We were Co-chairs of the WBF Appeals Committee. One of Edgar's favorite people, Mike Becker, whom Edgar had known since he was a young boy, was playing with Ronnie Rubin. Mike admitted to psyching one of their conventions with intent to steal the hand from unsuspecting opponents. They had been chastised for similar action at the 1992 ACBL Toronto Nationals and mild disciplinary action was taken with a severe admonition not to attempt it again. The Chile incident occurred at the end of a match that Rubin/Becker had lost, knocking them out of the tournament, but nevertheless, in my opinion, they deserved severe censure. I am usually like the proverbial dog with a bone when the rules have been defiantly violated (especially after a warning) but Edgar protectively whisked them out of the room and soft-soaped me into letting the issue go. How he accomplished that, I don't know to this day, but Edgar was a charmer and had his way as I went quietly.

Unfortunately, Edgar and I did have some clashes, owing mostly to my strong convictions and my tendency to defend my point of view with an excess of zeal at times, but it never tarnished our close friendship, our mutual respect or our joint efforts to uphold the honor of the game. I always wanted Edgar on my side. The world of bridge was truly blessed by Edgar's unique brilliance and talent on so many fronts. Despite our differences, or perhaps because of them, I learned much from Edgar. Debby was extremely fascinated by Edgar's eloquence and charm and our frequent contacts caused our friendship to flourish. We would visit Edgar at his West Side brownstone while Edgar and I discussed the laws. Edgar had a delightful charm, and women especially were captivated by him. Over ten years later Judy continues to mourn his death, recalls tender moments they shared, still quotes some of his wonderful 'Edgarisms' and sings his praises to the sky. She still cherishes her 1967 Montreal Mixed Pairs victory with him; she was a near-novice, and bragged that her only responsibility had been to try to count trumps. Debby, too, was one of his biggest fans. Edgar just had that affect on women — especially *my* women!

Edgar had a sweet, tender side rarely exhibited to his adoring public. He was respected by the masses for his countless contributions to the game in many venues, but he was not readily accessible to his fans and intimate with very few. Edgar was a very private person and abhorred engaging in small talk. He did not like his privacy invaded and made no secret of it to outsiders. This soft, sensitive side was rarely visible, but it did surface in 1983 in an incident involving the legendary Oswald Jacoby. Edgar was close with the Jacoby clan and had received a call from Ozzie's son, John (Jim's younger brother). It was no secret that Ozzie was suffering from cancer and his days were numbered. John asked Edgar if there was any possibility that his team for the upcoming Reisinger in Florida (Kaplan/Kay and Root/Pavlicek) could be augmented to include his dad. John discreetly offered to ante up some money to accomplish this, but Edgar (speaking spontaneously and unequivocally on behalf of the entire team) dismissed such a suggestion, professing it would be an honor to add Ozzie. The event was held in Bal Harbour and there was not a dry eye in the room when the Oswald Jacoby team emerged as the victor, coming from miles behind in the last session. It was a miraculous finish, as if ordained from above. Judy claims that Norman equated that resilient Reisinger triumph with Ozzie to the thrill of his 1997 ACBL Hall of Fame induction — every expert's fondest dream!

Edgar was, of course, the Chairman of the Laws Commission, and as stated earlier, was the person credited with increasing the penalties for undertricks after the famous Jeff Meckstroth out-of-the blue 7♠ save during the 1981 World Championships. When Edgar died in 1997, I was one of the logical choices to succeed him, but by that time my enemies had escalated in number and I didn't have a chance. I remained on the Laws Commission until my shocking dismissal, without cause, by Board President Bruce Reeve in 2004.[1]

As I have already noted in Chapter 14, Edgar was involved in the distasteful case in the 1990 World Championships involving Germany and Canada. At the appeals hearing, he was the only one to speak up for the Canadians. As I explained, I was not notified of the meeting and even when my absence was noticed, no great effort was exerted to locate me although I was in a logical place — having breakfast in the coffee shop. Unfortunately, as powerful as Edgar was at the time, his voice by itself was not enough to sway a group which in my opinion had already predetermined the outcome. I think even the great Edgar Kaplan was resigned to the fact that he did not have enough support to buck the European forces on the Committee.

As much as I admired Edgar myself and believed in his wisdom and vision, I didn't agree with everything he did or wanted to do. Perhaps, had I yielded to his wishes on one occasion, the infamous personally humiliating 1992 Toronto Incident could have been prevented. In the story I am about to relate, we will call the suspected culprit 'K' (as he was referenced in a *Bridge World* Editorial reprinted below). As a bridge player, K manifested signs of being a very troubled and troubling person. At the point that he came into my view — in the early 1990s — he was in hot water in several arenas. In bridge, he pretty much ran the gamut of offenses. He was accused of changing scores in at least one club game in New England; of trying to get one of his partners to use illegal signals; of playing cards from his discard pile as declarer; and of being very abusive to his partners and rude to the opponents.

All this resulted in charges being laid against him and a hearing being scheduled before a Disciplinary Committee at the 1991 Spring Nationals in Atlantic City. K was notified by registered letter of the hearing, and the receipt bore his signature. Later he said he had never received it — that a girlfriend had signed for it in his absence. A tournament director who knew something about the case told me that several people were fearful of K because of his erratic behavior. (Someone once joked, 'If you cross this guy, watch out for a falling safe as you walk along the sidewalk'.)

---

1. People such as myself, with experience, knowledge, confidence and a track record for doing the right thing for bridge, pose a threat to those in power — enabling them to infiltrate the Commission with members more beholden to them and less vocal. My dismissal (without any advance notice to me) was defiantly outrageous. I attribute it to the fact that in many nooks and crannies of ACBL-land, personal revenge has replaced equity and reason.

Whatever the reason, K did not appear to answer the charges in front of the Committee. Edgar didn't believe we should hold the hearing in the defendant's absence and argued that it was not due process. However, two witnesses had been called to the hearing at the ACBL's expense and had gone to considerable trouble to be there, traveling by train from New York to Atlantic City. At my urging, we went ahead without K and ended up suspending him for six months. That led, I believe, to the much-publicized letter that appeared out of nowhere during the 1992 Summer NABC in Toronto.

Before we get to the letter, I would like to address the editorial written by Edgar in *The Bridge World* in response to the defendant's appeal to have his story told in an upcoming issue — and my response to it as Chairman of the Appeals and Charges Committee. The two documents read as follows:

EDITORIAL (The Trial)

Last year, a young graduate student, whom we shall call "K"[2], made the mistake of going to Europe to work on a research paper. He returned several days before he was scheduled to play for his school in the last stage of the ACBL'S Intercollegiate Championship, to be contested towards the end of the Atlantic City Nationals. K was greeted by a registered letter from the League (someone at the school had signed for it). It was both mysterious and alarming: the case against K would be heard by the ACBL's Appeals and Charges Committee in Atlantic City on a specified date; K could appear and be heard, along with any witnesses he wished to call.

Now, it can be useful, in presenting a defense and assembling witnesses, to know the crime of which one has been accused. Still, if K were guilty he would presumably know what he had done, so you may feel that the ACBL's notification was not greatly flawed. More serious was the timing: the date set for the Trial had already passed, which made it yet more difficult for K to demonstrate his innocence of the nameless crime. Still, if K were guilty, how could he demonstrate innocence, even if allowed to attend his Trial?

In a panic, K started making phone calls. Eventually he reached the Chairman of Appeals and Charges. Yes, the Trial had taken place on the appointed day: K had been found guilty of whatever

---

2. Edgar, always the man of letters, chose the name 'K' for the protagonist here in homage to Franz Kafka, whose classic novel 'The Trial' was being alluded to in the Editorial.

it was, and had been sentenced to a short suspension (short, despite the heinousness of the crime, because it had been committed so many years ago — K should consider himself lucky!). K, now under suspension, would not be permitted to play on his Intercollegiate team. Could he not, K asked, come to Atlantic City for a new hearing, so that he could take his place on his team if cleared? No, to reassemble the committee members and complainants would be far too much trouble (anyway, how could K be cleared if he were guilty?). If K wanted to, he could apply for a hearing at some future Nationals.

So, K's team competed without him. K wrote a long letter to the ACBL, presenting what he considered evidence of malice on the part of his accusers, and asking for a rehearing. In reply, the League asked K whether he wished to file a formal appeal against the discipline that had been imposed, the appeal to be heard at the Indianapolis Nationals. If found not guilty, K would have the whole matter expunged from his file, but if the Atlantic City discipline were reaffirmed then K would be liable to additional penalty, "the maximum being permanent expulsion from the ACBL."

K answered that he was asking for an entirely new process, not an appeal of the old one. "In an appeal, the burden of proof would be on me... When it comes to decade-old accusations unsupported by specifics or even a shred of evidence. What evidence, short of a videotape of my entire life would exonerate me? ... although my letter has not proved my innocence, it has cast substantial doubt on my accusers and their accusation... A new hearing would imply that the evidence will be considered afresh, without prejudice. And how could anyone object to that? I am aware that a new hearing may result in a more serious punishment, but I am more than willing to take that risk in order to clear my name." At a new hearing, though, it would be unavoidable to listen to both sides — everyone knows that this makes decision-making much more difficult.

The Appeals and Charges Committee of the ACBL Board meeting in Indianapolis took action: "The request... for a hearing is denied."

(NOTE: Perceptive readers may have detected in our presentation a note of disapproval of ACBL PROCEDURES. Mind you, we have no opinion as to K's guilt or innocence — how could we? (How could anyone have?) If K happens to be guilty of some dire deed, he has not been harshly treated. However, we find it difficult to disagree with K when he writes, of the ACBL, "They did not inform me of the accusations until after my conviction; they have never told me exactly what I was convicted of; they give no reason for not granting me a new hearing. Is this how a supposedly democratic organization is supposed to treat its dues-paying members?")

In response to the Editorial:

We showed this Editorial to the Chairman of the ACBL Appeals and Charges Committee. This was his reply:

TO THE EDITOR:

I am not surprised to see criticism of the procedures in the case of "K". ACBL procedures are often barely adequate, and so they were here. What is the trouble? In the Memphis office, there is no investigation division. No one is charged with the responsibility for disciplinary procedures; no one has incentive to improve them. So, everything has to be done by volunteers. And very, very few of those with the expertise and experience to judge a bridge case do choose to volunteer. The top players have proven unwilling to patrol our game.

It is important to keep in mind the differences between the disciplinary hearings in our own little world and criminal trials in the world at large. Juries in normal criminal cases typically have to judge who is being truthful, a task for which their ordinary life experience has schooled them. In bridge cases, though, "jurors" need specific, technical bridge knowledge and experience, understanding of the workings of the criminal bridge mind, as well as of the possible evil motivation and competitiveness of the accusers.

In normal criminal cases, the penalties following conviction are severe enough to have a major impact on all aspects of a defendant's future life. In contrast, the penalty in bridge cases, suspension, merely affects the bridge reputation and participation. Most likely, suspension keeps a guilty defendant from playing a game he hates, anyway.

For more than 30 years I have been observing disciplinary bridge cases. Perhaps, over that time, there may have been an instance of an innocent player wrongfully convicted of something serious — but I have never heard of one. Rather, many of those convicted of something serious have since confessed, relieved that it is all over, happy to have their rehabilitation begin.

Sadly, there are probably some out there still practicing their evil art. Perhaps they are relying, if caught, on the ACBL's poor procedures.

BOBBY WOLFF

And now, back to the infamous letter referred to earlier: The host hotel for the Toronto tournament was the Royal York, where the major championships were being played. On the first Friday of the tournament, I was playing in the Open Pairs with my old friend, Morris Chang. We finished our game and went back to our hotel rooms. Later that day, before the evening session, I returned to my room where my wife Debby accosted me with these unexpected words: "Bobby, I've got news for you. Sit down." It sounded ominous!

The word was that between sessions someone (and it might have been more than one person) had distributed several thousand copies of a photocopied anonymous letter outside the playing area near where the hand records were placed for players to retrieve after the session. This is what the letter said:

To: All A.C.B.L. Members
From: A Concerned and Disgusted Parent

Last fall my teenage son went to his first national tournament. He was very excited to meet all of the famous players he had read about and maybe even to play against them. At a gathering for young players, my son met a man named Bobby Wolff, who claimed to be responsible for selecting and coaching the US Junior Team. Mr. Wolff seemed to take a strong liking to my son, promising him that if he really worked hard, he could someday play on this team. Of course, that's just what my son wanted to hear. He said "Hi" to Mr. Wolff at every opportunity for the next few days and swapped bridge stories with him.

One evening, Mr. Wolff invited my son to his suite for a "Junior Team practice session". When my son arrived nobody else was present. Mr. Wolff told him that others would arrive soon, and sat down next to my son on the sofa. The next thing my son knew, Mr. Wolff was groping his private parts and propositioning him with foul language. Thank God my son was alert and strong enough to break Mr. Wolff's grip and run out of the room.

My son told me about these events when he returned from the tournament. I was shocked, and I wrote to the A.C.B.L. I got a letter

after a few weeks, telling me that my complaint had been forward-
ed to the Chairman of the Appeals and Charges Committee. I
didn't hear anything more for several months, so I called the
A.C.B.L. Imagine my shock when I asked to speak to the head of
the Appeals and Charges Committee and I was told to call a certain Robert Wolff!

I have nothing against gay people, but this particular one seems
to have lost control of himself. I hope that the A.C.B.L. does something about this problem soon and that parents of other young
bridge players take warning.

Obviously, no one owned up to authorship and little credence is ever
given to unsigned accusations, but it was embarrassing nevertheless!
Over fifteen years have elapsed since that time and the ridiculous
aspects of the preposterous accusation seem to overshadow the humiliation of the incident. I can now laugh as I recount the horror of the
moment, but there was nothing funny about it at the time.

No one who really knows me took it seriously, but most of my
friends were furious. When Bob Hamman found out about it, he directed, "You've got to do something." Under different circumstances, I
would have considered the pathetic attempt to smear me laughable, but
the charges were serious, and I did notice some people at the tournament — all of them strangers — giving me awfully funny looks.

Zia Mahmood, a good friend, joked about it. Peter Weichsel, more
serious in nature, whom I respected but was not one of my closest
friends at that time, was very upset that someone would make such
ridiculous charges. Not one person who knew me believed it, of
course, but it was depressing to have to deal with something like
that. Brad Moss, at that time a Junior player, wrote a note in my
defense, dismissing the charges in the letter as 'ridiculous'. I will never
forget Brad's loyalty and his initiative in protecting my image. It was
a very responsible and touching gesture, particularly for one so young
at the time. The late Christy Jones, at that time the liaison between
ACBL Headquarters and the ACBL Board, contacted the office in
Memphis and verified that there had not been one single call accusing
me of such conduct.

All the copies of the letter were scooped up and trashed, but another wave of them appeared the next morning in different places around
the hotel and playing area. The cowardly perpetrators of this con-
torted attempt to smear the allegedly Big, Bad Bobby Wolff were per-
sistent. Naturally, there was a flurry of activity and meetings to decide
what to do about it, if anything. Joan Gerard, ACBL President and a

longtime member of the Board of Directors, argued quite persuasively that the letter should not be ignored, although there was some sentiment that a response would only call more attention to the shameful personal attack.

It was decided that the indignity I had suffered should not be ignored in the hope it would die a slow death and eventually go away. On the contrary, the NABC *Daily Bulletin* prominently displayed the following communication from the Board the next day.

> An Open Letter
> To ACBL members
>
> Some of you at this tournament may have seen a despicable, anonymous letter accusing Bobby Wolff, one of our most respected members, of disgusting conduct. In the same letter, the ACBL was accused of a cover-up.
>
> On behalf of the ACBL, we would like everyone to know that all of the accusations are totally false, and that no complaints were ever received by the ACBL. The letter is a pack of lies — the product of a sick mind.
>
> It is sad that any of us has to be subjected to such conduct. If anyone having any knowledge of the perpetrator of this vicious hoax can provide information leading to the identification of the coward involved, a privately funded reward is being offered.
>
> Please contact the ACBL's Executive Office (Royal York Hotel — Algonquin Room) if you can be of help.
>
> Joan Gerard
> ACBL President
>
> Denis Howard
> ACBL CEO
>
> Debbie Zuckerberg
> World Junior Champion

Was this hoax perpetrated by K? I can't prove it, but he was in Toronto, and his hatred for me is well known.

Another indication of his resentment of me pertained to the release of a publication by K. He had authored a book, a humorous work with a collection of bridge deals. It was reviewed in *The Bridge Bulletin* in a not-very-complimentary fashion (the reviewer, who was not me, said the bridge deals were good but the rest of the book was just silly). When the review was published, an angry K telephoned Henry Francis, *Bridge Bulletin* Editor at the time, to demand that another review be published — "By anyone," K said, "except Bobby Wolff." One more finger pointed at me by him!

We will never know for sure who distributed that assault on my character — more copies were found lying around later in the tournament but quickly picked up — but the coincidence of K's being in Toronto makes me and everyone else wonder.

I had other differences with Edgar, including the handling of what turned out to be one of the least known, but most spectacular, failures in the history of our sport. It involved the introduction of formal bridge education in the schools of China, something that could affect the whole future of the game. In 1993, there was a historic meeting at the People's Hall of the Republic on Tiananmen Square, where visiting foreign dignitaries were hosted. I, as President of the WBF, was accompanied by Jeff Polisner, who was doubling as Attorney for both ACBL and WBF, and Patrick Choy, the Zone 6 (Asian) representative to the WBF. Representing China were all of their important decision-making VIPs. We were treated like very special people, indeed.

We presented a commemorative medal to Chinese Premier Deng Xiaoping, and during later discussions with other Chinese officials, I talked about the wonders of bridge. Deng himself was a keen player, and had certain high standards involving the game. Apparently, he forced his military people to learn bridge, without which skill they could never attain the rank of general. The Deng influence was a very cogent argument for our cause. As a token of goodwill and to exhibit our great appreciation for the royal welcome we had been accorded, Jeff and I played several exhibition matches with many higher-up Chinese politicians, including the Foreign Minister. One evening we were taken to the Great Hall where a local section of the Epson Worldwide Pairs was being played. We were staggered to see hundreds of tables taking part under one roof!

At one point the Chinese ministry asked what they could do to assure that bridge would provide a greater influence on their cultural environment. My direct answer was easy. "Teach bridge in your primary and secondary schools as an accredited course!" Their spokesman asked that they be excused for a brief caucus and, within a few moments, returned and advised it had been overwhelmingly approved. I was asked to make the appropriate arrangements. I was delirious with joy that such a momentous decision had just been made!

Deep in my heart, I knew that what we accomplished that day could affect the perpetuation of bridge around the world. A suggestion was made that we should send our most qualified American teachers to familiarize the Chinese players with the best methods of instruction. We would provide all the textbooks needed and would translate them into Chinese. They accepted our offer for teaching assistance but felt they could handle the translation themselves. A lot of handshaking ensued and the atmosphere was one of accomplishment and determination. However, our celebration turned out to be a bit premature.

That evening I discussed with Patrick and Jeff at our hotel what I thought our best *modus operandi* would be to accomplish the endeavor with a minimum of cost and a maximum of efficiency. Audrey Grant was the author of the ACBL's official series of textbooks, used by bridge teachers throughout North America. My idea was to contact Audrey and ask her (along with her husband, David Lindop, and Julie Greenberg, the capable head of the ACBL Educational Department) to travel to China that fall (possibly November) to start the ball rolling.

I returned to the United States with great pride in our accomplishment. Can you imagine the magnitude of that Chinese decision? Overnight, there would be millions of new and upcoming bridge players, *just because the Premier said so*. A short time following my return, the WBF had its Management Meeting in Aspen, Colorado. My goal, besides keeping costs way down, was to arrange for the royalties from books and teaching (profits) to be earmarked for the WBF to promote bridge. What could be more appropriate? I was on a roll, bursting with pride, when I arrived in Aspen and was looking forward to discussing it with Edgar, whom I had invited to attend the meetings as my guest.

I was in for the letdown of my life! While the consensus of the participants was very positive, everyone seemed to have their own dance card in mind. Edgar, whom I thought would be my greatest ally, felt strongly that the USA (with all the experience and sophistication of the New York bridge teaching scene) should take over and offered to organize the enterprise. Jose Damiani, on the other hand, felt that France with their French Standard sound 5-card major system should have a strong positive influence on the teaching and, of course, be chosen.

The truth be told, it turned into an ugly competition of self-interest and sheer greed. During the course of the discussion, which lasted all day, it became evident that I had become only a messenger. Everyone had their own agenda and the introduction of bridge into the primary and secondary schools of China was destined, because of the overwhelming disagreements, to plunge into oblivion! Bridge missed the opportunity of a lifetime. The Chinese program could have skyrocketed bridge to being one of the most popular sports around the world, beginning with 200 million children in the primary and secondary schools of China. That's a lot of players in any language.

It is disheartening experiences like this one that have caused me to travel the road of the Lone Wolff. I will go to my grave with the knowledge that in my anxiety to handle the project in a sensible, non-greedy, democratic fashion, by not resorting to unilateral decisions, I missed the opportunity to have bridge permanently showcased all over the world, enabling future generations everywhere to enjoy the beauty of the game. I will always consider this as one of my greatest failures in life — allowing this unprecedented boon to the world of bridge to slip through my fingers. I can blame no one but myself for not circumventing the WBF and just making an executive decision, along with the accompanying private arrangements. Some may think that such a course would have bordered on dictatorship. So be it — dictatorships have redeeming features as long as the so-called dictator is a benevolent one.

One of Edgar's greatest senses of accomplishment was the role he played as Editor of *The Bridge World*, the oldest continuously published magazine dealing with contract bridge. This bridge monthly was founded by Culbertson back in 1929, run by Morehead from 1943 and taken over by Sonny Moyse in 1956 as sole owner and editor. McCall Corporation assumed the reins in 1963 with Moyse retaining the Editorship. In 1966 when Moyse retired and McCall divested itself of its interest, it became a welcome joint challenge to Edgar as Editor and Jeff Rubens as Co-editor. After Edgar's death, Jeff assumed sole ownership of *The Bridge World*. It had always been a sounding board for new and improved theories with a variety of fascinating columns and challenges. Today *The Bridge World* is one of the most highly acclaimed monthly bridge journals in the world. Jeff's innovations, ingenuity and diligent work habits have propelled it to the number one choice of bridge aficionados — catering to the above-average and superstar subscribers. Edgar would be delighted with both the strides it has made since his death in '97 and Jeff's total dedication to Edgar's pride and joy, which they began working on as a twosome some forty-one years ago.

I do regret one confrontation I had with Edgar. I have often had misgivings that I spoke before I thought in this particular case. Most people who were there were nonplussed by the course of events, as there were few who dared to challenge Edgar. Here's what happened. Edgar and Brian Glubok were playing in the World Open Pairs at the World Championships in Geneva in 1990. The play was behind screens and, at one point, Brian opened 1♠. Brian's screenmate passed, and Edgar, holding three spades to the jack, another jack and a king, also passed.

Edgar's screenmate, Michel Perron, had pulled his 'Pass' card out of the bid box, when Edgar said, "Wait a minute, I didn't see the one spade bid. I want to change my call."

A tournament director was called, but the TD would not let Edgar change his bid. It turned out that Glubok did indeed have a big hand, something that was indicated by the fact that both opponents probably were short in spades but took no action, neither of them bidding or making a takeout double. There was a clear inference for Edgar that his partner had the goods. Under the circumstances, Edgar's knowing about Perron's pass gave him an unfair advantage, and it wasn't right to let him re-enter the auction, which is what he had tried to engineer. Well, Edgar appealed, and I was on the Committee with about twenty other people. Patino showed up to speak on Edgar's behalf and was making some points when I interrupted.

Of course, a legal situation such as this involving Edgar was very sticky. Who would dare to challenge the uncontested master, Edgar Kaplan, on a matter of bridge law? Probably no one — and perhaps I shouldn't have either. It was embarrassing to Edgar when the Committee ruled against him. It wasn't at all complicated to me and, in fact, the matter probably would not even have made it to committee if Edgar hadn't been the one appealing the director's ruling. I personally have no doubt how Edgar would have viewed the position of the player in his seat had he been on the outside looking in, but that will never be proven. I suppose I was a fool to speak up because if the Appeals Committee wanted to give Edgar something, perhaps I should have let them... but I couldn't make an exception, not even for Edgar. And when all is said and done, I would like to think that Edgar respected me for it.

CHAPTER 20

AN APPEAL TO REMEMBER

WHENEVER I AM ASKED which phase of bridge administration I enjoy the most, I invariably respond, "Appeals". In this area not only am I the Lone Wolff, but the Black Sheep as well — because three generations of attorneys enhance my family tree (my father, brother, niece and late nephew).

Bridge appeals have always piqued my interest, causing me to do my damnedest to get it right for all parties involved. Mediating an appeal requires bridge logic, absence of bias or prejudice, knowledge of the laws governing the game, and most important of all, understanding the human element. I am proud of my track record, which has been built through decades of experience by having the courage of my convictions and an open mind to listen to both sides. This combination fortifies one's judgment and has enabled me, without fear of criticism, to go the whole nine yards to see that justice prevails. In bridge, there is no greater cause. *Equity* is the bottom line and should not take a back seat to anything!

With this in mind, allow me to recount an infuriating episode which struck home (actually *my* home) since it involved my wife, Judy. Though the case took a decided toll on her long-range health, there was a happy ending for Judy, her partner and all fair-minded bridge players, and the affair proved to be an embarrassing 'first' for the ACBL and its appeals process. Unfortunately, the joy of the girls' victory was immediately dampened by a retaliatory action by the Board of Directors, sadly relegating the success to the proverbial good-news, bad-news category.

Admirably, Judy is an activist about many things, bridge justice merely being one of her passions. Over the years, she has witnessed countless shenanigans at the table, mostly at the club level where many proprietors (or the directors in their employ) do not want to reprimand their regular customers for wrongdoing. They look the other way and, by allowing bridge unorthodoxies to go unpunished, actually foster unethical behavior. The tendency to give 'club rulings' arises out of fear of losing customers and, more specifically, their precious card fees. This kind of policy, which reigns in many clubs across North America, has caused us to boycott a local club because of their indifference to handling table indiscretions.

The same concept (sometimes with different motivations) sadly trickles down (or should I say trickles *up*?) to the tournament level as well and Judy's personality precludes her from sitting idly by and observing from the grandstand. I respect her all-out way of attacking a problem, never compromising her personal ethics (either at the table or in real life) — but more impressive still is her unyielding, undaunted determination to right a ship if she sees it listing.

The scene of this particular crime was March 11, 2005 at the Pittsburgh NABC, during the Silodor Pairs — coincidentally named for her late husband's first celebrated partner, Sidney Silodor. She was playing with her own favorite longtime partner, Jane Segal of Philadelphia. Here is the deal that caused the ruckus:

```
Dealer: North          ♠ 9 6
Vul: Neither           ♡ Q 7 5 3
                       ◇ Q 8 2
                       ♣ J 7 5 4
        ♠ K 10 8 7           N          ♠ Q 4
        ♡ A 8 6         W         E      ♡ J 10 4
        ◇ K 9 7 5            S          ◇ J 4 3
        ♣ K 9                           ♣ Q 10 6 3 2
                       ♠ A J 5 3 2
                       ♡ K 9 2
                       ◇ A 10 6
                       ♣ A 8
```

West	North	East	South
	pass	pass	1♠
pass	pass	2♣	all pass

According to Judy, after she opened 1♠ in third seat, the person on her left (LHO) looked perplexed, squirmed, made a hand gesture, labored a bit as he contemplated action and finally decided to pass, the break in tempo (BIT) being quite noticeable. Jane (who was looking down and preparing the pickup slips) passed and it rode around to Judy's right-hand opponent (RHO), a good-looking, well-dressed man who held the not-so-robust East hand. RHO studied long and hard (forty-five seconds or more), perhaps wrestling with his conscience and losing the battle as he slithered back into the auction with 2♣.

Judy tactfully advised her opponents that to 'protect the table' against a possible irregularity, she was going to summon the director. When he arrived, she related the facts. However, while everyone agreed RHO had paused, the opponents didn't agree that West had broken tempo. Jane, unfortunately, had been preparing the score slips for the round and had not paid any attention to what was going on. The director did not look at the hands, but simply instructed Judy to call him back at the end of the hand if there was a problem.

After this, the auction concluded with three passes and declarer eventually scored up +110 in 2♣. It was no surprise to Judy that when the dummy was spread, it revealed a full opening bid (with good spot cards to boot). To any objective, experienced individual, the West hand proved conclusively: (1) the huddle, gesture and eventual pass influenced his partner to balance; and (2) it was now unnecessary for West to take further action as he had 'shown' his values earlier.

At the conclusion of play, Judy called the director back. The opponents denied that any hesitation had taken place by LHO and only corroborated that Judy's RHO *did* hesitate before balancing with 2♣. Since the director felt that the vote was 2 to 1 against Judy's claims of a delayed pass, hand gesture and squirm by Lefty, he ruled there was no 'unmistakable hesitation' and that the result should stand. He still did not look at the hands in order to ascertain whether Judy's LHO had a problem or see that RHO had a hand with which most, if not all, players would not consider bidding.

Judy immediately requested an Appeals Committee. To her way of thinking, regardless of Jane's inability to corroborate her account, it was an open-and-shut case before a fair, knowledgeable, experienced committee. The hands would speak for themselves and act (in a documentary fashion) as her irrefutable, silent witnesses!

The Appeals Committee that met that evening was composed of a non-voting Chairman, Ron Gerard, along with Dick Budd, Doug Doub, Mike Kovachic, Bill Passell and Eddie Wold. Curiously, West did not show up for the hearing. Judy was given the floor. She described what she witnessed at the table: (1) LHO, by his break in tempo and body (actually hand) movement made it blatantly obvious he wanted to take action, but did not; (2) balancing by RHO was an action almost no player, good, bad or average, would take, unless influenced by other forces. (If the committee agreed with the second point, it would immediately result in a directed verdict for the plaintiffs.) Jane repeated her own statement — that she was North, making out the pickup slips and wasn't paying much attention to anything else, so in good conscience she could neither confirm nor refute Judy's claim. She was simply guilty of not watching.

The committee spent its time worrying about whether or not West had or had not created a BIT, and paid little or no attention to other issues. But even in this discussion, Ron Gerard told me when I approached him the next day, no consideration was given to the important concept of 'precedent': the idea that when a reputable person (or at least one who is not known to be disreputable) calls the director during play, *it is reasonable to conclude that something untoward must have happened.* Reflect on your own experiences at the table. How often is a director called because of a break in tempo or some other irregularity when absolutely nothing actually happened? You might find an isolated case, but it doesn't ordinarily occur that way. A contestant does not summon a director to the table to adjudicate a figment of his or her imagination. That is the justification for the concept of 'precedent'. Unfortunately for Judy, it was a concept with which her Appeals Committee was apparently not familiar.

Eventually the committee upheld the director's decision, deeming that Judy could not prove that an unmistakable hesitation had occurred. Surprisingly, there was no discussion of the possible unauthorized information (UI) from East's own admitted BIT. Even more astoundingly, the Committee also censured Judy and Jane by awarding them an Appeal Without Merit Warning (AWMW) for a 'frivolous' appeal. An AWMW flatly states that the offenders will be subject to discipline if this happens twice more.

Now, you may ask, censured for *what*? For following the correct ACBL appeals procedures? Their appeal had been scrutinized in the usual way before going to committee, and never had it been suggested that it might be 'without merit' or 'frivolous'. It appeared the AWMW was designed to discourage and ward off potential appellants with similar complaints — trying to dissuade them from challenging a director's ruling and wasting the time of a busy Appeals Committee with such trivia! Jane certainly felt that way, and immediately after the decision was rendered, she wrote and delivered a compelling letter to the ACBL Chairman of Appeals. Jane accosted him the next day, urging him to communicate her feelings to the committee and have them reconsider their AWMW. He replied that he was too busy to attend to the matter during the tournament, but assured her he would address it when he returned home a week later. Apparently playing bridge and writing articles for the *Daily Bulletin* took precedence over his responsibilities as Appeals Chairman. He did follow up when he arrived home, but the damage was already done. It was too little, too late.

Jane and Judy were not so easily dissuaded. They peddled the hand to every sympathetic ear available and were given tremendous encouragement by such luminaries as David Berkowitz, Larry Cohen, Bob Hamman, Gary Hayden, Eddie Kantar, Mark Lair, Mike Passell and Paul Soloway. The list of supporters read like the *Who's Who* of the bridge world. Some even offered, if push came to shove, to speak on their behalf, criticizing the horrendous ruling and the AWMW. Of course, it never came to that, but it is of interest to note that Eddie Wold, who had himself served on the infamous Appeal Committee, now commiserated with their plight, admitting it had been a bad decision all around.

In fact, many more disturbing things were to happen as Judy continued to pursue justice. After reviewing the series of blunders below, you will understand her desire (and mine) to modify the Appeals procedures, restoring equity and credibility to a process which has suffered in the wake of unjust decisions by less-than-stellar Committees.

Judy and Jane took issue with the following:

1) Neither during the screening process nor during the hearing was any mention made of the possibility of censure (or reprimand) for bringing the appeal if it was judged to be 'without merit'. The onus is surely on whomever does the screening to notify the appellants of their rights and possible jeopardy.

2) In similar situations, when a player's hand does not justify his bidding, that is almost always considered by the committee to be *prima facie* evidence that improper information has been conveyed. This committee apparently ignored the evidence of the hands.

3) There were factual errors in the Committee's writeup of the case, as it appeared in the *Daily Bulletin*. Firstly, the list of members of the committee was both incorrect and incomplete. It was also reported that 'The director was called at the end of play', whereas Judy had called him after the 2♣ call and before she had seen either opponent's hand. He was *recalled* at the end of play. Errors like these are inexcusable. Even worse is the fact that when a write-up appeared online in the ACBL Case Book internet site several

months later (which is the next horror story I'll relate), the mistake about the timing of the director call still had not been corrected.

The proverbial shit hit the fan at the Denver NABC when Judy, who had been anxiously awaiting coverage of their travesty in the official ACBL Pittsburgh Case Book, learned that the writeup of their appeal had been *omitted*! For those of you unfamiliar with the Case Books (the publication of which I had helped to implement some years before), each of them contains a detailed written account of *all* ACBL appeals from a designated NABC tournament. The writeup includes the actual hands and auction, the names of all four players involved, the names of the directors, the names of the Appeals Committee members, the pleas and defenses, the rulings and the reasons behind them. Most enlightening, however, is the addition of commentary from an 'Expert Panel' who give their opinions on the rulings and assess the quality of the work of each committee — as close to Checks and Balances as we get, but unfortunately with no official standing. It is a very useful concept, as the case is seen through different eyes in a less heated environment than the actual hearing, where all the participants can get caught up in the emotion of the moment.

When Judy realized their case had not been included, it was no surprise she went ballistic! Who wouldn't? There was no doubt it was a deliberate omission — the ACBL's personal version of Watergate. She was told it had been the decision of the Chief Tournament Director to omit the case from the Case Book. His reasoning was that 'It had little instructional value', and he alleged he didn't want to offend or embarrass her (Judy) further by reviving the issue and putting it in print.

C'mon. Spare me! A genuine copout in all its glory. First of all, to claim 'little instructional value' is preposterous; it is a landmark case if ever there was one. As for not wanting to embarrass her — well, knowing Judy as I do (and the CTD obviously knew her too), I can tell you she is no shrinking violet and has broad shoulders. It was a slam dunk that she was savoring the opportunity to expose an incompetent committee, and looking forward to the Expert Panelists' views on the ruling and the ridiculous AWMW. The CTD's action was obviously directed at protecting the egos and reputations of the Appeals Committee members.

Jane and Judy were so incensed with this cover-up that they pressured the ACBL to place the writeup on their website (printed Case Books were becoming extinct, the Pittsburgh book being the last of its kind). It did eventually appear — but in the Denver Appeals section, marked *Omission*. However, no one was expecting a Pittsburgh case to appear on the Denver page, so few knew where to search for it, or that it even existed. You can still go look at it if you have enough determination, but let me save you some trouble by including an excerpt here.

Goldsmith: When the facts are disputed, the director should do one of (a) judge the accurate facts and rule accordingly, or (b) make an interim ruling and notify the contestants of their right to appeal. Which did he do? I can't tell from the write-up; it seems as if he did neither.

I believe North-South. Add another queen and West would have overcalled 1NT. Many would double just to show their values, so I don't agree that West's hand doesn't suggest a hesitation. Moreover, does anyone really believe that East would balance at the two-level with a 5332 pile of crap without UI? Edgar Kaplan once said, "If I have no aces, no kings, no singletons, and no voids, I have nothing." East has nothing and bid. That sure suggests UI. Finally, can you imagine passing 2♣ with the West hand? No way, unless you've already shown your values somehow.

This was That Old Black Magic in action.

The AWMW was unreasonable, even if you buy the East-West story. North-South believed that East had agreed to West's BIT. East admitted that he might have let them believe that. For East-West to claim that there was a misunderstanding about the agreement later is perhaps plausible, but North-South couldn't know about it until the committee, so to claim their appeal is without merit is quite unfair.

East-West 1/4 board penalty — blatant abuse of UI.

Zeiger: I think the Committee may have missed something here. West has less than 1000 points. For a less than expert player, the West hand may not be an easy pass. The AWMW is only warranted if the Committee would have allowed 2♣, even in the face of UI. I suspect this isn't the case. Did the Committee think South made up the BIT out of whole cloth?

Wildavsky: Both the TD and the AC seem to have missed the second UI issue here. East acknowledged a hesitation before his 2♣ call. Surely this hesitation suggests that West's pass will be more likely to succeed than any bid, and surely 2NT by West is a logical alternative, even opposite a passed hand. One likely result in this contract, perhaps the most likely, is seven tricks to East-West, so contract ought to have been adjusted to 2NT by West, down one.

While this ruling would have rendered moot South's claim that West hesitated let's examine it on its merits. With conflicting testimony I like to let the cards speak for themselves. Unlike the AC I find that many players would hesitate with a hand like West's. With a poor hand they would pass. Were they short in spades they would double. Some would need only a fourth heart to double. As is they'd like to show some sign of life but have no reasonable action. Yes, they ought to pass in tempo, but rulings like this one give them no incentive to.

Meanwhile note that South called attention to the irregularity before she had seen the East hand and before she knew the result. Calling the TD over would have been better, especially given the apparent confusion as to South's contention. [She did, of course, although this was not reflected in the writeup. RSW] Many players are hesitant to call the TD as often as they should, spurred in large part by the mistaken impression that calling the TD is somehow an unfriendly act.

On to the East hand. Yes, with no UI he may bid as he pleases, but his hand suggests to me that he had a clue otherwise. West's conservative pass of 2♣ could also be a sign that West has already shown his values. This reasoning is speculative, and is not meant to cast any aspersions on the East-West pair. To assess an AWMW, though, is beyond the pale. Had the AC found South's account of the facts likely they would have ruled in her side's favor. Bringing out the facts is the precise reason to appeal cases like this one, and it is not appropriate to assess an AWMW simply because the AC finds that the TD's determination of the events at the table is likeliest.

The unresolved nature of their case had caused mounting pressure (especially for Judy who had recently been diagnosed with uncontrollable, irreversible hypertension) but they were determined to make another stab at clearing their names by setting up an informal meeting at the Dallas Nationals with the ACBL President, the CEO of the ACBL, and the League Counsel. I accompanied Jane and Judy, expecting (from something the President had said earlier) that everything was going to be resolved at the meeting and the AWMW was going to be dropped — which is all the girls had been campaigning for from Day One. Not so.

After Judy and Jane informally pleaded their case, Counsel conferred privately with the President. When they returned to the group, the attorney innocently and matter-of-factly stated that he represented the ACBL and in said capacity, he was advising the President to do nothing at this time. Jane snapped back at the attorney, asking. "Aren't *we* the ACBL?" Sometimes people lose sight of the indispensable role the membership plays in the overall scenario. If it were not for their enrollment, there would be no organization. If not for their dues, there would be no building in Memphis, no salaries for the staff, no perks, free trips and per diems for the Board of Directors, and so on. Lest we forget — without the members, the ACBL is *nothing*.

However, suspecting Judy and Jane were considering taking legal action if the AWMW was not removed, the attorney for the League recommended they go before the Appeals and Charges Committee at the Chicago NABC. It was the first time, in a yearlong grievance, that anyone had mentioned that they *could* appeal to a body with legal standing which had the authority to take positive action.

At the end of the Dallas tournament, Judy and Jane returned to their respective homes and immediately hired an attorney, who contacted the League Counsel. It was confirmed by him that suit could not be instituted until 'all remedies were exhausted'. That meant appearing before the A&CC, which was scheduled to meet before the Chicago Nationals actually began. Since Jane had previous commitments and Judy had been admonished by her doctor to avoid stressful situations, I was designated to carry the ball.

The A&CC, chaired by Georgia Heth, was originally a seven-person committee, but was reduced to five for this hearing by two recusals. The night before, Judy handed over to Ms. Heth a rather lengthy, detailed account of the sixteen-month ordeal to acquaint the Committee with the events leading up to the request for the hearing. The hearing was basically well-coordinated and Ron Gerard, the chairman of the original Appeals Committee, attended by speakerphone.

I must say that Ron was trying to be extremely fair, describing as objectively as he could the process and the decision of the Committee. He admitted that the issue of 'precedent' had not come up. I was attempting not to be judgmental, having served on hundreds of committees, almost always as chairman. The reality is that sometimes, in the moment, fatigue or emotion takes over and careless decisions are reached. We are all human. However, the real problem, at least to my way of thinking, is not the making of a bad call in and of itself. What does disturb me is that it is unthinkable not to try immediately to do whatever it takes to right the wrong. Pretending otherwise, and holding out to the world that one is incapable of error, is what happened here and is indicative of a far more serious problem — ego protection!

Getting back to the A&CC hearing, I merely recounted the actual events leading up to the situation, giving three distinct reasons why the issuance of an AWMW was in direct conflict with the facts — any one of which should have automatically precluded the AWMW from being issued. It was not a question of a bad decision — that was a given. It was just a question of degree.

When the smoke cleared, the A&CC unanimously recommended to the Board of Directors that they approve the 'vacating' of the AWMW against Judy Kay-Wolff and Jane Segal. Several members of the Board recused themselves when it was brought before them, but the recommendation was approved and the matter was put to rest. As the unofficial word leaked out, we were pleased to hear the motion was passed by the Board with only one dissenting vote — Sue Himmel. Of greater interest: it was the first reversal of an AWMW in the history of the ACBL — an optimistic sign for change!

How refreshing to see justice triumph after such a seemingly never-ending uphill struggle and to witness a ray of sunshine peeping through the clouds in the Board's willingness to concede that the Appeals Committee had made an injudicious call. But don't uncork the champagne quite yet — you are about to learn what further evil was brewing in the devil's workshop.

My admiration for the Board's about-face was very short-lived. I soon discovered that they had immediately changed the rules so that (similar to the finality of an Appeals Committee ruling) an AWMW would no longer be open to discussion, review, reconsideration or removal. This leaves no recourse for an innocent dues-paying ACBL member in the matter of an AWMW. I won't bore you with the wording of the actual resolution. If you are curious, you can check it out yourself. It is *Item 062-03: Recourse from a Bridge Appeal Committee Decision* from the July, 2006 Chicago BOD Meeting. I guess my Judy was too much for them! After the favorable verdict (which forced the Committee to eat crow since an account of the 'vacation' of the AWMW was published in the *Daily Bulletin*), those in control must have vowed never again to be placed in such a helpless and embarrassing position. They were having to cower publicly to two LOLs — and all because of an inequitable decision rendered by their own Appeals Committee!

With the passage of the above resolution, pray tell — what options are left to a wronged ACBL member? He or she has deliberately been rendered powerless. It is similar to jailing an accused person and tossing away the key. Unconscionable! Since there are no internal remedies left to pursue, the only alternative appears to be to fight such a suppression of human rights by litigation. The ACBL cannot have it both ways. Either it must repeal Item 062-03 and allow its members to protect their own good names against unfounded accusations or they must outlaw the issuance of AWMWs. As a Board Member, I would be embarrassed to have lent my name and support to such a loathsome violation of a member's democratic right to appeal what he sees as a wrongful punishment. Yet it was passed *unanimously*, an egregiously indefensible blunder.

Before we finally leave the subject, I want to repeat one remark which was made during the hearing and continues to haunt me. In defense of the Committee members, we were reminded that, after all, Appeals Committees are *volunteers*. So what? Does that relieve them of the responsibility of doing the job they have taken on? Of doing it properly, and conscientiously, and with due regard for the facts of each case and the rights of those who appear before them? I think not.

There is no doubt that that our appeals structure is in serious need of an overhaul, to strengthen and enhance it. The ACBL, by their decision here, may have finally righted this specific wrong, but the ensuing Board resolution took us backwards once again. Devoid of any real leadership, the organization continues to tread water, making no constructive effort to rescue the slowly sinking ship or acknowledge the deafening distress calls for change.

CHAPTER 21

THE "C" WORD

CHEATING AT THE BRIDGE TABLE and the alternative methods of dealing with the problem are age-old dilemmas. Cheating comes our way in a multitude of sizes, shapes and dialects — and surfaces at all levels of the game, in varying degrees and in many venues. But bridge does not own the exclusive on cheating. Such aberrant behavior has been exposed everywhere in the realm of sports — with race-fixing, game-fixing, the use of steroids and other performance enhancers, as well as various recent shocking chess/earphone scandals.

Recently the World Tennis Association found itself facing the possibility of match fixing at the very top levels. A legal British gambling organization (Betfair) was notified that in a match in an important Polish tournament upwards of $7 million had been wagered on Argentinian Martin Vassallo Arguello who was rated #87 in the world — while almost nothing had been bet on the favorite. The favorite, Nikolay Davydenko of Russia, was ranked #4 in the world and later in 2007 reached the semifinals of the US Open in New York. Much of the betting occurred after Davydenko had already won the first set with ease! The British firm canceled all action on the match immediately and — sure enough — Davydenko retired in the third set, claiming to be injured. In addition to that match being investigated, the US Open organizers hired an expensive security team to monitor the goings-on a few days before and, of course, while the event was in progress.

If this can happen in tennis, it can occur anywhere; it should serve as a warning and alert the bridge community to patrol our own game. With all the recent money involved in sponsorship, and the relative ease in which a bridge match could be fixed, our group has to band together, taking a firm stand to make sure similar happenings cannot disgrace our beloved game. Though incidents like this tennis abomination may sound like happenings from another planet, do not be so naïve as to think that any sport where significant money and glory is involved will not prove a fertile ground for temptation.

I can comment on this from my own personal experience. Not too long ago an opponent (whom I know very well) openly tried to suggest to me the possibility of his team winning their match against mine (translated to our 'throwing it'). Before he had a chance to elaborate or discuss the monetary worth to, him, I, in no uncertain terms, showed my disdain and contempt at such a suggestion and immediately changed the subject. I was embarrassed for him but more horrified that such an idea should enter his mind and, even worse, that he would entertain the thought of my being a party to it. Perhaps I should have caught him in a sting, but I was nonplussed by his gall and so to avoid a confrontation with him, I took the cowardly stance of letting it pass. What frightened me was that if an individual like him was considering involving someone like me, what would happen if he had the *chutzpah* to approach someone else — someone who, because of the absence of an investigative division in our game, had little to lose and much to gain.

Indiscretions at the bridge table can be categorized simply: *unethical conduct* and *actual cheating*. The latter is a far more devastating crime against bridge humanity, but both are viewed unconditionally as totally unacceptable behavior.

Unethical Conduct

It's different strokes for different folks. Unethical conduct falls under the broad category of 'improprieties' (a rather euphemistic term with a hideous connotation) and emerges in countless formats. It is any unorthodox technique used to help your partner or your partnership or your team illegally, usually embarked upon by the amateurish player desperate for success (although not beyond tempting some expert players to be sure). These acts of falling from grace are fostered by many incentives: monetary gain, fame, ego satisfaction, seeking the limelight or simply the challenge and thrill of getting away with some untoward action without detection.

Some no-nos are worse transgressions than others, but falling prey to any of the following measures is hardly considered cricket in the eyes of the bridge gods. Let us count the ways...

There are breaks in tempo (BIT). Such deviations indicate that someone has bid either extraordinarily quickly or slowly, allowing partner to draw an inference from the timing. Similar in nature to BITs are the ramifications of hand and body gestures. The other side of the coin is taking advantage of said actions, which impart unauthorized information (UI) — they gift you with additional (extra-curricular) knowledge to which you are not legally entitled.

There is also the issue of lack of full disclosure or failing to alert a conventional bid, which most of the time will adversely affect the opponents' judgment. How about craning one's neck to sneak a gander at one of your opponent's hands (or both, for that matter, if you are blessed with height and agility), not to mention gazing at a careless opponent's open scorecard? What about catching a glimpse of a board on a neighboring table as yet unplayed by your partnership as you non-chalantly saunter toward the restroom or the water station? That is known in bridge jargon as 'copping boards' — being the recipient of gratuitous information in advance of the board's arrival.

It doesn't end there. Let's not overlook *accidentally* (?) recording an erroneous score on the traveler or pickup slip — in your favor, of course (not to be confused with insidiously reporting a totally wrong match outcome score as in the Double IMPs scenario, which falls into the 'C' word group). Or straining your ears to catch a result being dis-cussed at an adjoining table. And don't skip over facial grimaces to express pleasure or displeasure with partner's opening lead or the ensuing switch.

There is a subtle inference to be drawn by observing from where in their hand your opponents detach their cards. That is known as 'clocking'; clever defenders who are aware of their opponents' detective work tendencies sometimes vary the placement of their cards so as to impart misleading information, thereby effectively countering the mon-itoring attempt. *Oh, what a tangled web we weave...* Shakespeare was really on target!

There is no end to the advantages that can be gleaned through shady moves by an individual with larceny in his (or her) soul. Believe it or not, though many would disagree, all the above are just considered minor offenses — little misdemeanors, summed up as *unethical con-duct* — as compared to the hard core stuff employed by some of the big boys (and girls), which is known as *cheating* (equated to major felonies). There, I've said it again — the 'C' word in all its 'gory'!

To sum up unethical conduct, its prevention and handling, it seems to me that in order for the fledgling bridge player to be taught how harmful it is to the development of one's bridge game, the bridge clubs of America must band together and stand ready to force young (or old) 'new' players to follow the straight and narrow. The club own-ers and directors should constantly (though tactfully) remind everyone (young and old, novice and experienced) that not following the prop-er path will lead to an immediate penalty, a checkered reputation, and — if not corrected — an eventual exclusion from competition. Sitting down with a culprit and explaining the seriousness of the charges may serve as a deterrent to repeating the crime, although human nature has evidenced the absence of willpower that pervades the good intentions of very competitive people.

Cheating

To my way of thinking, 'cheating' is preconceived and deliberate (with malice aforethought). For example:

(a) Using stealthy prearranged illegal signals (known only to the partnership);

(b) Garnering information on hands not yet played by your partnership via either a chance or prearranged clandestine meeting and using that illegally transmitted information to the benefit of your partnership or team;

(c) Deliberately reporting an incorrect score or result, with or without the collusion of your opponents;

(d) Playing on the internet while having deviously planned access to partner's holdings via telephone, cell phone or another computer, etc.

(e) Helping someone else illicitly achieve good results which, in turn, will work to your material advantage in the form of money, favors or any other contrived personal gain.

(f) Stacking the deck or introducing stacked decks in games where that is possible, like Swiss Teams. Believe it or not, there are several documented instances of this kind of criminal behavior.

Unfortunately, bridge does not enjoy the luxury of DNA testing to nail the culprit beyond any doubt, but it has employed the use of hidden cameras and 'live' monitors to break codes and confront the perpetrators. The methodology and distorted rationale behind *any* underhanded tactics matters not. *Putting an end to such unacceptable behavior at the bridge table should be of universal concern* — regardless of the potential shame, the scandals and the consequences that blowing the whistle may bring upon our game. Making sure that bridge is contested on a level playing field should be our only objective. It is time we stopped closing our eyes and turning the other cheek, finally asserting ourselves and taking decisive action to police our own sport effectively. We have swept the dirt under the carpet long enough!

It may be a startling revelation to many unsuspecting readers but it is important to recognize and acknowledge the major role foreign cultures have played in the cheating arena. Some of them have actually *encouraged* such insidious acts. The curious aspect of this is that those at the helm do not necessarily disapprove of their players helping each other. However, they do frown upon the clumsiness of getting caught!

World championships have been won and lost through cheating — with the losing side being mere pawns in the game. If I were to name individuals, partnerships, teams and dynasties, and elaborate on the bloody details of their deceitful maneuvers, it would undoubtedly propel sales of *The Lone Wolff*, but it would offer no practical solution to the gravity or the depravity of a situation which still exists today. The cheats know who they are and most of the bridge players at large have shared that knowledge for a long time. Most of the newer offenders have been nipped in the bud as the world of bridge has finally started rising to the occasion and taking strong vocal action to rid itself of these undesirables.

Before continuing, I want to share the bewildering saga of last-resort desperation faced by a frustrated group of top Austrian players. At one time in the late sixties, they felt they were being 'had' by players from another European nation and found it necessary to seek a remedy. The situation was brought to my attention by a good friend and excellent player who moved to Munich in the early seventies and had compiled a dossier on a certain coterie of players.

Understandably, the Austrians wanted to be on equal footing with this neighboring nation of questionable bridge standards. Provoked and exasperated by continually getting the worst of it when not competing on a level playing field, the 'disadvantaged' countrymen assembled to consider their options. Twenty-two frustrated individuals gathered in the hope of seeking a palatable solution. They concluded that realistically the only effective solution would be to adopt the same tactics used against them... *a shameful decision to say the least*. However, after much contemplation they reluctantly resisted the temptation.

A few days later, though, after thinking more about their ongoing plight, they decided to fight fire with fire and the entire group agreed to cross the line. However, one concession was made: said 'measures' were only to be used *against the enemy* (a term that happened to include everyone who wasn't in that room), but never employed *against each other.* I guess it could be considered the classic example of honor among thieves! It may be worthy of note that the next World Open Pairs (Stockholm, 1970) was won by an Austrian pair (Fritz Babsch and Peter Manhardt) with a ten-session score averaging over 70% against excellent competition. Amazing.

In my career spanning over fifty years serving the WBF, the ACBL, the ACBL Board, the former Ethical Oversight Committee (EOC), Appeals Committees and other official groups, I came face to face with many of these deluded practices and the lurid nuances of the torture perpetrated against the game we all love. I served as Chief Recorder for the ACBL and the principal Liaison for the EOC, a position I created and held from 1985-1992. The 'recorder slip' process was the sole vehicle used for investigating and prosecuting all serious cases that came before the ACBL disciplinary courts. As mentioned before, when I stepped down, I appointed Bob Rosen to replace me as Chief Recorder. He was a worthy successor because of his passion for his responsibilities, his excellent judgment and superior work ethic. Some time later Bob was disgustingly forced to bite the dust in a political boondoggle starring the Board of Directors, who fired him as Recorder for just daring to do his job in the Ace of Spades case, which will be discussed in detail in Chapter 22.

Whenever I was able, I exhausted every logical remedy at my disposal to put an end to some of these bad practices. However, one person alone cannot accomplish such a Herculean task. There are obvious forces working against that goal. People either fear that individuals with whom they are close will be exposed or they are afraid of a scandal. The fact that there is yet to be an adequate resolution of these issues rests squarely upon the shoulders of the ACBL. It is they, and they alone, who could have wielded the necessary power, but for reasons better known to themselves over the years, they have chosen to assume a passive stance — more accurately viewed as wimpiness!

The actual solutions resorted to were warnings, suspensions (temporary or so-called lifetime), dissolution of partnerships, taps or slaps on the wrists or even in some cases (which I find inexcusable) looking the other way. Obviously, the primary cause of the failure to initiate strong positive action stemmed from the dreaded (though realistic) fear of legal retaliation. *Perhaps if we had had the gumption way back then to rise to the occasion, armed with indisputable evidence of wrongdoing and unafraid of the consequences, these situations would not exist today.* When guilty people are publicly tried, convicted and hanged from the highest gallows, it has the legitimately frightening affect of discouraging others from testing their luck (especially those with fear of heights).

But, possibly due to the laid-back attitude of those in power, both unethical behavior and actual cheating are still alive, though somewhat more subtle and less blatant, as more caution is being exercised to avoid detection. It may surprise you to learn that many known culprits (reformed or active) still participate in the game today. They play in major ACBL events and Team Trials and some are even eligible to participate in world championships. Others hold or have held exalted positions with the ACBL at the national, district or unit level.

I would like to recount several historic bridge incidents with which you may or may not be familiar — but which provoked whisper campaigns over the years. Make up your own mind how criminal you believe each of these acts was, and whether the punishment, if any, fit the crime.

Some of you veterans may recall the occurrence where a player, after the conclusion of her match, discovered that her teammates had been sitting in the same direction (a situation covered explicitly in the rule book). Such a violation of protocol results in a loss (forfeit) for both of the offending teams (with the score of 'zero' given to each team). Heads-up thinking (a nice term for terribly shady tactics) prompted her to suggest to her opponents that they record the match as a tie, thereby salvaging 10 of the 20 Victory Points each would have lost. Unfortunately for both teams, someone ratted on them, reported the ruse and justice triumphed. The result: no Victory Points for either team — although incredibly the players involved got off scot-free with no disciplinary action against them. A similar incident took place at a Toronto Regional some years ago, proving our northern neighbors also have problems abiding by the rules.

Of course, probably the most ingenious attempt to undermine actual match results was the insidious 'Double IMPs' distortion which came to light several years ago, described in an earlier chapter. To briefly refresh your memory, it was preagreed when two professional teams were playing each other in the final round of a team game that the loser (regardless of the actual difference in the score) would take a dive, reporting the score as a blitz against themselves. Thus the winning team would come home with all the marbles, almost surely emerging as the victor in the event, impressing the sponsor and most likely assuring rehiring at a future date. It worked for a time — at least until the scam became public, bringing Double IMPs to a screeching halt!

Another distasteful practice (and I use the word 'practice' advisedly as it has been perfected in many partnerships) is what I refer to as

Hesitation Disruption. This is something that is just as damaging to innocent opponents as any of the other forms of germ warfare. Let us say a player takes a long time before passing and the bid rolls around to his partner. What is his or her ethical obligation? There are several options based on the balancer's hand: (1) Automatic action based on his or her cards to bid on; (2) Automatic action based on his or her cards to pass; (3) Though not etched in stone, the balancer would almost surely have bid again even if partner had not huddled; and the trickiest of all (4) Balancer does not have a clearcut pass/bid decision, but now the hesitation suggests bidding. Obviously Options (1) and (2) can rectify themselves. I would like to recommend altogether different resolutions to the turmoil and sensitivities created by Options (3) and (4).

Since the problem is created by Hesitation Disruption by partner, in the case of the third option balancing should be allowed (as probably the field would take the same action so balancing would stand to protect the field). It would not be right to force the player to pass and possibly give the undeserving opponents an edge. The decision made on that specific board would not affect the field, so it would be scored as played. However, hesitation disruptions must be stopped to avoid giving the huddling side unfair advantage. So, after the scores are entered, a serious procedural penalty at the discretion of the director (half a board, a whole board?) is taken off the offenders' score at the end of the game. Thus justice is served — and hesitation disruption will soon disappear from the bridge scene because of the harsh loss it entails!

Option (4) imposes an obligation on balancer to lean over backwards *not* to do whatever he thinks his partner wants him to. This will tend in and of itself to protect the field. However, I would not give the opponents a windfall in this case (unless for some reason they clearly deserved it), but rather tend to give them an average or the equivalent of the rest of their game. If someone bids as a result of his partner's hesitation, they should not only get a bad score on that board, but be subject to a procedural penalty in the case of a flagrant violation.

A humorous incident involving revered Hall of Famer, Alvin Roth, comes to mind when one talks about hesitations. Al, who recently died at ninety-three after retiring to Florida, had an overpowering persona at the table. Co-author of the Roth-Stone System, he and Tobias Stone enjoyed an exemplary partnership in the 40s, 50s and part of the 60s — effective and very ethical, though at times somewhat intimidating. I cannot document where the situation occurred, but Alvin, who was defending against a grand slam, was playing with neither Stoney nor one of his regular partners. In order to make the hand, with three cards left, declarer had to locate the missing queen. Dummy held K32 opposite declarer's AJ10, providing a two-way guess. After studying both hands for a considerable length of time, the inspired declarer led the jack from his hand. LHO, holding three small, paused briefly (an action that has come to be sarcastically referred to as a 'professional study'), played low — and *the jack held!* Declarer claimed the rest of the tricks and scored up the beatable contract. Al's partner leaped across the table, asking why he didn't win the queen. A straight-faced Roth replied, "You had me convinced *you.* had it." A commendable performance by Al — one way to punish a larcenous partner! Score one up for the good guys in an all-too-rare tribute to the way the game should be played.

Another book-worthy story on the subject of sharp practice, but not as admirable as the above tale, involved a pair of now-deceased world-famous superstars, both winners of the McKenney Trophy (currently known as The Top 500, this is the award for garnering the most ACBL masterpoints in a given year). They were the central characters in an incident that became the subject of much attention. Winning was *every-thing* to this notable twosome and on the deal in question, in an auction showing a spade fit, Blackwood was used to check on the number of aces (making sure they were not off two of them). This was followed by a jump to 6♠ which would end most auctions... but *hold everything!* Partner now committed the unthinkable act of overruling the intended final bid, bidding 7♠ and contracting for all thirteen tricks. When you do that you had better be right... and indeed he was! Imagine that.

It turned out the trump king was missing, but, as you would expect, it was onside and thirteen tricks came home. Ugly rumors spread like wildfire that the partnership had a wire on the board. The grand slam bidder was too expert a player to chance winning all the tricks when that hinged on a finesse, especially since their percentage score in that event was in the very high sixties. The question remains to this day — did they have advance information or did someone spot the trump king onside? If the latter were true, who is to say that if your opponent unwittingly flashes a critical card in your face, you are not allowed to take advantage of it? But the expert community, and with good reason, concurred that someone knew the result in advance. A candidate for *Unsolved Mysteries*? I don't think so.

Another renowned cheating case which is worth revisiting is that of Steve Sion and Alan Cokin. In the late 1970s, Cokin and Sion were a successful pair — perhaps too successful. Opponents began to be suspicious of too many unusual bids or leads that always seemed to be right. Eventually they were watched carefully, first at the Spring Nationals in March, 1979 in Norfolk (where they won a major title, which has since been vacated), and then, a few months later, at the

1979 Grand National Teams finals in Atlanta. Finally, the code was broken. They had devised a simple but ingenious signaling method which involved the placement of their pencils on the table — using this code, they were able to signal information about their distribution, especially the location of short suits.

The case was an ugly one, and at one stage threatened to spill over into a lawsuit against the ACBL — one which would see a bridge cheating case tried by a judge and jury who knew nothing about the game. This would be to nobody's benefit, I thought. While I wasn't involved in the earliest stages of this affair, I had by this time become the main actor. Using my own forceful methods, not always winning the Good Housekeeping Seal of Approval, I got Alan Cokin to confess, persuading him that his future in bridge offered more that way than contesting his guilt. After that, Sion, a classic sociopath, had no alternative but to confess also.

The pair were barred for five years, after which they were reinstated with the stipulation that they could no longer play together. However, in 1997 Sion was caught on video stacking the decks in a teams event, and this time he was permanently banished from bridge. By contrast, Alan Cokin became a reformed man, devoting himself to expunging the blemish on his record, and has given a great deal back to the game. Prior to his recent bouts of ill-health, he has been much in demand as a coach, and has contributed enormously to the Junior program, *pro bono*.

Getting back to other sources of violations of ethics, let us examine deportment at the table. Many top players have been accused of using the *intimidation card*. It is unfortunately common practice for 'experts' to arrive at the table ten minutes or more late for a Swiss match, then try to get their less experienced opponents to play quickly in an attempt to catch up. But the top experts have a built-in advantage without shenanigans of this kind. Their fame, reputation and perhaps a coterie of kibitzers all are disconcerting to a lesser, inexperienced player. The superstars should make an effort to exercise damage control, but it rarely happens. Why give up a cozy advantage for which you're not responsible? Being overmatched is already a liability, but to be unnerved by a gallery of onlookers who are rooting impatiently for you to fall on your face creates an uneasy feeling for weaker players. Whatever the discomfort of the visiting pair, the ACBL's rule is that a traveling pair may have only one kibitzer per session (not per table!) removed without showing cause. *Removing one kibitzer is negligible.* Yet there is nothing more one can legitimately do about it. It may fall under the heading 'inadvertent psychological warfare' but it is a real advantage for the high-level group and all too often comes into play in the final rounds of a major event.

Another distasteful practice, although one which occurs rarely in the high-level game, involves unsolicited commentary at the conclusion of a deal. It is prevalent at the club level and often occurs when the score slip is opened and the previous results are made public. It ranges from serious gloating to simple poor manners — or perhaps just plain ignorance of protocol. If the latter is the case, the blame belongs with the director for not educating the players as to proper etiquette.

Protocol at the table clearly dictates that all four parties should make like children — and be seen but not heard. It is considered improper to make comments about getting a good board or to allude to anything negative concerning the opponents. In duplicate games, the problem is easily solvable — though the solution is a shade more costly and involves additional manpower. That solution is the use of pick-up slips for each individual round rather than traveling score slips — a policy which some high-level duplicate clubs have already implemented. Another positive result of this is that if you have a non-playing director, the scores can be entered in a timely fashion and final scores can be posted immediately after the last round is entered.

With regard to gratuitous, unsolicited negative remarks — they are considered offensive and equate to gloating or hot-dogging. It is tantamount to making a 'high-five' hand gesture over the opponents. Such exuberant self-aggrandizement is considered unsportsmanlike conduct at bridge and falls under the heading of *excessive celebration* (routinely punishable in soccer matches, for example). Bridge players, just like athletes, should assume a humble demeanor in the presence of their opponents. While the enemy is present, you may if you wish direct a *complimentary* remark in their direction. After they have left the table, you may silently gloat or acknowledge your success to your partner out of earshot of others (especially your previous opponents). To be on the wrong side of a poor result is one thing; to have your nose rubbed in it is inexcusable.

And now to a much more modern problem: internet bridge (another arena that lends itself easily to cheating). With its growing popularity, online bridge has mesmerized a multitude of former duplicate devotees, who can play with their regular partner(s) or with new ones picked up at a moment's notice with the click of a mouse. (One negative aspect of this format of bridge activity, totally unrelated to the complaints of unorthodoxy presently under scrutiny here, is the impact it has had on local duplicate clubs, where attendance is dwindling.) Bridge on-line is a lifesaver for many, who because of age, infirmity, time, the weather or geographical challenges, prefer to play bridge via cyberspace from their offices or dens. It is a lazy, convenient, stay-at-home source of comfort and enjoyment to the masses and is conducive to instant bridge gratification — but not without problems or challenges.

Security issues have escalated with the advent of new and more sophisticated computer techniques. One such *acknowledged* problem which presents a real and present danger is that online bridge competition takes place in what is essentially an unprotected, unsecured environment. Don't think for one minute that hanky-panky does not occur in many homes, especially where there are two computers side by side or in nearby rooms. And what about the easy accessibility to contact with partner by telephone? Knowledge of partner's holding may be within earshot or eye contact. Is it paranoid to think in this vein? Certainly not! Remember, many online games now award ACBL masterpoints — to some, more precious than life itself. For years there have been complaints about masterpoints being issued online when there is absolutely no security in place to prevent exchange of unauthorized information by various illicit means. It is ludicrous that nothing has been done to counter such potential and probable debauchery, but the lust for masterpoints rules the world.

Understandably, the ACBL is in a precarious position. Why look a gift horse in the mouth? This issue has been a thorn in their side for some time now. The internet is an extraordinary promoter of bridge and the lure of masterpoints is hard to resist, but is it worth encouraging deceptive practices which equate to the "C" word? No one wants to discourage any kind of bridge playing but this issue presents a real dilemma! Playing bridge on a computer hardly has the same safe parameters as playing in a controlled environment with a monitor or director in place to oversee compliance with the rules of the game. It allows and encourages unbridled actions and assumes that the glorious *honor system* is in place — a naïve assumption, at best. With such relaxed standards, we are bastardizing the dignity and sanctity of the game, selling it short, or perhaps, more to the point — selling it down the river as we cruise through the canals of cyberspace.

The problem doesn't stop there. Because of recent advances in live internet reporting on major tournaments from the four corners of the globe, the marvel of relaying up-to-date information to an audience thousands of miles away — including hands and scores — allows for the leaking of crucial information to parties with vested interests. What (or who), without cautious monitoring, is going to prevent a person from excusing himself or herself from the playing room and contacting someone with access to a computer who can describe boards that have yet to be played?

Many remember an incident that occurred about a decade ago at a major national team event. The wife of one half of a world-famous duo was seen kibitzing their teammates at the other table. The match ran into overtime and halfway through the twelve-board playoff set, she departed the playing site. Shortly thereafter, at perhaps 2 a.m. or so, her husband left the table unaccompanied and was seen at the bank of telephones speaking to someone. Perhaps it was all perfectly innocent, but what a strange time to be making a call, before the match was officially over. No one should place himself or herself in that position. People do talk!

There is no end to the amount of subterfuge that can pervade the bridge scene. Suffice it to say that even groups like Wells Fargo, the FBI and the CIA which specialize in security and classified information would have their jobs cut out for them policing online bridge. Without such monitoring protection, certain challengeable events are inevitable. What happens if, after an absence from the table, someone plays or defends a hand in an unusual manner (successfully, of course) as if he or she knew where certain cards were. Or, during the bidding, he or she arrives in a very aggressive contract that just so happens (because of the lucky lie of the cards) to be cold. The combination of extracurricular meandering away from the site in conjunction with extraordinary luck in reaching a fortuitous contract or the amazingly good fortune of 'guessing' the cards right outweighs the element of coincidence and realistically points to the possession of unauthorized information.

The enforcement of more rigid regulations regarding freedom of movement during a live contest should be mandatory. As described earlier, at the 2006 Open Trials in White Plains, the fire alarm sounded during play and the building was evacuated, offering the Directors in Charge no alternative but to throw out the results of the last three boards in play. It may not have seemed fair to some because undoubtedly the outcomes of some matches, through no fault of any of the players, were affected by the substitution of new boards, but *protecting the honor of the game at any cost* should be the sole objective of those in command.

Familial ties as well as cultures have played key roles in promoting and encouraging cheating. Bridge produces strange bedfellows and you don't have to search any further than some unholy matrimonial alliances who led the way — far surpassing other unkosher liaisons such as siblings, boyfriends/girlfriends and significant others who have played starring roles as well. The classified records of the ACBL are filled with documented information and lengthy dossiers on some of the perpetrators of bridge crimes, perhaps an effective deterrent to reformed offenders not to falter and revert to their former tactics.

To me, overt cheating (not that any other kind is acceptable) is unconscionable. The victim is the game of bridge itself, usually all for the distorted purpose of self-aggrandizement and the unwarranted acclaim that stems from being credited with an honor that one does not rightfully deserve. Professionalism has added material advantages to winning, making cheating an even bigger temptation than ever before. Cheating at bridge is the stealing of one's ego, by illicit means, which moralistically is about as bad as it can get. It destroys the integrity of the game, victimizes the honest players and creates false and despicable results which benefit no one but the cheats. It is a lose-lose proposition for the millions of honorable participants. I cannot imagine anything worse. Can you?

It makes sense to me, as it did to Gilbert and Sullivan's Mikado, that the penalty for being caught should fit the crime. Yes, I am unyielding in my philosophy about crime and punishment. Because of the seriousness of deliberate cheating, I feel *lifetime expulsion* should be the automatic penalty. The sad fact is that for every cheat that gets caught, there are many more who escape detection, prosecution and punishment. Perhaps those considering the possibility of cheating will be turned off by the severity and irreversible nature of the consequences and the realization that the bridge police mean business — once and for all. I recall reading the opinion of some psychologists regarding the permanent expulsion of bridge cheats from the game. Expulsion was actually viewed as a blessing — the cheaters were being barred from participating in an activity that they must hate or cannot master. If the psychologists are correct, it is no penalty at all, but rather the relief of a burden! Of course, we need to examine each case and determine the exact circumstances. If the jury determines that one partner or the other was intimidated or forced to cooperate, perhaps some mitigation of punishment could be considered (although it takes two to tango and I doubt if anyone ever brandishes a weapon). However, where both partners are equally guilty — or worse yet, where teammates cooperated — then a lifetime suspension should be issued.

Allow me to close this chapter by describing a deal that almost cost Bob Hamman and me the World Open Pairs in Tenerife, Canary Islands, in 1974. That is over three decades ago, but it is still so vivid in my memory I can envision the hands as if it happened yesterday. Needless to say, this incident took place before screens became the order of the day.

The auction had proceeded:

West	North	East	South
Culprit	**Wolff**	**Accomplice**	**Hamman**
1◊¹	1♠	pass	1NT
pass	3NT	all pass	

1. Playing Precision.

West held:

♠ A 5 3   ♡ K 9 2   ◊ Q 10 4   ♣ K 9 8 2

What would you lead?

I'll relieve your suspense by shocking you with news that our opponent led the diamond ten — finding his partner (who obviously got the message across loud and clear) holding the following dog:

♠ 8 7 6   ♡ 10 7 5   ◊ K 9 7 6 5 2   ♣ 4

Bob held ◊A4 and I had ◊J3. This 'inspired' lead beat the contract two tricks when we were cold for 4♠, which would have made ten or eleven tricks. Without a diamond lead in notrump we would have made eleven tricks, but no such luck. Our opponents were right on target.

In the high-level game, when you take unusual actions which *more often than not* turn out favorably, your skill is recognized and acknowledged. Sometimes taking such positions turns out wrong and you live with the consequences of your unfortunate decisions. However, when somewhat unusual actions (actions that might even be considered aberrant) turn out advantageously 100% of the time, it sends up a Red Security Alert and observers can discount the element of luck. This East-West pair, who for years had a suspect reputation, had worked their magic once again. To make matters worse, at least from my personal standpoint, I am ashamed to have to admit that they were Americans. Their *lucky* lead could have easily cost us the championship, but although we survived their pitifully shameless behavior, it left an indelible impression on me as to just what kind of people they were and the depths to which some will sink.

Perhaps I am in the minority, but I liken cheating at the bridge table to treason against my country. There is no upper limit to the contempt that is directed toward the perpetrator and, in my mind, there is no punishment too severe.

RESTORING EQUITY AND METING OUT PUNISHMENT

ABERRANT BEHAVIOR AT THE BRIDGE table is not restricted to top players or specific foreign nations. Sad to say, as we saw at the end of the last chapter, the United States has crosses of its own to bear — with both the average players as well as high profile ones. I must remind you that a major problem for bridge administrators is the possible negative effect of a cheating scandal on the game. It could be so injurious to bridge as to discourage many from taking up the game or continuing to play. In any event, it's certainly not a great endorsement for our exciting pastime. Most dedicated players wanted to preserve the dignity of the game at all costs, sometimes compromising certain ideals to avoid an international incident and simply exerting greater precautions to avoid a recurrence. *I personally am not of that mind, preferring to deal with hideous problems directly and in a timely fashion.*

'Helping' your partner at the table, otherwise known as *cheating*, is not restricted to the rank and file player. Years ago (before screens were introduced), it went on at the highest levels as well. Discreet hearings were held and the guilty persons confronted. In many instances they confessed. In one celebrated partnership, information on gradations of hands (strong, average, weak) was relayed to partner by the height at which the cards were held. The same methods were used to indicate which suit they wanted led. Luckily the methods were crude and the code was easily broken. Not all violators were treated in the same manner. Some became *persona non grata* in ACBL events. Others were asked not to play together. Some voluntarily dropped out of sight. The rest returned to the game with other partners.

Keeping these incidents quiet by treating them as classified information was judged by many to be in the best interests of bridge. Perhaps it was. Perhaps not. Our only consolation is the assurance that the game is patrolled much more conscientiously today and stringent measures have been taken to discourage and deter such despicable behavior. The Code Level today would be classified as one step below *severe* according to the current terrorist chart.

The implementation of screens was in large measure successful in preventing partnerships from relaying information across the table. However, nothing has been invented to prevent copping of boards and stealing a look at your opponents' open scorecards to learn the results of hands yet to be played by your side. The method called Double IMPs really took the cake for originality... but it was just one more in a long line of underhanded measures that has infiltrated our game.

Let me call your attention to another disgusting and worsening situation involving cheating and ethics. This concerns the ACBL's Ethical Oversight Committee (the EOC), which at one time had a firm grip on resolving those alleged ugly improprieties equitably. However, the situation is directly affected by the relationship between the Ethical Oversight Committee and the ACBL Board of Directors. Each year the Board becomes more and more immersed in politics — to the absolute detriment of the organization itself and of bridge in general.

You may never have heard of the Ethical Oversight Committee, but I assure you it has been busy since its creation in the mid-eighties. You may also wonder why I care and am so familiar with this issue. Here are a couple of important reasons. First, bridge desperately needs a *non-political* way to deal with certain issues, notably those involving cheaters. Second, this was my baby! I conceived the Committee, oversaw its creation and take great pride in the purpose it was designed to accomplish — to protect the honor of the game... unquestionably a pretty stalwart objective!

It came into being during my tenure as National Recorder for the ACBL. You may recall from a previous chapter that the National Recorder system provides a way for players to deal with sensitive issues without uncomfortable confrontations. It seemed to me that, in addition to this position, bridge needed an unbiased, knowledgeable, nonpolitical group of individuals to deal with actual cases of unethical behavior, including outright cheating.

My idea was to assemble a group of experts who would, without influence from the political Board of Directors, perpetuate themselves. If, for any reason, a seat was vacated, the other members of the committee would vote on his or her replacement. That way, none of the members would be unduly influenced by politics. I envisioned an Ethical Oversight Committee that served a vital purpose in the ACBL — not another plum appointment for a Board member to utilize in an effort to further his or her own agenda.

Let me give you an example of a case that would have been ideal for the Ethical Oversight Committee. In the 1987 Team Trials to select an ACBL representative to the Bermuda Bowl, there were four teams in the event, meaning the competition started at the semifinal stage. My team (Chip Martel, Lew Stansby, Hugh Ross, Peter Pender, Bob Hamman and myself) played against Malcolm Brachman, Ron Andersen, Mark Lair, Bobby Goldman and Paul Soloway. The Conditions of Contest put a time limit on play. These limits were imposed mainly because slow play in major events had gotten completely out of hand. It was not uncommon, for example, to see the last set in a Spingold or Vanderbilt match concluding at 3 a.m. Anyway, on this occasion it was clearly spelled out that there were to be penalties for slow play, and time monitors were in place.

Late in the match with the Brachman team, Bob and I were defending a 3NT contract being played by Lair, and the only question was whether he would go down one or two. Unfortunately, Bob failed to follow suit at one point in the deal — I think it was diamonds — and I knew he had a diamond, so I asked, 'No diamonds, partner?' I had forgotten that the Trials were now run under what we called WBF rules, which stipulate that you are not allowed to ask if partner is out of some suit — and if you do (and if he has indeed reneged), it is an automatic, established revoke. The revoke allowed Lair to make his contract and we lost 10 IMPs.

As we were leaving the room, the time monitor told everyone the Brachman team would be penalized 3 IMPs for slow play. With the 10-IMP loss on this board, we were about to lose the match by 3 IMPs but the slow play penalty gave us a reprieve, which meant we were going into overtime. We won in overtime by 1 IMP and went on to win the Trials and the World Championship. At the Trials, the Brachman team appealed the slow-play penalty — but lost. Later, with lawyers present for both sides at the next NABC, they appealed to the full ACBL Board for relief and again lost. More ludicrous than the appeal itself was the body from whom they sought relief. By their own admission, the Board was not qualified to judge this kind of case. Besides, if the ruling had been reversed at that stage, the Trials would have become a total farce and have to be replayed from the start. Because of this absurdity, my team came within a hair of losing. Not only did we barely win the real match, but we almost lost the appeal. Double jeopardy seemed to have been the order of the day.

I've seen the Board take some ludicrous actions and I guarantee you that politics reared its ugly head in the deliberations, but justice did prevail. The Brachman team, of course, had the right to appeal, but the case should have gone to the *qualified* Ethical Oversight Committee, whose members would not cast their votes based on whom they liked or whom they wanted to get revenge against — or countless other extraneous personal unrelated issues. An expert committee would understand the competition and the importance of Conditions of Contest. Even if such a committee had voted against us, I would have felt better about the process.

Anyway, I conceived of the idea for this committee during a time when my influence with the ACBL Board of Directors was very high. I was in the enviable position of being indebted to no one, and my action was, as always, directed at promoting what I thought was good for the game itself. To get the committee off the ground, I arranged a meeting in New York City with several influential figures. I don't recall all of them, but the group included Roger Stern, a successful businessman, Edgar Kaplan, Mr. Laws himself, Bob Hamman, Ralph Cohen and Jeff Polisner, who was legal counsel to the ACBL for twenty years. Ira Zippert, who represented New York on the Board, was also there. We hammered out the details, including the appointment of Michael Aliotta as Chairman, and soon it was presented to the Board. It was a done deal.

I intentionally omitted myself from the Committee because, as National Recorder, I knew I would be presenting cases to (and sometimes personally prosecuting them before) this group. I am a big proponent of recusing oneself from situations or committees where there is the potential for conflicts of interest to appear. Unfortunately, conflicts of interest surface in several ways. An enormous amount of that exists today — particularly where husbands and wives or sponsors and professionals sit on the same body, making it virtually impossible to make pure decisions without considering personal advantages. You can't go to bed together and wake up on the same committee. It is simply against the democratic process for which the ACBL should strive.

I pushed for Aliotta, a professional player out of Oklahoma City, OK, to be Chairman of the Committee because he had his ego in check. He was also a hard worker, extremely organized and experienced with cards and card cheats — in fact, he was my 'official' code breaker to blow open cheating cases. I needed the kind of person who would be willing to round up Committee members when a case needed hearing. Aliotta is no longer Chairman of the group, but he did an exemplary job while at the helm and helped successfully catapult the project into acceptance and respectability. I envisioned the Committee as having a maximum of fifteen members, a kind of insurance (I hoped) against its use by politicians to reward their cronies or to grease the skids for something they wanted.

Some years ago, after taking inventory, it was discovered that considerable cheating was going on with both husband-wife and sibling partnerships — all at about the same period of time. During my tenure as official Recorder, I was able to help process four crooked twosomes out of the League — some for a set period of time and others for life. One of the most notorious cases heard by the Ethical Oversight Committee involved a married couple from the West Coast. At the time, about ten husband-wife pairs were suspected of cheating, but one couple was a standout. They were indeed using secret signals. An expert from Los Angeles, Danny Kleinman, kibitzed them for a few sessions and presented a dossier on their activities. Six or seven members of the Ethical Oversight Committee were assembled at the Las Vegas NABC in 1991 to hear the case. They were found guilty. The Committee's mandate was to recommend punishment to the Board of Directors, which usually went along with the recommendation.

I went to talk to the wife to try to work out a plea bargain of sorts. My idea was to have her admit guilt and express regret publicly. My theory is that when cheaters are caught and exposed, it has a chilling effect on other potential miscreants. A cheater who gets away with it is emboldened to do more. At first, she denied any wrongdoing, but eventually admitted their guilt. I arranged with her to publish a 'confession' and apology in the ACBL *Bridge Bulletin*, and she was suspended for three years along with her husband. Because she had cooperated, I gave her some hope that she would be able to return to playing bridge with someone other than her spouse before three years were up. As far as I know, the husband has never played duplicate bridge again.

Of course, I was not in a position to give her any *guarantees* about when she would be able to resume playing in ACBL-affiliated bridge clubs and tournaments, but I thought the arrangement was reasonable and plausible. It turned out that the signals were not her idea, and although that does not relieve her of guilt for going along with the cheating, it was a slightly mitigating factor in my opinion. Two years after the suspension took effect, the wife asked through a well-known player if she could resume playing — with a girlfriend at a local bridge club. She said she never intended to play with her husband again. I was no longer on the ACBL Board of Directors, but I saw to it that her request was submitted. Was I shocked that there was opposition? No, but I was still disgusted. It got back to me that of all people, Howard Piltch, in a sanctimonious harangue typical of him, bitterly opposed reinstatement for a confessed cheater. The motion to allow the woman to return to the game was defeated.

I was embarrassed, of course, given that I had talked her into confessing and publicly apologizing, but there was nothing I could do. She had admitted guilt, paid her penalty and was committed to turning over a new leaf. She had done everything that was asked of her and I personally was saddened by the Board's decision. Interestingly, Piltch eventually faced the Ethical Oversight Committee himself. He managed to extricate himself from a difficult spot with some political maneuvering, but it was not a shining moment for Piltch or the ACBL Board of Directors. Here is what happened.

At a Las Vegas Regional, Howard and another New Englander were competing in the semifinal round of a knockout when they had a bidding misunderstanding and landed in a hopeless spade slam. Piltch, attempting to make the contract, went down two; as North, he then sent the boards to the other table. When the boards arrived, the players noticed that the ace of spades was exposed in the board on which the ill-fated slam had been reached. Imagine that!

A tournament director was summoned. The rules stipulate that when a card is exposed face up when it arrives at the other table, the board must be thrown out and a substitute board put into play. Therefore, the TD returned it to Piltch's table, explained the procedure and informed the players they would have to replay the board. One of Howard's opponents was Kyle Larsen, now a veteran professional player and a tough competitor. "No way this board is being replayed," muttered Larsen, pointing out that Piltch had gone down in a slam. The TD then assigned a score of plus 450 at one table and minus 100 at the other — an 11-IMP loss. Howard's team lost by 10 IMPs and he appealed unsuccessfully.

I had attended that tournament, but I did not hear about the incident until I was at the Las Vegas airport about to leave town. I ran into

Bob Rosen, ACBL National Recorder at the time, and he told me about it. I asked him what he intended to do, and he told me he was going to prepare formal charges against Piltch to take to the Ethical Oversight Committee. Cecil Cook, ACBL President that year, immediately contacted Rosen and ordered him *not* to take the case to the EOC. It seemed Howard had enough allies on the Board of Directors to sway the President. However, Rosen was not to be dissuaded and admirably pursued the matter.

In his letter referring the matter to the EOC, Rosen was accusatory in tone though the facts spoke for themselves. What actually happened next was that the case was brought before the EOC, chaired at the time by Edgar Kaplan. Piltch was *unanimously* found guilty of intentionally facing the ace of spades. Rosen now wrote to the full Board of Directors notifying them of the EOC finding. The unsurprising result was that Cook fired Rosen as National Recorder and the Board of Directors exonerated Piltch without a hearing. Sickening... but true!

In 2000, the Board passed a motion expanding the EOC to a maximum of twenty-five members, directly in violation of the intent of its creator (*moi*). Further, each new ACBL President would have the power to appoint up to three new members to the EOC. That meant in four or five years a once-pure committee would become overwhelmingly political. In essence, it was to become just another appointment plum for one of the Board's politicos to dangle in front of someone a favor was wanted from, or to whom a favor was owed... known in history as the Spoils System. That's how it works, folks! Make no mistake about it.

What once was a viable, important entity in the ACBL is fast on its way to becoming nothing more than another trash receptacle for political appointees. Because the composition of the group has been changed, I consider its name to be an offensive and misrepresentative misnomer. Perhaps said committee should be renamed 'The President's Advisory Committee' or something similarly inept, innocuous, useless and limp. I don't want the once-descriptive name of my brainchild to be used as it no longer carries the same dignity and meaningful stature it had when I organized it. The influence and appointments of the Board relegates it to being merely another one of its political pawns.

If you don't think politics infuses just about every phase of the ACBL, consider the famous 'Oh shit!' appeals case from the 1999 Spring NABC in Vancouver, which has been alluded to briefly earlier. Before I fill you in on the details of the case, let me set the stage by acquainting you with the two individuals who co-chaired that infamous Appeals Committee.

First, there was Doug Heron, President of the Canadian Bridge Federation. As I recounted in Chapter 18, Doug and I did not see eye to eye over the propensity of the Canadian Federation to deliberately fashion their team trials in such a way that the politicos, rather than the best players, often ended up representing Canada in world championships. This had resulted in embarrassing showings by Canada (last or next to last in at least six Bermuda Bowls in a row), and Doug and I had clashed over the selection process more than once — never head to head, but rather indirectly.

The other co-chair of the Appeals Committee was Robert Gookin, a good player from the Washington-Virginia area. My run-in with him was much more serious. This is the story. A few years earlier, in a Regional Pairs event at an NABC, Gookin held something like

♠ 8 ♡ 6 3 ◊ Q 9 7 2 ♣ K 10 7 6 3 2

His left-hand opponent opened 1NT and his partner, an experienced player, went into the tank before passing. RHO bid 2♣ and Gookin passed. LHO now bid 2♡ and Gookin's partner again sank into the tank, emerging some time later with another pass. When RHO passed, Gookin was right there with a bid of 3♣; that became the final contract, and it was made. It turns out that Gookin's partner had a 16-point hand (surprise, surprise)!

Naturally, the opponents called the director, and the contract was duly rolled back to 2♡, making. Gookin argued rancorously with the director that he was only making the bid he was always going to make and that the auction, not his partner's hesitation, made his balancing bid of 3♣ virtually mandatory. The TD thought that Gookin's overall behavior was so out of line that he filed a recorder slip; this resulted in a Conduct and Ethics hearing for Gookin. At the request of Bob Rosen, the Recorder, I agreed to sit in at the hearing. With the blatant breaks in tempo (agreed to by everyone), it was clear Gookin had no ethical business balancing, and — with encouragement from both Bob and me — the committee chose to issue a strong sanction against Gookin for his behavior.

This, of course, did not endear me to Gookin. Given our history and his natural resentment of me for coming down hard on him, it had to be difficult for him to render an impartial opinion in any case involving me. Nevertheless, he was asked to serve on the Appeals Committee when the 'Oh, shit!' case came up. In Gookin's shoes, I would not have trusted myself to be disinterested, and I would have declined to participate in the appeals hearing. Did Gookin think of that? Who knows? Is it paranoid of me to think that in Vancouver he was getting revenge for my part in the earlier case against him? Maybe. Maybe not!

Lest you think I'm being unreasonable in expecting people who have a potential conflict of interest, like Heron and Gookin, to recuse themselves in such circumstances, let me add one more fact. Both Ron Gerard and Henry Bethe, who were playing on teams in my bracket in the same event, were asked to serve on the Committee, and both refused.

The verdict in the 'Oh, shit!' case drew an amazing outcry from players who read about it in Vancouver. Later when an article about it was published in the *Bridge Bulletin*, Bob Hamman deemed it the worst ruling he had ever seen. There was strong dissent within the committee itself. Was it coincidence that two people with whom I'd had altercations voted against my team? Was I wrong to expect a different result? My wife Judy places the blame squarely upon my shoulders for expecting that the potentially prejudiced pair sitting in judgment would have the decency to step down voluntarily. In retrospect, perhaps she was right. Maybe I should have suggested that they recuse themselves in light of the past history we had shared. However, that is not what I am about... and if a similar situation arose again, I am not certain I would act differently. Some people never learn. In case you are among the few who are unfamiliar with the hair-raising 'Oh, shit!' case, here are the very gory details. You be the judge!

Basically, my team was playing in the Vanderbilt against a group which included JoAnna Stansby, a good player and a good person. At one point, she and Michael Shuster bid to 6♣. We were in the first quarter of our match in the second round of the event, which typically lasts a week as a field of sometimes more than 100 teams is reduced to 64, then 32, and so forth until they reach the championship round. Once the event gets to the head-on matches, the No. 1 seed plays No. 64, No. 2 goes against 63, etc., so you can see there are quite a few mismatches. That's not to say that the favorites always win, and nowadays it's a huge mistake to take any team for granted. Most players these days bid well enough that they can cause some damage — plus most players who enter the Vanderbilt know what they are getting into, so there is no intimidation factor to speak of.

Anyway, this is the deal that set the bridge world on fire. I have rotated the hands to make it easier for you to follow:

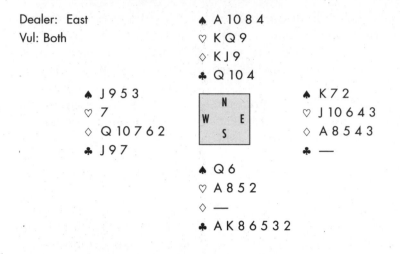

Dealer: East
Vul: Both

	♠ A 10 8 4	
	♡ K Q 9	
	◇ K J 9	
	♣ Q 10 4	

♠ J 9 5 3		♠ K 7 2
♡ 7	N	♡ J 10 6 4 3
◇ Q 10 7 6 2	W E	◇ A 8 5 4 3
♣ J 9 7	S	♣ —

	♠ Q 6	
	♡ A 8 5 2	
	◇ —	
	♣ A K 8 6 5 3 2	

West	**North**	**East**	**South**
Wolff	Shuster	Morse	Stansby
		pass	1♣
pass	3NT	pass	4♣
pass	4♡	pass	6♣
all pass			

I led my singleton heart, which JoAnna took in the dummy. When she played a low diamond from dummy at Trick 2, Dan went up with his ace, which was ruffed. At that point, had she extracted trumps, she had twelve tricks — seven clubs, three hearts, a diamond and a spade — but she didn't do that.

Instead, JoAnna played a low club to dummy's queen, paused, appeared to be considering the 3-0 club break and then said, "Low spade." Dummy complied. Dan, naturally, went up with his king, at which point JoAnna said, *"Oh, shit!"* It was a phrase that was to become so famous that those two words will always be synonymous with the most ludicrous appeals decision that ever came down the pike. JoAnna might not have been able to count to twelve right at that moment, but Dan was astute enough to realize what had happened and returned a heart. I ruffed for down one — a real gift considering that even without a trick from the ◇K, which Dan set up by playing the ace at Trick 2, the contract was cold because Dan had the ♠K.

When the deal was over, JoAnna's partner, Michael Shuster, suggested that she call a tournament director since she had meant to call for a club but had said 'spade' inadvertently. The TD summoned to the table was the popular veteran, Stan Tench, who ruled the result would stand, but about ten minutes later he reversed his ruling, after consulting with the Chief Tournament Director, Henry Cukoff, with whom I have had several run-ins over the course of time. JoAnna was permitted to change her play long after the fact, and the result was scored as 6♣ bid and made. Talk about bad rulings. This one *unquestionably* falls into a class of its own. We appealed the ruling, but we lost the case, and perhaps with the presence of Gookin and Heron on the Appeals Committee I should not have been surprised.

Appeals cases are reported in the *Daily Bulletin* at NABCs. Couple that with the fact that the *Daily Bulletins* are posted to the ACBL web site overnight every day and you can understand the furor and shock that went around the bridge world, from expert to relative newcomer. The day after the decision reached public awareness, ACBL headquarters in Memphis was bombarded with emails from outraged players. One person wrote to say that the ruling by the Appeals Committee "seems to set a precedent which will save my partners and teammates much aggravation. As long as I say, 'Oh, shit!' shortly after I make a bonehead play from dummy, my partner can call the director when the hand is over if he doesn't like the result and have my play declared a misspeak."

Is that what happened with JoAnna? In the aftermath of the deal, she claimed that she did not remember calling for a spade, but she conceded that she must have because everyone else at the table recalled her doing so. An English observer noted that had Stansby said, "Oh, shit, I didn't mean to call a spade, let's get the director," things would have been very different. His view was that her exclamation seemed to indicate that she realized she had made a mistake and that it was telling that she made no effort to correct her play. Indeed, she said later she didn't think she had any recourse.

What it boils down to is that if she had been thinking 'club' but inadvertently said 'spade', it would be permissible for her to change her designation and, therefore, her play. On the other hand, if she had gotten ahead of herself or simply made a poor play, she would not be allowed to change the play. Former ACBL Recorder Richard Colker, commenting on the controversy, said there was no evidence that she had misspoke rather than misplayed. It was a bitter pill to swallow for me, especially considering the makeup of the committee — and I am far from the only one ever to be victimized by a miserable Appeals Committee decision.

Another disgusting appeals verdict involved a bit of maneuvering. I recall that at the 1993 Fall NABC in Minneapolis, one of the top foursomes in the Reisinger Board-a-Match Teams narrowly failed to qualify for the final of the three-day event. Their battle plan was to survey their convention cards from the previous qualifying sessions to see if there were any results they could get changed through the appeals process. In fact, they took two or three 'cases' to the appeals screeners before they were allowed to take one to a committee. Thus did they burrow their way around their results and crawl back into the Reisinger final.

That such a devious, unconscionable plan could have been conceived, carried out and succeeded is a monumental indictment of the system in place. Imagine the New England Patriots, having lost in the Super Bowl, going back to the NFL and asking to appeal a play where they suffered an interception, saying the defender was guilty of pass interference — after the game was already over. Even worse, imagine them getting away with it! That's the same thing that happened in Minneapolis — and in countless other situations. Further, imagine that the Appeals Committee was composed of supporters or owners of their most bitter rivals in the NFL. Can you imagine anyone tolerating such a situation? Of course not. One of the keener observers of the 'Oh, shit!' case commented on the system itself being rife with conflicts of interest. The committees, after all, are populated with players who are competing for the same awards or clients as the appellants. In my case, of course, I had Gookin and Heron on the committee with a chance to exact revenge for our previous run-ins.

Another issue, rarely discussed, is the enormous amount of influence and power both Floor Directors and Chief Tournament Directors have amassed over the years. The obligation of a biased or prejudiced committee member to recuse himself or herself has been discussed. However, is it not just as improper or imprudent for a Floor Director or Chief Tournament Director to hand down a verdict involving players with whom he has had a track record... either favorable or unfavorable? Failure to recuse oneself for good reason seems to be a matter that is passed over lightly though it often has an overwhelming impact on the result of a match or an event.

One person who comes to mind who was affected by favoritism, or in his case the reverse, is the late Barry Crane, the TV producer and matchpoint superstar. For some reason Barry would not have won a popularity contest with the directing staff. He often got the worst of the draw in Swiss matches and came to the realization that it was not by coincidence, chance or an act of God — but rather because of deliberate mismatching, making sure his group faced the toughest opponents regardless of the standard criteria normally used in pairing up opponents. At one point, late in his career, nearing the end of a team event,

Barry, without compunction or shame, would defiantly pull a chair up directly in front of the Directors' Table where the matchups were being decided, to protect his team's interest. *Mission Impossible*? Not for Barry Crane. He found a way to get a fair shake!

CHAPTER 23

WHAT'S TO BECOME OF AMERICA'S TALENTED YOUTH?

In the very late eighties I turned my attention to the plight of the Junior players. The USA had been fielding a Junior team internationally for a few years, but up until then, and continuing through 1990, our young people never finished in the top half of the pack — a pretty sad commentary with such a plethora of rising stars.

A few people exhibited concern — perhaps better summed up as *curiosity* — but without any burning desire or effort to rectify the problem. At that time, I was still on the BOD and my reputation for not being a spendthrift allowed me more or less to call the shots and accomplish what I thought was best for the game. My goal was to eventually hold a Junior Pairs Trials, but I was more interested in being able to get a handle on the potential candidates who would be competing for spots on the team.

I conceived and created a Bridge Aptitude Test. It was presented in a format somewhat similar to the LSAT (the aptitude test used for law school admissions) and afforded me great insight into their talents, resourcefulness and problem-solving abilities. It amounted to picking their fertile young brains. From my simple idea of pretesting the candidates, the process took off. The exams were monitored and the venues were set up all around the country, wherever interest in serious bridge among the Juniors surfaced. My two best students were a sometime partnership, John Diamond and Brian Platnick, both from the D.C.-Virginia area. On a potential perfect score of 99, both John and Brian exceeded 100 on the strength of extra credit gained from on-point answers and suggestions that showed initiative (never prompted or considered by me).

By this time the process had borne fruit. The 1990 Boston Summer Nationals were soon upon us and we were readying for the Junior Pairs Trials. The rules governing this event were totally different than many were accustomed to and expecting. I had unrestricted power to exercise my judgment concerning the selectees. But the decision would not be made without the groundwork necessary to scout the field and learn in advance about the players. I had done my homework, indeed! Because I was unfamiliar with many of the players, my detective work entailed kibitzing, speaking with friends (and in some cases, enemies) and also researching each candidate's individual availability.

I would be remiss if I did not express my thanks for the extraordinary help I received from the Memphis office, particularly from Becky Rogers, who was then the Chief Operations Officer at League Headquarters. She was a tremendously positive force behind the movement. Becky was the principal person with whom I discussed my intentions, often running them by her for approval. Her view usually supported my thinking, making our liaison very workable and productive. Reinforcing the program, she made certain her office oversaw the administration of the aptitude tests — providing the supervision that was vital for the proper operation of the testing program.

Working with the younger generation was a revelation and a learning experience for me. Some of the incidents during the workshop seminars were eye openers and worthy of mention. An introductory meeting was held to welcome all the participants and in an effort to glorify what we were attempting to accomplish, I encouraged any and all questions from the youngsters (ranging from middle to late teens to twenty-five years of age). One direct question came from a young lady who didn't mince words. Her query: "Would females be treated equally to males in their attempts to make the team?" My reply was candid. "Of course," I replied... but addressing the hard and cold facts: at the highest level, almost all the top players in the world were men. I further assured her I would be objective and we would try to overcome that reality. I went on to say that women have made great strides and that there are many more top female players today than in the early days of bridge. It was true and perhaps that appeased her. I further stressed that the skills necessary to reach stardom had nothing to do with physical strength, except perhaps endurance, and I was optimistic that with good training and the right education, the heretofore chauvinistic situation would change.

No sooner had I convinced myself that I had assuaged the young woman's reservations and prepared to move on, than I was confronted by a second female candidate. In no uncertain terms she lashed out, "It is conversations like this which tend to make what you are saying a self-fulfilling prophecy, making that fact true. The less one expects from us, the less we will deliver." Believe me, her ranting gave me pause. I have since come to believe that her words were on target. Working with these youngsters was a tremendously exhilarating and invaluable learning experience for me!

The Junior Pairs Trials lasted about two days with thirteen twosomes participating. The USA was slated to furnish two teams (six pairs plus two non-playing captains) for the already-scheduled World Junior Championship to be held on the campus of the University of Michigan in Ann Arbor during the summer of 1991. After extensive staff work and advance planning, I wound up choosing the first, second and third high finishers for USA 1 (David Rowntree/Michael Klein; Brad Moss/Lenny Holtz; and Mike Cappelletti, Jr./Rav Murthy). However, USA 2 was made up of Brian Platnick/John Diamond; Joel Stuart/Jeff Ferro; and Martha Benson (now Mrs. Ralph Katz)/Trish Thomas, who actually finished *fourth, fifth and thirteenth* respectively. At the time of the Trials, Trish was studying theatre at the University of New Mexico and expected that acting offers would soon be on the table; it was unlikely she would be available to play in Ann Arbor.

More shakeups were on the horizon. Debbie Zuckerberg (now Mrs. Michael Rosenberg) was playing in the 1990 Grand National Teams in Boston, an event that was being held concurrently with the Junior Trials, precluding Debbie's participation. Debbie had much more experience than any of the other Juniors, probably because of the always-tough, rock'em sock'em competition in the Greater New York area. My nose suggested that Debbie would be a valuable addition to one of our teams. And so, predictably, Debbie replaced Trish on USA 2 and Martha and Debbie developed a partnership which emerged as a crucial factor in the final results.

With the announcement of the teams' formation, we got down to serious business. Just as professional sports teams prepare for an upcoming season, so did the Juniors. A travel schedule was prepared which included attending the Reno Regional during the Christmas holiday period and a practice match in Dallas. Joining three ACBL Junior squads (USA 1, USA 2 and Canada) was the Jimmy Cayne team, who duked it out with them to whip them into shape. The Cayne team (besides Jimmy) included Chuck Burger as his partner, Bob Hamman and me. This team (with Mark Lair and Mike Passell) were coming off highs after winning both the Open BAM teams and the Reisinger at the 1988 Nashville Fall NABCs and the following summer we triumphed in Chicago in the Spingold. It was a tough workout for the kids... but a necessary exercise nonetheless. The schedule would not have been as effective had it not been for the colossal efforts and cooperation of the Memphis staff, coordinated by Charlotte Blaiss, who was both a super organizer and a decisive leader in her role as Junior Coordinator. No one could have been more perfect or more willing to tie it all together.

Each of the twelve selected American Juniors was encouraged to attend a few Regionals of their own choosing, and if practicing with their partner for the upcoming Trials, they were subsidized by the program. I had spoken to Peter Pender, who was known to be dying at the time (and was later posthumously elected to the Hall of Fame), and he graciously agreed both to help fund the program and donate the impressive trophy for the winners of the Junior Trials. I also convinced Peter to leave an additional $50,000 to the Vugraph development program, and (unbeknownst to him) it was decided to rename it the Pendergraph in gratitude — although come to think of it, I have not heard that name used in quite a while.

Essential to the success of any team (and especially these inexperienced youngsters) was the selection of competent non-playing captains. I commandeered USA 1 myself and my choice for USA 2 was Chip Martel, of Berkeley, California, one of the top players in the United States. Chip is not only a great player, but he is a long-time college professor and his student-related talents have often been employed (when he was not playing on international teams himself) as a coach. The responsibilities of a coach are to impart to the team the opponents' methods and to make suggestions to his players regarding defenses against the opponents' conventional methods. If necessary, it also involves preparing and improving a pair's own methods for maximum effectiveness. Chip turned out to be the perfect choice for the job as he not only led his Junior Team (USA 2) to victory, but his interaction with the Junior players earned him tremendous respect. An all-around great liaison!

This was a one and a half year adventure, beginning with the introduction of the Junior testing program and culminating in the Junior World Championship in Ann Arbor, Michigan in 1991. It was not without chaos, aggravation and problems, but one end-product emerged from the operation that justified our efforts — success! The three ACBL teams (USA 1, USA 2 and the Canadian Juniors) finished fourth, first and second, respectively, whereas in the previous seven years not one of the ACBL teams ever finished higher than fifth. I can't claim personal credit for the Canadian success, but the ACBL did provide some funding for their training and travel.

It is interesting to trace the whereabouts today of those ground-breaking Juniors from the early nineties. Without detailing specifics or actual names, it should be noted that all of the American players (except one, Rav Murthy, who tragically died about the time of the new millennium) have pursued their love of bridge either as an avocation or a major hobby. Many have continued to play bridge on a conservatively limited basis (keeping it in its proper prospective, which is admittedly a hard thing to maintain) while assuming a traditional station in life, earning a living in their own fields of endeavor and supporting their families. Others have moved on to the lucrative professional bridge circuit — to the exclusion of all other enterprises. There is no denying that once smitten, bridge is a tough habit to kick!

As I was writing the first draft of this chapter, the 2006 Reisinger Board-a-Match, possibly the most difficult and prestigious team game competition in the world, had just been completed at the Fall Nationals in Hawaii. Dozens of world-class players from many countries were in attendance and nothing could be more gratifying than to recognize many present and former Junior players and their places in the order of finish. On the winning team was Joe Grue; finishing second were Brad Moss and Fred Gitelman; in eighth place were Eric Greco and Geoff Hampson; and in ninth were Gavin Wolpert, Joel Woolridge and John Hurd. Hats off to the young US and Canadian stars who are making their mark in the annals of bridge!

At this point, it is also appropriate to send some accolades overseas to a special friend (and former Junior player) — a now much respected world bridge personality and teacher, Andy Robson of the UK. Andy is a graduate of the Junior wars, having been the leading player on the UK team that won the Junior World Championship in 1989. It is now almost twenty years after that triumph, and Dame Fortune ordained that Judy and I stop over in London on the way to the World Championship in Verona during the fall of 2005. While there we decided to (what else?) find a bridge club and play in their regular game the evening before we departed for Italy. We chose Andy's club and were treated to an unforgettably positive experience. Andy and I have always enjoyed a cordial relationship, having competed against each other many times during the last number of years in the American Nationals, invitational events in Europe, World Championships and a celebrated £50,000 challenge match in London. We looked forward to patronizing his club and it was obvious from the moment we arrived that his workplace was his labor of love.

He was particularly flattering and extremely kind to both Judy and me in our stand-up introduction. We played the three-hour game and then everyone was presented with the hand records (pre-dealt hands which were duplicated earlier) replete with analysis! To think — it was just a little duplicate game, but that did not deter Andy and his staff from expending a great deal of time to enlighten his patrons and offer them much expert guidance. Andy (and perhaps other skilled analysts) had taken the time to critique and explain what ideally should have been done on every deal.

In addition, the scorecard that was used was the best I had seen for clarity, convention notification, and for helpful information to facilitate the scoring. On the front was a list of conventions for partnerships to check; inside was the actual scorecard to record one's results with all sorts of scoring aids — slam scores well as the scores for failed contracts (double and undoubled) at different vulnerabilities. What appeared on the fourth side of the scorecard warmed the cockles of my heart! It dealt with ethics, propriety and manners — three areas over which many tiptoe. Whoever had written it suggested that both partners were expected to know their conventions and, of course, be able to describe them accurately.

Also the alert procedure was tied to a 'need to know' theme which applied common sense to why the alert procedure existed in the first place. Sure it could be somewhat threatening and initially intimidating to complete newcomers, but it wouldn't take long for those rookies to learn their accountability and responsibility to their opponents, a factor prominently lacking in our game today. The 'need to know' concept will be dealt with in the next chapter, where I discuss the necessity for knowledgeable administrators and directors to understand alerts and the inferences drawn from non-alerts.

There are no STOP cards in the bidding boxes. Again, pragmatic application is expected, suggesting that when one player either jumped or perhaps made a competitive bid at a high level, that person's left hand opponent should (like the three bears) not bid too slowly nor too quickly, but in perfectly consistent tempo with his previous bidding.

I am not embarrassed to admit that I was so taken with Andy's efforts, I pilfered a few convention cards bearing the inscription THE ANDREW ROBSON BRIDGE CLUB and brought them back to the USA. Upon my return, I presented a sample convention card to a person in authority in Memphis, hoping it might trigger some improvements and help tidy up our own process. As of this writing nothing has changed, but hope springs eternal! By the way, if you are ever in London and a free night presents itself, a trip to Andy's bridge establishment will be an evening well spent. Hats off to Andy Robson! He is a refreshing credit to the game.

It is appropriate now to continue to address the status of our young players. I understand the ACBL BOD has recently downgraded support for the Juniors. The worldwide approach currently seems to favor 'Schools Teams' to supplement Juniors Teams. I, very predictably, am for spending money to encourage young players to learn and become proficient at the game. We witnessed the great strides made with the Juniors in the early nineties. I believe that furthering junior bridge is mandatory (not optional) and perhaps more so now than ever! The BOD prefers to concentrate their energy promoting Seniors bridge. On the surface, that choice appears prudent and more practical since the average age of the ACBL membership is now in the high sixties. However, no one can deny that the future of our game is in the hands of our youngsters. We must hope they will choose to learn bridge because it is *cool* rather than exercise other available options in this fast-paced society that envelops us today.

One big disadvantage is that the positive influence for bridge present in the homes of America some forty or fifty years ago is now history. As my generation was growing up, we watched our parents and grandparents playing amongst themselves, or with their neighbors or other invited guests. Kitchen bridge, as it was often called, was a way of life in many homes. It was an inexpensive and enjoyable way to socialize and pass the time of day (or night). At one time, young girls were encouraged to learn how to play — if for no other reason than to acquire knowledge of the game as a social grace. Now here we are in the twenty-first century, and the game of bridge, once considered one of our country's favorite pastimes, has been supplanted by the internet, video games, professional sports, fantasy football, HBO, Direct TV, reality shows, soap operas, movie rentals and dozens of other forms of entertainment. It is up to us to do whatever is humanly possible to perpetuate the game via the youth of America, lest it fall by the wayside.

Bridge is becoming more popular universally. It is prevalent throughout Europe and an explosive upsurge in bridge has been witnessed in China at all levels of play, but without the ACBL's support, enthusiasm and dedication, it seems inevitable that bridge, as we know it, will eventually die here in America. In Italy, France and several Scandinavian countries bridge is going great guns in their primary and secondary schools. Yet, here in the United States, in our colleges and universities, many Special Services Directors in charge of curricula pooh-pooh bridge as old hat. They think of it as that ancient game of pasteboards once played by their grandparents.

Those of us who cherish the game feel it is incumbent upon ourselves to muster up every ounce of strength we possess and keep battling to captivate the interest of the Juniors and stimulate their passion for bridge. The time is now! Without our support, the game will gradually fade out and eventually disappear. To me it is obvious that new blood is imperative if bridge is to survive, but it is evident our bridge politicians are not of like mind.

In bridge, the definitions of 'Youth' and 'Junior' players encompass people from teenagers through to young adults in their early twenties. As a result, an ever-present concern and responsibility of the ACBL must be the moral fiber and lifestyle of those in charge of our youth program and the rules and regulations guarding the safety of the physical Junior camp sites. In the past, loose standards have been maintained. No one foresaw the possibility of interlopers showing up and invading the camps, bringing booze or drugs and hitting upon some of our younger players (of both sexes). This caution is directed to the monitoring and coaching personnel of the ACBL Junior Teams. For the most part, the attendees are starry-eyed, in awe of the famous bridge personalities on hand, easily susceptible to influence, ever mindful of getting ahead in the bridge world and naturally fearful of offending or stepping on the toes of those in a position to further their careers. Moreover, their zeal to impress those in charge, and to do *whatever it takes*, may cause them to relax their standards and fall from grace in an effort to gain favor and garner brownie points from those at the helm.

You may wonder what all this is leading up to. Let's cut to the chase!

The list of key personnel handling our Junior program includes the coaches, monitors, teachers, mentors and any other aides slated to work closely with our youth groups. All of these individuals must be screened, interviewed and impeccably scrutinized, with a thorough background check on their past history, morals, lifestyles, etc. We owe this responsibility to the Juniors as well as to the parents who have entrusted them to our care. In the age in which we are now living, corruption and depravity are not uncommon. Let's not forget all the much publicized situations involving clergy and scoutmasters or the recent sordid stories involving Senator Foley and the young congressional pages. Why are our bridge youth immune to possible predators? I am certainly not accusing anyone of, or alluding to, any current or previous wrongdoing, but why tempt fate? There is no justification for wearing blinders when the cards are on the table for everyone to see. Let's consider my admonition along the lines of a safety play!

CHAPTER 24

WHERE DO WE GO FROM HERE?

OVER THE CENTURIES, 'crying wolf' has been synonymous with falsely energizing the public to a non-existent danger. But when the danger is very real, it is important that someone accept the task of arousing public awareness. Otherwise, the potential perils on the horizon will lurk unknown until, predictably, lightning strikes. The coincidental heritage bestowed upon me by my surname grants me poetic license to publicize the process of slow decay which is damaging our game and then talk about the changes that need to occur if we are to salvage it. *The Lone Wolff* is simply a subjective stab at setting several errant records straight, awakening and enlightening the bridge-playing public regarding some well-guarded secrets and — of utmost importance — thinking ahead and offering a number of constructive suggestions.

If bridge is to advance, and survive the many controversial issues with which it has recently been plagued, those charged with its management and administration must do some crucial soul-searching. There are warning signs everywhere but no one seems to be paying them any attention. After reading and considering my suggestions for preserving the game for generations to come, I invite you to judge for yourselves. You are already aware of my candid concerns about politics and the ACBL's apathy toward world bridge, as well as my uncompromising determination to maintain the integrity of the game at all costs. I suspect that, as a result, in some quarters the Lone Wolff will be in the running for Public Enemy Number One. So be it!

I have reached the three-quarter century mark and, except for failing hearing, I am more than holding my own and still performing capably. I will be forever appreciative of the thousands of pleasure-filled memories which the game of bridge has afforded me. The sheer satisfaction and pride that swells my heart is derived from a sense of accomplishment — both in competition and administration — but equally as meaningful is the profusion of longtime loyal friends, associates, acquaintances and bridge allies I have acquired all over the world. A debt of this magnitude is virtually impossible to repay and I would be remiss if I didn't share with the world of bridge my concerns for the future of our game.

Other than the basic concept — fifty-two cards, minors, majors and notrump — little in our game has remained constant since its inception. Let us examine some of the issues head on and consider how to cope effectively with revolutionary changes and the direction in which bridge is moving. They are picking up momentum even as we speak. Our organization, the ACBL, is slightly over seventy years of age and we have come a long, long way. God bless the geniuses who conceived the idea of masterpoints (attributed to William McKenney and Ray Eisenlord). No other single lure can rival its popularity. Our progress has been mind-boggling, but as society advances and methodologies change, we must be prepared to follow suit.

I am going to address 'The State of the Game' from three vantage points: where we are now; where we should be heading; and, of greatest significance, the areas in which we must concentrate our energy — revamping our organization but always keeping an eye on protecting our democratic principles. Let's look at each of the issues as I see them.

1. System Treatments

The handling of 'Brown Sticker Conventions', both by the ACBL and the WBF, has improved markedly through the years. The current rules clamp down on their frivolous use and abuse — applying certain minimum restrictions if such bids are to be employed. They cannot be used except in a few very high level events, and their users are required to provide adequate written defenses, to which the opponents can refer at the table. An improvement for sure — but far from ideal! Because of the conditions imposed upon the users, Brown Sticker conventions have lost much of their appeal; they are not as damaging to the opponents as they were originally intended to be. In all fairness to both sides, it is perhaps appropriate to discuss the pros and cons of the issue.

Proponents point out that in the early days of bridge, the use of any convention was regarded as cheating. Takeout doubles and Blackwood, for example, came under heavy criticism when they were first introduced.

However, over the years, most types of bids have become accepted, and there has never been a fundamental philosophy that suggests making certain bids off limits. To some it would logically follow that any legal bid or sequence developed by creative minds should be acceptable. They would argue against restricting any attempt within the rules to reach a par result or make it difficult for the opponents to achieve that same par result. The scoring system has been essentially the same for many years, and any legal method that takes advantage of the system should be given a proper blessing.

On the other hand, one can argue that yes, the fertile minds of bridge players should be encouraged to innovate, but not when those minds are dedicated to conjuring up poison gas type bids that are simply disruptive. An example of these is an opening bid showing a very weak hand, which does not specifically name one suit but could be any of a number of two-suited hands.[1] Such gimmicks can be very damaging to innocent opponents. However, the scoring system, especially at favorable vulnerability, encourages such flights of fancy.

As I mentioned in Chapter 17, bridge is a relatively new game, and most of the original scoring system is still intact. The penalty for each non-vulnerable undertrick is only 50 points, though according to many experienced bridge aficionados, in a perfect world it should be 75 or 80 points. Unfortunately, altering such a fundamental number could set bridge back a long way as most people resist change. Instead, those who want to take advantage of that defect should not be catered to, but rather chastised for trying.

Much of what has been done by the poison-gassers was geared to changing the game, as most of us know it, to something quite different. Their methods were deliberately designed to prevent their opponents from exercising superior judgment and to disrupt the all-important psychological aspects of playing bridge at a high-level. The only way to retain these beautiful qualities is to police the auctions and render the methods of destruction endorsed by the radicals totally off-limits by outlawing them.

2. Alert procedures — keeping up with the times

With the enhancement, upgrading and modifications of systems, conventions, and treatments, our alert procedures must be updated right along with them to educate unsuspecting opponents about nuances of which

---

1. One that comes to mind showed one of three pairs of such hands: majors/minors, pointed/rounded suits, red/black suits.

they may be unaware. Apropos of this, Danny Kleinman recently cited an on-target example. Think about the following in the context of Andy Robson's concept of 'need-to-know' alerts, which I described in Chapter 23.

Let us assume North-South, in the auction below, are playing Intermediate Jump Overcalls (IJO), as opposed to Weak Jump Overcalls (WJO) — the method suggested years ago by Charles Goren and still the majority choice.

The bidding proceeds:

West	North	East	South
1◊	1♠	3◊¹	pass
pass	3♠		

1. Either weak or limit.

South has an obligation to alert East-West to the fact that since North-South are playing IJOs, North's rebid of 3♠ should preclude his having a hand that fit the qualifications for the conventional call that he chose *not* to make. Since North must be trusted to know what he is doing, it appears that North may have wilder distribution, with at least six decent spades and possibly a four-card or maybe even a five-card side suit of lesser strength. In any event, since he didn't make his conventional IJO at his first opportunity, the opponents should be alerted that he probably has a slightly different type of hand.

There is good reason to discuss the above situation. It has been called to my attention recently that some ACBL tournament directors have concluded that an alert of this type is not only out of order but possibly subject to penalty, since it is not included on the 'accepted' Alert Procedure list. It is time we clarified the existing set of rules. Unfortunately, 'clear rules' in this area is an oxymoron; indeed, there are many instances in bidding where 'clear rules' will keep the TD from being able to give an equitable decision. TDs need to hear and accept looser rules; 'up front' bridge players should be rewarded as opposed to the ones with larceny in their hearts. Here's my first new rule: *NEVER penalize anyone, if possible, for trying to do the right thing.*

Rather than making alerts like the one suggested above off limits and subject to penalty, our TDs should be educated to understand the real reason for alerts and strongly encourage our players to take the extra step to try and practice active ethics. You will, I hope, have noticed the admonition that I created and that is printed on every ACBL scorecard:

Always Disclose! Never Abuse! Don't Intimidate! Practice Active Ethics! If all our administrators and tournament directors take the time to get on the same page, our players will get the picture of what is expected of them. It is only when there is confusion and disagreement among our rule makers and implementers that our system suffers. Bridge is not only a thinking man's game for a player, it is also one for our administrators.

We must encourage alerting on a 'need-to-know' basis, applauding when alerts are appropriate, and reserving criticism (and maybe even penalties) for the time when alerts may be used either to help partner and/or disadvantage unsuspecting opponents.

My experience tells me that when more is expected from a player, he will deliver more — striving to live up to the old adage, 'Bridge is a Gentleman's Game'. (Sorry, Judy, my chauvinism is showing again.)

3. The Handling of Bridge Appeals

This topic relates to the age-old question: which group is better able to handle bridge appeals: distinguished, experienced players or tournament directors? The former is the time-honored method that has been employed, but recently there has been a movement to abandon appeals committees composed of players in favor of directors. The ACBL BOD chose recently to continue with the traditional method by a 13-12 vote — hardly a show of solidarity, and suggesting to both appeals committees and directors that their foothold in that area is tenuous at best. The jury is still out as far as I am concerned, but the primary determinant is undoubtedly the competence of the individuals involved.

More training is the key in both fields, but that is easier said than done as Memphis is unwilling to press the issue and be more exacting on the persons involved in the specific processes. Proper education is a must. Being a good player, in itself, does not qualify one to serve on appeals committees nor does expertise in the rules alone make a director able to handle appeals. The crucial element is a *practical* knowledge of the laws: understanding how to temper justice with mercy and above all how to assure an equitable final result — that the guilty be punished and the innocent be protected — even if it means bending the rules.

On the brighter side, two individuals stand out in my mind as making great contributions to high-level bridge in the field of directing. They are Solly Weinstein, from New York, and Chris Patrias, from St. Louis — who have shared the Director-in-Charge title at the annual US Team Trials. Both gentlemen always do everything right during that event — showing the players proper respect in making well-thought-out decisions at one of bridge's most prestigious competitions. Even more admirable is the temperament displayed in handling their daily responsibilities — always a smile, a wonderful sense of humor and a touch of class. We are blessed to have them on hand to sort out the many issues — both big and small — that arise every year. Their demeanor is outstandingly professional and I have never heard any player challenge their knowledge or integrity. In the bridge world of today, that is a rarity.

4. The Function of the ACBL Board

The ACBL Board is composed of twenty-five Directors, each elected from one of the twenty-five Districts of the League. However, it does not function as a Board in any normal sense. The CEO is required to bring most decisions to the BOD for approval, so the result is micromanagement by twenty-five bosses, each with his or her own personal and political agenda. No wonder so few have been able to make a success of the CEO position.

I propose the entire business of the ACBL be conducted out of the Memphis office (at least for now) with three principal executives, all of whom must have had some previous experience (plus a positive connection) with the game of bridge. Below is a very generalized description of the proposed roles they would play; it is not intended as a specific job description for each — merely a starting point.

The *Chief Executive Officer* would be ultimately responsible for and oversee the whole business as well as being the main liaison with the ACBL BOD.

The *Chief Operations Officer* would be responsible for all the activity in the home office as well as being the chief liaison with all tournament directors.

The *Chief Marketing and Public Relations Officer* would be responsible for increasing membership and promoting ACBL activities, ensuring the right image for the continued future of bridge.

These three executives would be able to call on two major Advisory Committees:

Business Committee: I see this as comprised of people such as Warren Buffett, Jimmy Cayne, Morris Chang, Bill Gates, Cliff

Meltzer, Peter Lynch, Nick Nickell and Jimmy Ortiz-Patino. Its members would be individuals who have achieved great business success and who are either passionate about the game themselves or are influenced positively by someone who is.

Bridge Committee: This advisory group would be made up of experienced old timers — individuals like Peter Boyd, Dick Freeman, Bob Hamman, Denis Howard, Zia Mahmood, Chip Martel, Eric Murray, Jeff Rubens, Tommy Sanders and Kit Woolsey. Memphis would have these people available to provide input on decisions that involved bridge know-how, such as system approval, the alert procedure, the appeals process, or even the format of an event.

The current ACBL BOD would stay at home and keep out of the day-to-day running of the League. It would seem logical for them to meet once a year at a National tournament to discuss overall direction and make suggestions for Memphis to consider. Perhaps one day should be designated for a meeting of the Memphis executives with the BOD to exchange thoughts and productive ideas. Memphis would basically have control of its own destiny, with two super-qualified committees to rely on for guidance in financial and business decisions respectively, and the BOD to consult when needed. However, in the event of a serious problem, the militia would be brought in and all resources of the ACBL could be brought to bear.

In other words, the ACBL BOD should function as a Board of Directors, allowing League management to run the business — just like any other business organization.

While this would go far towards eliminating today's system of pork-barrel politics, in the end it is the ACBL Directors themselves who have to clean up that particular act. Being a loyal follower has its place, but being an independent thinker is far more important. Make no mistake, when a person is elected to any executive position, those who supported this person want him (grant me my chauvinistic gender reference for simplicity's sake) to exercise his energy and cast his vote toward what he thinks is the best course for the common good. Anything less is shameful, and fear of retaliation by rogue members is as bad as politics can get.

Furthermore, when someone is elected President of the ACBL, it is that person's duty, among other things, to right obvious wrongs, even when he or she could be criticized and chastised by angry associates.

Doing the right thing should be a matter of course and falls within the mandatory duties and responsibilities of the presidency.

5. Keeping the Foxes out of the Henhouse

Liberty and equality are the foundations upon which America was built. However, those two normally cherished qualities tend to suffer when conflicts of interest surface — and in the game of bridge these conflicts are a given.

Neither professionals nor sponsors should be members of any group involved in ratifying or selecting players or teams to represent the USA in international competition.

Similarly, anyone with a potential conflict, such as the husband or wife of someone playing on a sponsor's team, should also be excluded from this powerful decision-making group — for obvious reasons. Preventing this from happening should not have to involve rocket science or brain surgery, but that is where we currently are with the USBF, the organization that has the ultimate power to approve all our teams and make far-reaching decisions. Let's leave the honor system to the military academies (though it's been no great triumph for them either) and be firm in policing our own behaviors and choices.

The worst danger is unavoidable built-in conflicts of interest. In a highly competitive bridge environment it is virtually impossible for people who have their own dance cards to show impartiality. Hundreds of years ago, Machiavelli described that theory in his signature book, *The Prince*. In a potentially corrupt society, a 'do-gooder' is always despised and done away with since he may deprive others from getting what they want. Thus the bad guys assume control until either time or war ends that regime. When we allow important committees like the USBF to function with too many birds of the same feather who have formed alliances for their common good, fairness flies out the door.

Furthermore, since the USBF does control our international play, it would seem that the group should be composed of highly experienced and knowledgeable people. Positions which involve dealing directly with the World Bridge Federation (WBF) should not be filled by individuals inexperienced in global bridge matters. Our present arrangement is reminiscent of the tail wagging the dog. However, since these are considered prestigious positions, understandably it is in the best interests of a professional — or anyone who may want to curry favor — to see to it that his or her sponsor receives the honor of such an appointment. Serving on this committee should not be about honor or patronage. The individual/s making the appointment should have one focal point: who is the best and most qualified person (or persons) to represent our interests in the WBF community. We need people who will stand tall — shoulder to shoulder — with some of the exceptionally bright, hard-working and experienced world bridge leaders they will be encountering.

In theory, the USBF elects its officers, but these elections (at least up until now) have been tantamount to appointments. Some of these new 'appointees' are very nice people as well as sharp, but unquestionably are unqualified to deal head on with the WBF's top administrators. This situation has led to the trouble 'right here in River City' and is strictly our own doing. We need to amend our loose policy toward the composition of such an important group, and recruit willing and dedicated qualified people (educated, respected and experienced in the workings of world competition) who do not carry excess baggage or conflicts of interest.

I have been talking about structural issues at the USBF. However, specific practices which result in much less productivity and lack of trust, not to mention downright irritating work ethics (or the absence of them), are delicate topics that must also be addressed. There must be no more *posturing from the podium*. Decisions must be made democratically in a very real sense. Too often I see 'surveys' from USBF that are obviously designed to produce a specific result, or discussions that are meant simply to rubber-stamp a decision the leaders want made. The process must not only appear to be unbiased: it must actually, beyond a doubt, *be* unbiased. To slither around and behave otherwise is very destructive to the process and it is repulsive to witness this allegedly democratic process in action.

Finally, we have *behind-the-scenes deals*. We don't live in a perfect world, and consequently we should not expect exemplary behavior at all times. But if one is supposedly heading the group, there should not be *any* deals made which might be considered against policy — either self-serving or for self-aggrandizing purposes. The charge of the leader is simply, in order to show leadership qualities, to appear to be, *and actually be*, above suspicion. All groups need to be able to trust the motives of the individual in charge; when doubt creeps in, harsh thoughts and therefore harsher words are sure to ensue. Only in dictatorships does anything else work — because the group has no effective remedy to stop it. Carrying it a step further, it is easy to realize that, at least in practice, leaders employing these unhealthy methods are just one step down from non-benevolent dictators — since traditional dictators never hold themselves out to be anything different.

While we are discussing world bridge and the USBF, it is time the USA hosted an important international tournament on our soil once again. Obviously there are a large number of the world's best foreign players who come here as many as three times a year for our NABCs. Traveling to our country has not proven to be a hardship — so why wouldn't it be practical for us to host a World Championship here in the States? The last time the ACBL independently ran such an event, in 1986, it was a financial disaster, but there's no reason that has to be the case.

United States pride would soar, not to mention the advantage to our Zone 2 participants (from Mexico, Canada and the USA) simply because they do not have to bear the high cost of international travel. Lagging behind in doing what others would expect of us is not the traditional American way, but it certainly has been true in bridge. The action of the ACBL BOD in vehemently stamping their veto on sponsoring a World Championship on our own turf has not bolstered our psyche or our world image. However, in my opinion, that in itself is an even greater incentive for us to take over the reins, initiate a plan of attack, select a site and show the world what we can do to present a world-class event on our own soil — with grace and style!

6. The 'C' word again

Power and money — money and power. Say it quickly — say it slowly — say it any way you want! In the long run, no one can deny they are most competitive individuals' ultimate goals (whether they admit it or not). It is a natural drive with which we are all endowed. That is where the temptation to cheat at bridge can rear its ugly head — and it has. Beyond the rank of actual cheaters, there are those who consider it and decide against it. For them, the risk of getting caught (which can occur in several different ways) plus the fear of humiliation, exposure, censure and severe punishment serves as a strong deterrent. Thankfully, the thought does not even enter the minds of the vast majority of players as self-respect far outweighs the lust for glory and booty. To me, personally, committing such a heinous immorality would render life not worth living. And, as has been proven over the years, the powerless victim of such insidious wrongdoing is the game itself.

We must maintain ceaseless vigilance against that small minority of players for whom no price is too high in the search for success. *The honor of bridge must be preserved at any cost!*

7. The History (and Changing Role) of Sponsorship

Fifty years ago sponsorship and professionalism made its debut in the USA on a small scale. A pro was paid to play with a sponsor — usually at a duplicate club. The concept caught on and spread to Sectionals, Regionals, and even Nationals, although at a National tournament, the side games were usually the setting, not the more serious events. After a few years, professionalism became better organized and acknowledged as a respectable, legitimate way of earning a living. Standard prices were quoted for a specific event and firm dates were made months in advance to reserve the pro's services for coming attractions.

As mentioned earlier, although it was a well-kept secret at the time (mainly because pride was a delicate issue), Charlie Goren was paying top players of his day to uphold his bridge image — an expense which could ultimately be charged against his cost of doing business. Charlie was a decent player in his own right but contributing toward their expenses guaranteed him top partners and teammates. It was sponsorship in its meekest form — and with far from the enormity of influence it has in the present day.

In the mid-1960s a new bridge phenomenon was introduced — sponsorship of teams by a *non-playing* captain. Non-playing captaincies were an admirable concept — honoring and recognizing support and sponsorship and leaving the playing to the super-experts. First on the scene was Ira Corn, followed by C. C. Wei: Ira captained the Aces while C. C. did the honors for the famous Precision Team. The Aces were formed for a dual purpose. Ira was intent on returning the Bermuda Bowl to American shores and thought he could accomplish this by creating a professional bridge team for profit. The gains would come from a contract with a well known successful corporation such as Hallmark or 3M, both of which made offers. On the other hand, the Precision Team's purpose was to show the effectiveness of the Precision System attributed to C. C. Wei — as well as to garner acclaim for C.C. (as the system's creator) and his energetic wife Kathie.[2] Money from the sale of books extolling the system's advantages would be earmarked for paying the expenses of the project, specifically the wages of his star players.

Both enterprises flirted with success in the early 1970s. The Aces signed a contract with Hallmark for all their future bridge products (bridge paraphernalia and books were to appear in special Aces sections

---

2. Kathie has contributed so much to bridge on her own merits too, and holds the position of Ambassador for Bridge from the WBF.

in all of Hallmark's stores). The Aces had bridge success, but failed in their allied business venture. Hallmark helped sponsor an ABC prime time one-hour TV bridge show on Sunday afternoons. However, they soon opted out of their contract because of a power struggle between the company and Ira Corn, who was intent on calling the shots. The Precision organization got the world champion Italian Blue Team to play, endorse and publish books on 'Super Precision', of which Garozzo and Belladonna were the principle architects. However, while their system worked to advantage, the business could not be supported by the book sales and the project eventually failed.

Many years later Maria Teresa Lavazza, from Italy, the impresario of Lavazza coffee, also assumed the role of a non-playing captain. An outstanding team of Italian stars bears her name, with the idea of popularizing her coffee product. Madame Lavazza's bridge enterprise is, as far as I know, still functioning. The aroma of Lavazza coffee has a great presence at European bridge tournaments, but I do not know if the venture has paid its way financially.

Professional bridge continued to grow from these beginnings and became more attractive to motivated individuals with a variety of goals. Prices per session were constantly escalating — the more prestigious the event, the higher the professional fee. In my opinion, Paul Soloway was primarily responsible for upping the ante for the pros by his unrelenting determination to upgrade and strengthen the process.

Allow me a moment of digression. Although I no longer play on the Nickell team, their record has proven them to be a breed apart. They fall outside the parameters of the standard 'sponsored team', as Nick Nickell has consistently been an integral part of the team (other than merely the one writing the paychecks). The history of their formation is a story worth telling. Dick Freeman and his wife Louise were friends of Nick from earlier days. In the fall of 1991, Dick received a call from Nick, inquiring about playing in an event. Dick said that without a 'good team' there was not much point to it. Nick asked what he would consider a 'good team'. Thinking it a moot point (as he was not anxious to play and thought the team was impossible to put together), Dickie replied, "Hamman and Wolff and Meckstroth and Rodwell." A couple of weeks later he received a message from Nick: "You've got your team." Sixteen years later they were still going strong, with Paul Soloway replacing me in 1998. Sadly, as this book was going to press, we were all shocked and disheartened to learn of Paul's sudden death on November 5, 2007.

Before I move on to another topic, let me recognize and pay homage to a very unusual gentleman whose concept of sponsorship may lead to an improved understanding among our many diverse cultures and continues to lead us in the direction of a united and peaceful world. Although his 'real' first name is Chen, he is simply known as Mr. Yeh. He and his friend and bridge partner Patrick Huang, both from Taiwan, deserve to be honored. For four consecutive years now Mr. Yeh has put on major invitational worldwide team bridge tournaments in various spots in mainland China and Taiwan. I have been lucky enough to be invited each time and the events themselves are a cut above anything in which I have ever played. The ambiance of the surroundings and generosity extended to the guests sets a standard which, at least up until now, has not been matched. The competition is as good as it can get — with representation by the best teams in the world, unequalled winning prize money and all (or most) of everyone's expenses being defrayed. Mr. Yeh is trying to afford players in his WBF zone, Zone 6, the experience necessary to improve faster and thus enable the Orient to rank up there with Zone 1 (Europe) and Zone 2 (North America) on a consistent basis. It already appears to have made a difference. In 2006 in Verona, for the first time, a pair from Zone 6, Zhong Fu and Jie Zhao of China, won a premier world event — the World Open Pairs.

Patrick Huang, Mr. Yeh's great friend (and also a close friend of mine since 1970), is one of the best players in the world. He is also a fine credit to the game with his outstanding talent, impeccable ethics and fair play, and above all his incredible love of bridge. He, together with his wife Grace, contribute mightily to the organization of Mr. Yeh's marvelous extravaganzas. Mrs. Yeh (known affectionately as 'Sugar') completes the foursome as a most gracious hostess to the visiting players. Neither Mr. Yeh nor Patrick have ever asked anything of anyone, other than to do them the honor of attending and by their presence enhance the standard of these unparalleled tournaments. I would have been remiss not to have acknowledged Mr. Yeh in a special way. He demonstrates what a kind, wealthy sponsor can mean to the future and improvement of bridge the world over — and, to think, his sole driving force is simply his *love of the game.*

8. Professionalism and the US Team Selection Process

With the growth of professionalism, and as fees have climbed to an all-time high (particularly in the premier National team events), we need to look at the overall influence it has had — not only on the game, but on the decision-making process which it undoubtedly has affected.

Many prospective ambitious sponsors now aspire to represent their country. Achieving this goal usually entails playing in the Reisinger,

Vanderbilt and Spingold as well as the Open Team Trials (or the Women's Team Trials) — and then, if successful, the World Championship itself. It should be no great shock to learn that the cost, including expenses, may range from $300,000 up to $500,000 or more per year — somewhat less for a women's team. Add to this the cost of regular practice at Regionals, which, besides being fun because of the likelihood of high finishes, is necessary to keep partnerships sharp. The meter continues to run and the total annual cost to the sponsor could approach or even exceed seven figures.

One of the sorriest days of my life was when I voluntarily relinquished my chairmanship of the US International Team Trials (the ITT) in 1997, which at that time was run objectively — with the best interests of bridge as its *only* consideration. I was Chairman at the time that my Nickell team was in the midst of winning four Spingolds and three Reisingers in a row. However, it will demonstrate the purity of my intentions when I tell you that despite our impressive track record, I saw to it that no team was either given a key 'bye' or advantageously placed in the ITT.

Since the team trials have grown in popularity mainly because of the mutual benefit to professionals and sponsors, it is time to examine some of the negative aspects objectively and realistically. Specifically:

> a) The USA team is unquestionably weakened by the inclusion of a sponsor, rather than being composed of six individuals forming three superior partnerships of expert caliber. It is doubtful that anyone can challenge that statement.

> b) Having sponsors fill very important USBF administrative positions inevitably weakens our relationship with the WBF. These people are inexperienced and, more to the point, lack knowledge of the history of the WBF and the events that have shaped its course. A sponsor should not be placed in that unenviable position. My career in bridge politics goes back more years than I would like to admit. I have no doubt that the best Executive Boards are composed of highly respected people who are well versed in the situation, endowed with experience, know-how and the ability to voice their own opinion without allegiance to anything or anyone other than what is good for bridge.

As I discussed earlier, at present not only do we have a high percentage of people deeply embedded in the professional lobby also serving on the ITT Committee, but the parent association (the USBF) also includes some with professional ties. Worse yet, the USBF involves some of the sponsors who energize and enable the motors that drive the whole process. The conflicts of interest abound and are obvious as our top administrators each year set the Conditions of Contest for the Trials, and two issues stand out glaringly.

First, determining the minimum playing time for a sponsor. In fairness, it must be said that at our Trials everyone on the team is required to play at least half of every match, whereas at the World Championship no one is required to play over 37.5% (3/8). This is because the WBF has always recognized the country that won, rather than the individual players. My point is that the players in charge of making these kinds of rules will certainly experience conflicts with their own personal situations and should not be in decision-making positions.

Second, the seeding of our Team Trials must take into account the ticklish problem of foreign professionals. These players often play a crucial role in enabling their US teammates to gain a high seed in the Trials by winning an event such as the Spingold — but of course, they themselves are not eligible to play. Indeed, without the foreign participation, who knows how far they would have gotten at all. What is even more bizarre is that if the team on which the foreigners was playing makes it to the World Championship, they may face each other as competitors. Should a US team minus its foreign mercenaries be entitled to any Trials seeding points whatsoever? I think not.

Maintaining personal detachment and objectivity on issues like these presents an impossible problem. *The practical solution is to make important administrative positions off-limits to both pros and sponsors.*

It should be mentioned here again that Pairs Trials (versus Team Trials) do not lend themselves well to sponsorship. For many years, Pairs Trials were used to determine our team and, although I am not one of those who really think so, arguably might be the most accurate method of selection. The process certainly enables up-and-coming (usually young) players and pairs to become visible and recognized. Prime examples in the past were Milton Ellenby, Bob Hamman, Eddie Kantar, Don Krauss, Mike Lawrence, Marshall Miles and Billy Rosen, followed in later years by Eric Greco, Bobby Levin, Brad Moss, Stevie Weinstein and many more of our current crop. But using a Pairs Trials is against the best interests of pro-sponsor alliances, so is unlikely to come up for serious consideration today. A sad commentary!

Some professionals claim that team qualification events are better than pairs because of the importance of camaraderie and team spirit. My view is that they are prompted by an underlying motivation tinted by the color green.

The situation is very different from earlier times when there were fewer acknowledged sponsors and the pay of the professionals did not approach today's high figures. Very little was at risk in the 'old days'. Now bridge is a serious, top-drawer business. To restore equity and non-favoritism to the process, we will need the cooperation of everyone involved to seek a happy compromise in the interest of making the process of playing bridge fairer for all, especially at high levels. Not a very likely happening!

Ask yourself the following question: if you were a top professional player, would you rather:

1) legitimately contend for a World Championship, playing on a team composed of three experienced expert partnerships?

or

2) have a guaranteed pay date waiting at the end of the rainbow, and be reimbursed — win, lose or draw?

In the present state of our union, the answer is sadly obvious. Assuming I am right (and I wish I weren't), I feel strongly that the game in the USA has been so tainted that unless someone rides in on a white horse, with a silver bullet and a friend named Tonto, its future is bleak.

To underline my point about human nature, consider two situations which in the summer of 2007 received more than their fair share of publicity through the US news media. Let us examine the main reason the American public has taken such strong stances against national heroes such as baseball star Barry Bonds and football quarterback Michael Vick.

Wasn't Bonds' alleged use of steroids attributable to his zeal to be the best at what he does — which goes hand and hand with the great American tradition? This has placed him under grave suspicion of achieving his home run records by resorting to harmful and illegal methods. He is therefore, in simple terms, a fraud. In Vick's case, his involvement in gross animal abuse caused the public to forget quickly his prior football hero status. Their former idol was deemed unworthy of their admiration and respect, proving once again that individuals are responsible for their own actions. This happens in all walks of life — but those in leadership positions make the headlines.

The bridge world can recount its own cases similar to the above indiscretions. However, it's important to recognize that the player's responsibility is quite different from the administrator's goal. The player has to live his life the best he can, keeping in mind that earning a living is usually a necessity for any kind of success. Playing professional bridge is certainly a respectable way of earning a livelihood and our bridge heroes should strive to uphold the dignity of the game.

However, from an administrative standpoint, the one and only consideration should be: *how do we select and send our three best, most hungry, talented and experienced pairs to represent us in the World Championships?* Nothing less should be appropriate or satisfactory. Perhaps at least a few of our thoughtful, caring, mega-rich sponsors, recognizing the fruitful opportunities they themselves have had in the highest-level bridge enclaves, may come forward. They could make it financially easier for our youngsters and other potential non-sponsor-connected stars to participate. By contributing toward their expenses, they could afford these heretofore out-in-the-rain players the opportunity to play at the highest levels, including the Open Trials and, of course, the World Championships too if they earn the right.

In Conclusion

I started writing this book in 1994, and on and off it has occupied much of my spare time during the years that followed. As I am winding down, though, many of you must be wondering — why did I write this book and what was I trying to do?

Here were my options:

1. Devote these thirteen years of my life to a more deserving and less stressful project and let the chips fall where they may;

2. Move forward with the book, but omit many unseemly things, naming no names and masking the truth — basically turning the story of bridge into a meaningless fairy tale with all sweetness and light;

3. Chronicle with accuracy what actually did happen — including names and details when appropriate — and let the reader decide the possible motives and reasons for what did transpire.

You probably know me well enough by now to expect that I would have been inclined to the last option in any event. However, what influenced my decision was a phone call I received from a concerned Alan Truscott some years ago, when he reminded me that many of the players and administrators who were our contemporaries were either dead or simply not interested in chronicling what had transpired. He felt strongly that before he and I checked out, we had a responsibility to all bridge devotees to share our up-close and personal knowledge of the history of the game. Sadly, Alan is now gone and since there is probably no one else left who has had the good (or bad) fortune to witness as many key events as I have, I considered myself elected to that task, keeping the vow I made to him.

Remember, too, that I was born and bred in San Antonio, Texas, where in 1836 the Battle of the Alamo was fought (a battle in which every real or adopted Texan present was killed). I have always found it sad that the most important single historical event ever to be associated with that city has no accurate contemporary documentation whatsoever. From that war, when Texas was still under the Mexican flag, came the following familiar quote: "Thermopylae had its messenger of defeat, the Alamo had none".

I was inspired by that sad realization to try to assure that, at least for bridge, history would not repeat itself. If *The Lone Wolff* is the only voice to go on record and plead for change, it will not be the first time I have stood alone for what I believe to be right.

And it may not be the last.

BOBBY WOLFF Achievements

ROBERT S. (BOBBY) WOLFF

Positions of Distinction (past and present)

Member ACBL Hall of Fame
WBF Grand Master
ACBL Grand Life Master
Member ACBL Board of Directors 1981-1992
President of ACBL 1987
Chairman of the ACBL Board 1988
Member of WBF Executive Council 1988-94
President of WBF 1992-4
Elected to WBF Committee of Honour, 1994

The only player to have won world championships in five different categories:

Winner Bermuda Bowl 1970, 1971, 1977, 1983, 1985, 1987, 1995
Winner World Mixed Teams 1972
Winner World Open Pairs 1974
Winner World Open Teams 1988
Winner World Senior Teams 2000

Second-place finishes:

World Open Teams 1972, 1980, 1992
Bermuda Bowl 1973, 1974, 1975, 1997

Third-place finishes:

Rosenblum Teams 1978, 1982
Bermuda Bowl 2003
World Senior Teams 2007

National championships:

Pan-American Invitational 1974, 1976, 1977
USBC (Team Trials) 1983, 1985, 1987, 1992, 1993, 1995, 1997, 2003
US Seniors Team Trials 2000, 2001, 2007

Spingold 1969, 1979, 1982, 1983, 1989, 1990, 1993, 1994, 1995,
1996
Reisinger 1970, 1978, 1979, 1988, 1993, 1994, 1995, 2002
Vanderbilt 1971, 1973
Men's BAM Teams 1968, 1972, 1973, 1988
Mott-Smith Trophy 1973
GNOT 1975, 1977, 1986
Fishbein Trophy 1979
Blue Ribbon Pairs 1984

Second-place finishes:

Life Master Pairs 1960, 1968
Reisinger 1964
Spingold 1967, 1970
Men's Teams 1969, 1980, 1984, 1989
Vanderbilt 1970, 1981, 1996
Men's BAM Teams 1989
Open Swiss 1992
Senior KO teams 2007

Marquis Book Printing Inc.

Québec, Canada
2008